VEGETABLE GROWING IN INDIA

VEGETABLE GROWING IN INDIA

PREM SINGH ARYA
and
SANT PARKASH

Himachal Pradesh Krishi Vishvavidyalaya,
Palampur–176 062 (H.P.) India

KALYANI PUBLISHERS

LUDHIANA – NEW DELHI – NOIDA (U.P.) – HYDERABAD - CHENNAI
KOLKATA – CUTTACK – GUWAHATI – KOCHI - BANGALORE

KALYANI PUBLISHERS

Head Office

B-1/1292, Rajinder Nagar, **Ludhiana**-141 008 • Ph : 0161-2760031
E-mail : kalyanibooks@yahoo.co.in

Administration Office

4779/23, Ansari Road, Daryaganj, New Delhi-110 002
Ph : 011-23271469, 23274393, 23278688 **E-mail :** kalyani_delhi@yahoo.co.in

Works

B-16, Sector-8, **NOIDA** (U.P.)

Branches

1, Mahalakshmi Street, T. Nagar, **Chennai**-600 017 • Ph : 044-24344684
110/111, Bharatia Towers, Badambadi, **Cuttack**-753 009 (Odisha) • Ph : 0671-2311391
3-5-1108, Narayanaguda, **Hyderabad**-500 029 • Ph : 040-24750368
10/2B, Ramanath Mazumdar Street, **Kolkata**-700 009 • Ph : 033-22416024
Arunalaya, 1st Floor, Saraswati Road, Pan Bazar, **Guwahati**-781 001 • Ph : 0361-2731274
Koratti Parambil House, Convent Road, **Kochi**-682 035 • Ph : 0484-2367189
No. 24 & 25, 1st Floor, Hameed Shah Complex, Cubbonpet Main Road, **Bengaluru**-560 002

KPP L 18826 05

Second Revised Edition, 2016

Gautam Graphic Printers
(VEGE-P15)

ISBN 978-93-272-5835-6

PRINTED IN INDIA

At B.B. Press, A-37, Sec.-67, NOIDA-201301
and published by Mrs. Usha Raj Kumar for
Kalyani Publishers, New Delhi-110 002

CONTRIBUTORS

1. Arya, Prem Singh
Senior Vegetable Breeder,
Deptt. of Vegetable Science and Floriculture,
H.P.K.V., Palampur-176 062
Distt. Kangra (H.P.), INDIA.

2. Azad Thakur N.S.
Ph.D (A.R.S.)
Joint Director,
ICAR, Research Complex for NEH Region,
Mizoram Centre, Kolasib-796 081.

3. Devadas, V.S.
Associate Professor, Kerala Agricultural University,
Vellanikkara-680 654 Thrissur-680 654, Kerala, INDIA.

4. Dhandar, D.G.
ICAR Research Complex for Goa,
(Indian Council of Agricultural Research)
ELA, Old Goa-403 402.

5. Dwivedi, Sanjai K.
Scientist
Government of India, Ministry of Defence
Defence Research and Development Organisation
Field Research Laboratory, 31 NF Div. C/O 56 APO

6. Fageria, M.S.
Department of Horticulture,
S.K.N. College of Agriculture,
Jobner (Jaipur) - 303329 Rajasthan.

7. Gaonkar, V.Y.
ICAR Research Complex for Goa,
(Indian Council of Agricultural Research)
ELA, Old Goa-403 402.

8. Gupta, Arun Kumar
Scientist Vegetable,
Division of Vegetable Crops,
Shere-Kashmir Univ. of Agriculture and Technology,
Shalimar, Kashmir, J&K, INDIA

9. Hari Har Ram,

Professor & Head
Department of Vegetable Science
G.B. Pant University of Agriculture & Technology,
Pant Nagar-263 145 (U.S. Nagar)
U.P., India

10. Hazra, P.

Reader
Bidhan Chandra Krishi Vishvavidyalaya
Department of Vegetable Crops
Faculty of Horticulture
P.O. Krishi Vishvavidyalaya,
Mohanpur, District, Nadia-741252,
West Bengal.

11. Kantha Swamy, V

Ph. D.
Asstt. Prof. (Hort.) & Vegetable Breeder (AICVIP)
Tamil Nadu Agricultural University
Department of Olericulture
Horticultural College and Research Institute,
Coimbatore—641 003, India

12. Laxminarayana, K.

ICAR, Research Complex for NEH Region
Mizoram Centre, Kolasib-796 081.

13. Naik, L.B.

Senior Scientists
Division of Vegetable Crops,
Indian Institute of Horticultural Research,
(ICAR), Hassaraghatta Lake Post,
Bangalore-560 089.

14. Parkash, Sant

Deptt. of Vegetable Science and Floriculture,
H.P.K.V., Palampur-176 062,
Distt. Kangra (H.P.), INDIA

15. Rana, S.C.

ICAR Research Complex for Goa,
(Indian Council of Agricultural Research)
ELA, Old Goa-403 402.

16. Reddy, Prabhakar

M.Sc. (Ag.) Ph. D. Horticulturist (Veg.)
Acharya N.G. Ranga Agricultural University,
Vegetable Research Section
Agricultural Research Institute
Rajendranagar, Hyderabad-500 030. (A.P.)

17. Sarnaik, DA.

Prof. & Head,
Deptt. of Horticulture, College of Agriculture,
I.G.K.V.V. Raipur (M.P.), INDIA.

18. Sood, Vishal

Deptt. of Horticulture,
Mahatma Phule Krishi Vidyapeeth (MPAU),
Rahuri-413 722, Maharashtra, INDIA

19. Thakur, J.C.

Senior Vegetable Breeder,
Department of Vegetable Crops,
Punjab Agricultural University,
Ludhiana-141004, Punjab.

20. Warade, S.D.

Senior Vegetable Breeder,
Deptt. of Horticulture,
Mahatma Phule Krishi Vidyapeeth (MPAU),
Rahuri-413 722, Maharashtra, INDIA.

21. Yadav, L.M.

Regional Research Station,
Agwanpur, Distt. Saharsa,
Bihar-852 201, INDIA.

22. Yadav, R.C.

Regional Research Station,
Agwanpur, Distt. Saharsa,
Bihar-852 201, INDIA.

23. Malhotra, S.K.

Senior Scientist (Horticulture),
Central Horticultural Experiment Station,
(Indian Institute of Horticultural Research),
Godhra-Baroda High Way,
Vejalpur-389 340, Distt. Panchmahal, Gujarat, INDIA.

24. Singh, Brahma

Director,
DFAS, Room No. 326,
'B' Wing Sena Bhawan,
New Delhi-110 011.

25. Singh, S.P.

Associate Professor,
Gujarat Agricultural University,
Sadar Krusinagar,
Junagadh Campus, Junagadh-362 001, Gujarat.

PREFACE

The book **"Vegetable Growing in India"** (Status, problems and prospectus) has been compiled by the authors keeping in view the increasing importance of vegetables in the country under varied agro-climatic conditions to meet the requirement of increasing population. However, India is the second largest producer of vegetables only next to China in the world. The information regarding vegetable area, production, productivity, vegetable/seed/off-season vegetables grown in each state, agro-climatic zones and export potential, etc. of each State and Union Territory of the country percolating from different sources have been compiled in the form of above mentioned manuscript. Though scattered information is available that too on cultural practices and other aspects of vegetable/seed crops but no such information is available. The detail information distilled from various sources will be quite useful to the students, teachers, scientists, research and extension workers and the planners, financing organisation, both in public and private sector.

The unique feature of the said book is that a special attention has been given to contain the detail information of each state regarding economic role being played, vegetable varieties grown, impact of environmental factors and zones and more so these all embodied does cut across the geo-ecological boundaries but most applicable in agro-climatic situations all alien to each state.

The book has been compiled for the benefit of all those who are interested in increasing their knowledge and understanding about detailed valuable statistics of vegetable/seed/production emanating from the above concerted efforts. We hope that the information contained in the book will be of immense value to the farming community especially vegetable/seed producer, students, researchers, extension workers etc. involved in vegetable industry in India.

The authors are thankful to Dr. P.K. Khosla, Hon'ble Vice-Chancellor, H.P. Krishi Vishvavidyalaya, Palampur for encouragement and the contributors who could spare their valuable time for supplying the detail information of their respective state. Special thanks to Dr. S.P. Ghosh for the material taken from the book 'Agro-climatic zones Specific Research'.

We also gratefully express our sincere feelings to our family members for sparing us to complete this book at their personal comfort and against heavy odds.

We welcome suggestions for the improvement of this real record of this mammoths compilation from the readers to send their opinion to the publishers .

2016

Prem Singh Arya
Sant Parkash

CONTENTS

ANNEXURES

CHAPTER 1

INTRODUCTION

Vegetable are the integral part of our daily diet in all walks of society. The population of India is increasing at a faster rate (1.8% year) and the vegetable production in our country cannot cope with what is needed for nutritional security particularly the developing country like ours. The Indian population being vegetarians since ancient times but the per capita consumption is very less as compared to the most advanced countries.

India is fortunate enough to have a varied agro-climatic conditions found throughout the length and breadth of the country which enables to produce both tropical and temperate vegetables. It is known fact that vegetables are important food and production, marketing and processing of vegetables are important source of income and nutritional security. During the last fifty years, there is tremendous increase in vegetable production and therefore, India is the second largest vegetables producer only next to China with an estimated production of about 82 million tons from 6.2 million ha. India contributes sizable share in terms of area and production under principal vegetable crops. This will make available 210 g. per capita per day which is less than the dietary requirement of 300 g per capita per day. Statistics in respect of Area and Production under principal vegetable crops in the world and India is given in Table 1.1.

If we see the vegetable production scenario of the country, the state-wise distribution of area under different vegetable crops, the maximum area is in UP (12.6 lakh ha), followed by Tamil Nadu (8.8 lakh ha), Bihar (8.4 lakh ha), West Bengal (4.5 Lakh). UP is the largest state contributing maximum share in country's vegetable production while Bihar and Orissa occupy second and third place respectively. (Pandey & Singh, 1998).

TABLE 1.1: Area (000 ha), Production (000 t), in the world, India and India's Percentage share.

Crop Share	Area (000 ha)		Production (000 t)		India's percentage	
	World	India	World	India	Area (5%)	Production (%)
Cauliflower	698	280	13420	5000	40.11	37.25 (1st)
Pumpkins & gourds	1130	335	13705	3200	29.64	23.35
Brinjal	1128	320	17415	3400	28.36	19.52
Beans	631	148	4357	400	23.45	9.18
Peas	849	148	7272	2150	17.43	29.36 (2nd)
Onion	2291	405	38146	4300	17.67	1127
Tomato	3167	350	88222	5300	11.05	6.00 (5th)
Garlic	1060	100	11795	430	9.361	3.64
Potato	17786	1140	295407	19240	6.41	6.515 (th)
Carrot	637	22	17977	320	3.45	1.78
Cucumber	1560	17	25827	115	1.08	0.44

Source: FAO Year Book, 1997 Ist,2nd and 5th position in the world.

There are variations among different states of the country with regards to productivity of vegetable crops. Karnataka recorded the highest productivity of 23.49/ha in the country, while Punjab ranked second. In India one of the major reasons of low production of vegetable is steep variation in productivity of vegetables among states. Only following states viz., Andhra Pradesh, Gujarat, Karnataka, Kerala,Madhya Pradesh, Meghalaya, Punjab, Tamil Nadu, Uttar Pradesh and Delhi are having productivity more than 10 t/ha. Our country has witnessed 2.6 per cent increase in vegetable production per year in last 10 years (1983-94.), which was at par with the region's growth rate (2.7 percent) and higher than the world growth rate (1.81 percent).

At national level, our country has been divided into 8 zones and area, production, productivity and future estimates are given in Table 1.2.

STATUS OF VEGETABLE PRODUCTION

India grows the largest number of vegetables in the world. Vegetables play a very vital role in the health and nutritional security of the human population of any nation and India is no exception to this statement. Vegetables give higher tonnage per unit area and time than the cereals, besides better food value. India is vast country bestowed with a wide range of agro-climatic conditions thus enabling

TABLE 1.2: Present Area, Production, Productivity and Future estimates for different zones in India

Zone	Area (000ha)	Production (000 t)	Productivity (t/ha)	Estimated area @10% increase	Enhanced estimated productivity (t/ha)	Production at present area with enhanced estimated productivity (000t)	Production at estimate of increased area and productivity
I	276.1	1838.7	9.087	303.71	16	4417.6	4859.36
II	678.4	6812.3	9.93	746.24	16	10176.0	11939.84
III	110.5	2946.3	6.36	121.55	12	1326.0	1458.6
IV	2185.1	30347.8	12.63	2403.61	20	43702.0	48072.2
V	1041.7	10950.0	10.73	1145.87	17	17708.9	19479.9
VI	238.3	2852.00	11.29	262.13	17	4051.1	4456.21
VII	243.3	4485.63	13.33	267.33	19	4617.57	5079.27
VIII	1445.03	10781.8	8.08	15.89.54	15	23120.48	23843.10
Total	6218.16	71014.53	10.18	6839.98	16.5	109119.7	119188.37

Source: Silver Jubilee National Symposium, December 12-14,1998, Varanasi U.P., India.

to grow fresh vegetables in one part or the other. The entire country can broadly be divided into temperate, sub-tropical and tropical regions for growing various crops but efforts have been made by the author (Singh, 1986) for the first time to delineate six agro-climatic zones for vegetable growing as shown in Fig. 2

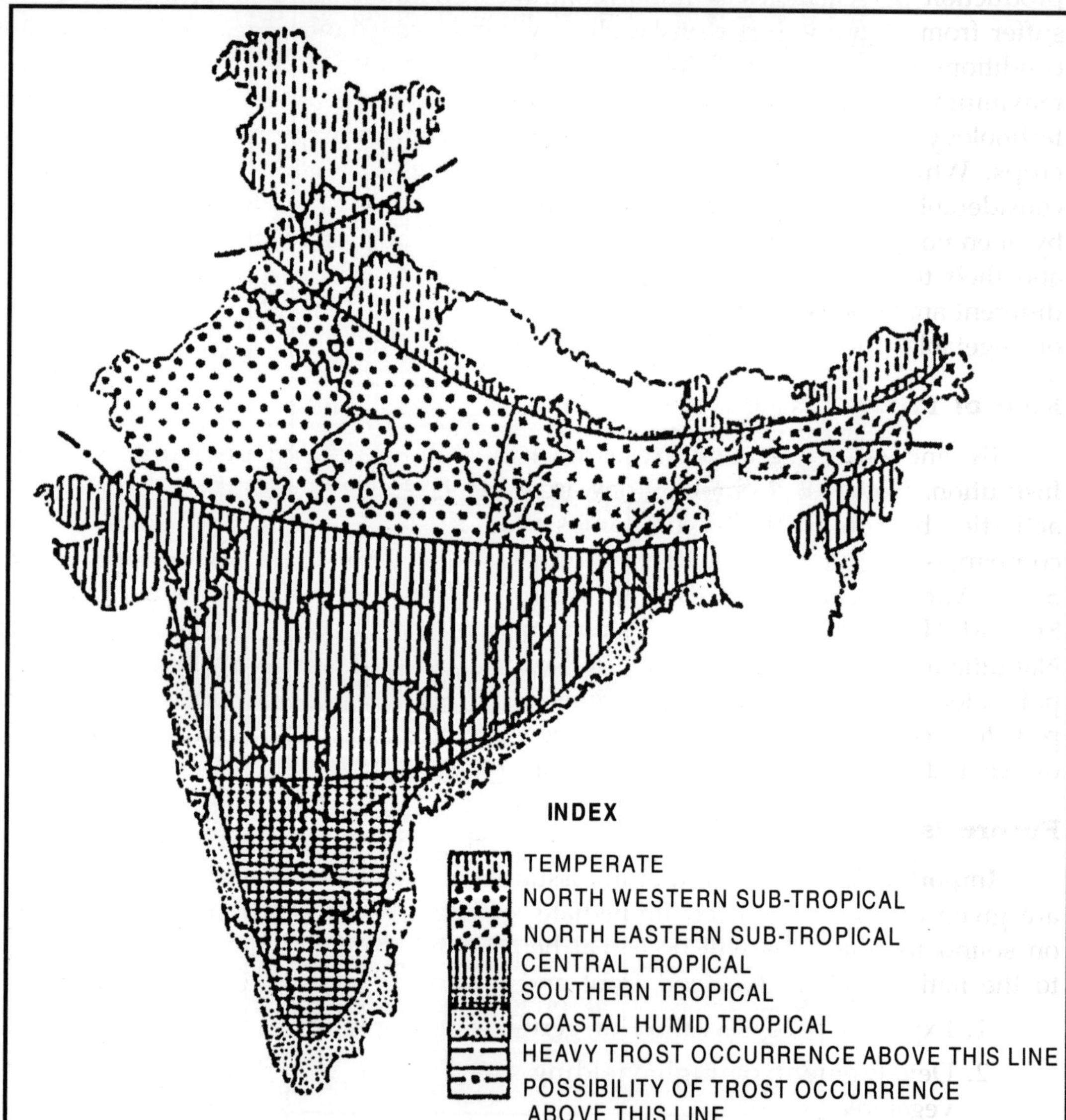

Fig. 1.1 Vegetable growing zones in India

Reasons of low productivity in India

Although India is second largest vegetable producing country in the world, productivity of different vegetables is comparatively low as compared to other developed countries. The average productivity of tomato in our country is merely

157.10 q/ha, while its productivity in USA is 587.62 q/ha, in Greece 498.6 q/ha, in Italy 465.55 q/ha and Spain 466.29 q/ha. The poor productivity of different vegetables in our country is due to several reasons. In developed countries, maximum production of vegetables is under controlled conditions and production does not suffer from severe weather onslaughts, while in our country area under controlled conditions till date is negligible. Similarly in developed countries hybrids occupy maximum area up to 95-100 per cent and advanced production and protection technology have been standardized to realise the maximum productivity in vegetable crops. While in our country area under hybrids vegetable has increased very considerably in last few years, however, maximum share in production is contributed by open pollinated varieties with the application of farmers own package of practices and their traditional vision. In recent past, concerted efforts have been made from different angles to boost the vegetable production pf the country. These new aspects of vegetable production are discussed under following heads.

Role of Private Organisations

By and large, vegetable research has been carried out in India by Public Institution. However, from 1969 onwards, there has been an effort to start R & D activities by some private companies with foreign collaboration. Some private companies conducting research include M/s Mahyco, Jama, Maharashtra; Nath Seed, Aurangabad, Maharashtra;, Sutton & Sons, Calcutta, West Bangal; Bejo Sheetal Hybrid Seeds, Jalna, Maharashtra; Biogene, Bangalore, Karnataka; Namdhani Seeds Pvt.Ltd., Bangalore; Novartis India Ltd.,Pune. A number of open-pollinated varieties and hybrids in vegetable crops have been developed by different private seed companies, which have performed well under multi location testing of All India Coordinated Vegetable Improvement Project.

Future Issues and Strategies

Important Issues: The important issues of vegetable/seed production in country are given below which need immediate solutions to bring the vegetable industry on sound footing. This will be a real help to the farming community and service to the nation both in the food front and nutritional security of the masses.

1. Exploration conservation of germplasm of vegetable crops.
2. Development of high yielding and quality varieties and hybrids of-vegetables.
3. Development of varieties resistant to disease and pests.
4. Development of multiple disease and pest resistant hybrids in vegetables.
5. Management of environmental stress conditions for growing of vegetable
6. Growing of vegetables under protected conditions.
7. Integrated nutrient management programme for growing of vegetables.
8. Development of production technology of vegetables.

9. Development of technology on organic farming.
10. Survey and surveillance of diseases and pests.
11. Development of integrated pest and disease management programme in vegetable.
12. Seed technology research.
13. Post-harvest losses in vegetable crops.

Strategies

1. In collaboration with NBPGR, survey, exploration, cataloguing, use, maintenance, and conservation of germplasm to be taken up with special emphasis on the exploration of germplasm of minor vegetables from the tribal belts in the country.
2. Generating breeding material and selection of lines and varieties having high yield and quality attributes.
3. Identification of sources of resistance to major diseases and pests and transfer of genes for resistance diseases and pests. Biotechnology approaches to be considered to develop such biotic stress resistance.
4. Hybrids resistant to multiple diseases and pests to be developed in tomato, brinjal, chilli, okra, melons and cucurbit, etc.
5. Development of varieties resistant to salinity alkalinity, high temperature, low temperature, excessive moisture and development of production technology for growing of vegetables under such conditions.
6. Identification of varieties suited to controlled conditions and development of computer programme for growing vegetables under controlled conditions.
7. Development of integrated technology for the use of biofertilizers along with other chemical fertilizers.
8. Generating information on the cropping system, weed management, use of growth regulators, drip irrigation system, sprinkler system, etc. on newly developed open-pollinated varieties.
9. Generating information on the organic farming and vegetable production without using any chemical on major vegetable crops.
10. Major diseases and pests to be surveyed in order to understand appearance and effective management. It will also facilitate to develop various predictive models.
11. Identification of biocontrol agents for the control of major pests and diseases, creation of facilities for large scale multiplication of bioagents and development of complete package for major diseases and pests.
12. Various aspects of quality of vegetable seeds to be undertaken and the research work on seed viability, seed packaging material, seed storage, etc. to be emphasized. Isozyme studies for all the varieties to be done.
13. The actual losses of post-harvest to be assessed and accordingly strategy for reducing the losses to be framed.

Tips for Realization of Maximum Productivity

1. Obtain high yielding varieties/hybrids from reliable source.
2. Treat the seeds with effective fungicides if they are not treated before sowing and storage.
3. Raise seedlings in polyhouse/greenhouse/shade/net houses or thatch-houses.
4. Sow the seeds in treated/sterilized growing medium @ 500,600 seeds per sq. metre.
5. Apply plant protection measures as per need of the vegetable/crop to control insect-pests and diseases in the nursery both in the open or controlled conditions viz. poly/green-houses.
6. Irrigate the nursery by watering cane attached with nozzle.
7. Prepare the field by chiseler for easy penetration of roots to a greater depth.
8. Transplants/seedlings at right age in rows either in flat beds or raised beds as per situation.
9. Always apply balanced doses of organic and inorganic manures and fertilizers.
10. Apply light irrigation after transplanting by means of drip system or watering cane.
11. Irrigation of the crops as per need and avoid heavy flooding.
12. Train the crops as per requirement through suitable devices.
13. Pinch the early flowers and fruit for proper growth of the plants.
14. Spray insecticides and fungicides as per need at right time.
15. Use micro-nutrients if there is deficiency.
16. Use plant growth regulators as per need of the vegetable crop to get early and high yield.
17. Harvest the fruits at ideal horticultural maturity stage and are frequent intervals to boost the yield.

Conclusion

Thus, it can be summarized that the vegetable research in India remained almost neglected in the first half of the century and gained momentum thereafter to acquire the present status having moderate infrastructure facilities and research priorities for vegetables in different institutions. Still there is a wide gap between production and availability of vegetables in our country. The strategies and suggestions given may serve as guidelines for our endeavors to bridge this gap (Chadha,1998).

●●●

CHAPTER 2

VEGETABLE GROWING IN ANDHRA PRADESH

Prabhakar Reddy

1.	Name of the State	:	Andhra Pradesh
2.	Total geographical area (ha)	:	2,74,40,000
3.	Area under cultivation (ha)	:	1,30,43,000
	(a) Net cropped area	:	1,06,37,000 ha
	(b) Area Cropped more than once	:	24,06,000 ha
4.	Irrigated area (ha)	:	53,04,000 ha
	Net irrigated area	:	41,23,000 ha
	Area irrigated more than once	:	11,81,000 ha
5.	Area under vegetables (ha)	:	4,54,030
	Production	:	32,50,8841
	Productivity	:	7.16 t/ha
	Anticipated in 2000 AD: Area	:	817250 ha
	Production		8172500 t
	Productivity		10.00 t/ha
6.	Area under each vegetable	:	As given in Table 2.1

TABLE 2.1: Area under different vegetables in the state of Andhra Pradesh

S.No.	Vegetable	Area in (ha)	Production (t)
01.	Tomato	52793	52730
02.	Brinjal	20175	403500
03.	Bhindi	21569	172552
04.	Cucumber	5451	51765
05.	Gourds	7792	77920
06.	Bottle gourd	276	4140
07.	Beans	8319	50346
08.	Peas	119	1190
09.	Cabbage	1640	41000
10.	Onion	27165	679125
11.	Garlic	672	3696
12.	Greens	5810	34860
13.	Chillies	262174	524348
14.	Sweet potato	2174	43480
15.	Tapioca	22033	440660
16.	Potato	1450	23200

7. Major constraints

TABLE 2.2: Production Constrains in Vegetable Crops

S. No.	Crop	Biotic factors		Abiotic factors
		Pests	Diseases	
1.	Tomato	1. Fruit borer 2. White fly 3. Root knot nematode	1. Damping off 2. Fusarium wilt 3. Leaf curl virus 4. Tomato spotted wilt virus	1. High temperature low fruit during summer 2. Susceptibility to salt 3. Susceptibility to drought 4. Susceptibility to herbicides
2.	Brinjal	1. Shoot & fruit borer 2. Jassids 3. Mites	1. Little leaf 2. Bacterial wilt	1. High temperature & low fruit set
3.	Chillies	1. Thrips 2. Mites 3. Pod borer 4. Aphids	1. Anthracnose. 2. Fruit rot 3. Die back 4. Powdery mildew 5. Cercospora leaf spot 6. Bacterial leaf spot 7. Chilli mosaic	1. Poor adaptation 2. Lack of improved varieties

S. No.	Crop	Biotic factors		Abiotic factors
		Pests	Diseases	
4.	Capsicum (Bell pepper)	1. Thrips 2. Fruit borer 3. Aphids 4. Mites 5. Nematodes	1. Fruit rots 2. Leaf spots 3. Wilt 4. Powdery mildew viruses 5. Mosaic viruses	1. low adaptability 2. salt susceptibility 3. low tolerance to high temperatures.
5.	Okra	1. Shoot & fruit borer 2. whitefly 3. Jassids 4. Root knot nematode	1. Fusarium 2. Powdery mildew 3. YVMV	1. Lack of varieties suitable for export market. 2. lack of processing industry
6.	Cabbage	1. Diamond back moth 2. Spodoptera	1. Black rot 2. Blight	1. Lack of varieties & hybrids which require mild winter. 2. Lack of varieties which could stay longer in field after head formation.
7.	Cauliflower	-do-	1. Black rot 2. Downy mildew 3. Alternaria blight	1. Lack of varieties & hybrids which require mild winter. 2. Lack of self in compatible and cross compatible lines.
8.	Garden bean	1. Pod borer 2. Pulse beetle 3. Leaf miner	1. Mosaic virus 2. Powdery Mildew 3. Fusarium wilt 4. Wilt 5. Bacterial leaf spot	1. Lack of Photo-insensitive bushy varieties.
9.	Cowpea	–	Bacterial leaf blight	1. Lack of bushy varieties.
10.	French bean	1. Pod borer 2. Stemfly thrips	1. Powdery mildew 2. Anthnacnose 3. Angular leaf spot 4. Beans rust.	
11.	Onion	Onion thrips	1. Purple blotch 2. Basal rot 3. Stemphyllium blight	1. Lack of varieties for export market 2. Lack of varieties for moisture stress.

S. No.	Crop	Biotic factors		Abiotic factors
		Pests	Diseases	
				3. Lack of varieties for dehydration industry 4. Lack of white colour bulbs with high dry matter.
12.	Cucurbits	1. Pumpkin 2. Fruitfly 3. Aphids	1. Powdery mildew 2. Downy mildew 3. Viruses	1. Lack of F_1 hybrids.
13.	Leafy vegetables	1. Spodoptera	1. Leaf curl 2. Mosaic viruses 3. Cercospora & Alternaria leaf spots	1. Lack of high yielding, quality and diseases resistant varieties 2. Lack of photo-intensity and late bolting types

8. Topographic regions and potential pockets for commercial production by depicting in the map of the state : Fig. 2 (*i* & *ii*)
9. Important vegetables and vegetable seed production areas : Given in Table 2.3 & 2.4

TABLE 2.3: Identified leading areas of major vegetables in the State of A.P.

S.No.	Crop	Districts Identified
1.	Tomato	Kurnool, Chittor, Ranga Reddy, Mahaboobnagar, Prakasam.
2.	Brinjal	East Godavari, Visakhapatnam, Guntur, Ranga Reddy Chittor.
3.	Okra	Guntur, Kurnool, Ranga Reddy, Prakasam, East Godavari.
4.	Onion	Cuddapah, Kurnool, Medak Mahboob Nagar, Nizamabad.
5.	Potato	Chittor, Medak vizag, Cuddapah, Ranga Reddy.
6.	Chillies	Guntur, Warangal, Prakasam, Khammam, Karimnagar.
7.	Gourds	Guntur, East Godavari, Rangareddy, Krishan, W.Godavari.
8.	Tamarind	Chittor, Anantpur, East Godavari vizag, Mahabobngar.

TABLE 2.4: Important Vegetable Seed Production Areas in the State

1.	Tomato	–	Kurnool, Ranga Reddy, Mahaboobnagar
2.	Brinjal	–	Ranga Reddy.
3.	Okra	–	Kurnool, Ranga Reddy.
4.	Chillies	–	Warangal, Khammam, Karimnagar
5.	Onion	–	Medak, Mahaboobnagar, Nizamabad.
6.	Cucumber & gourds	–	Guntur, East Godavari, Krishna.
7.	Watermelon	–	Guntur, East Godavari, Krishna, Cuddapah

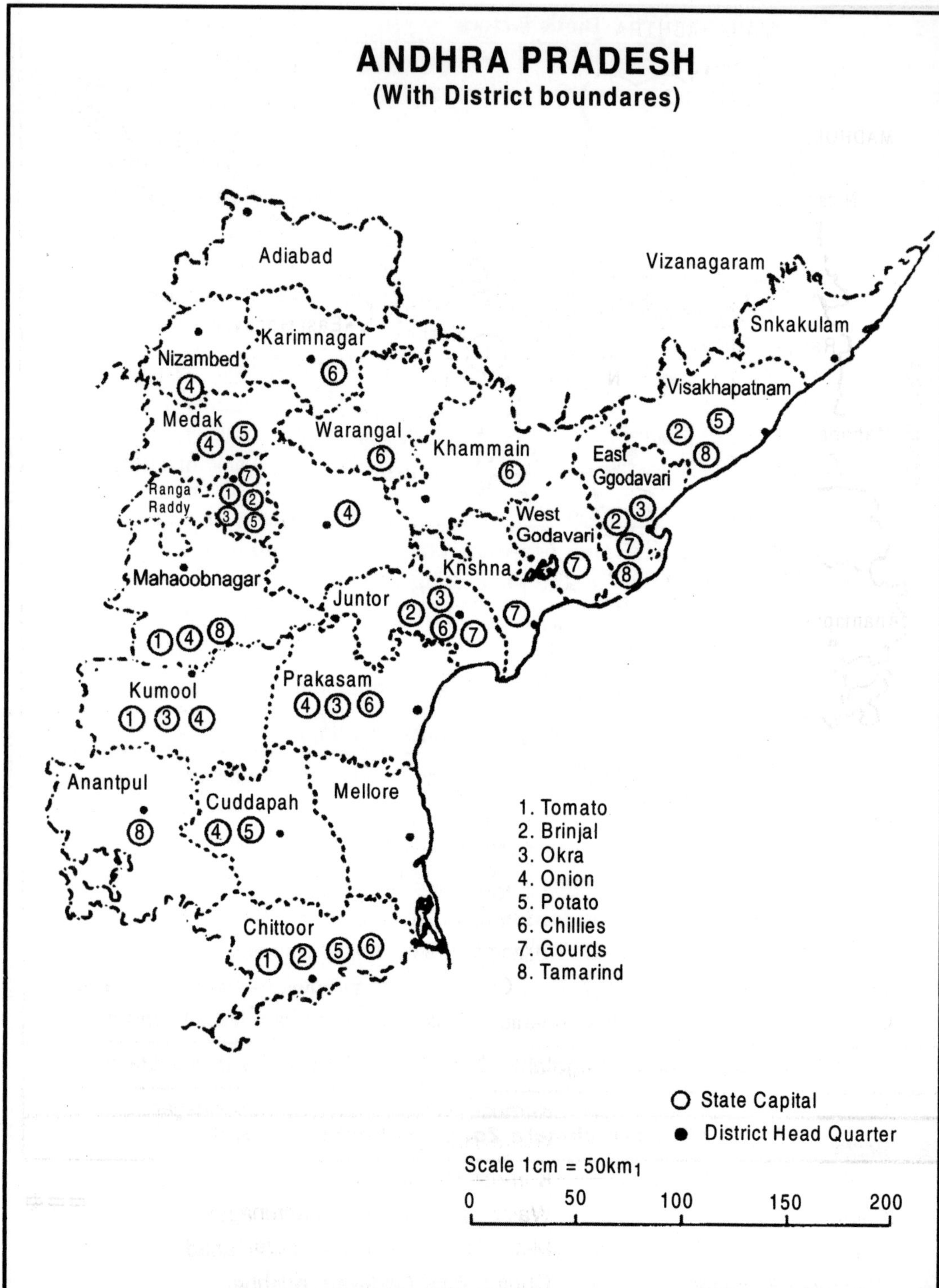

Fig. 2. (i) Identified Leading Areas of Major Vegetables in A.P.

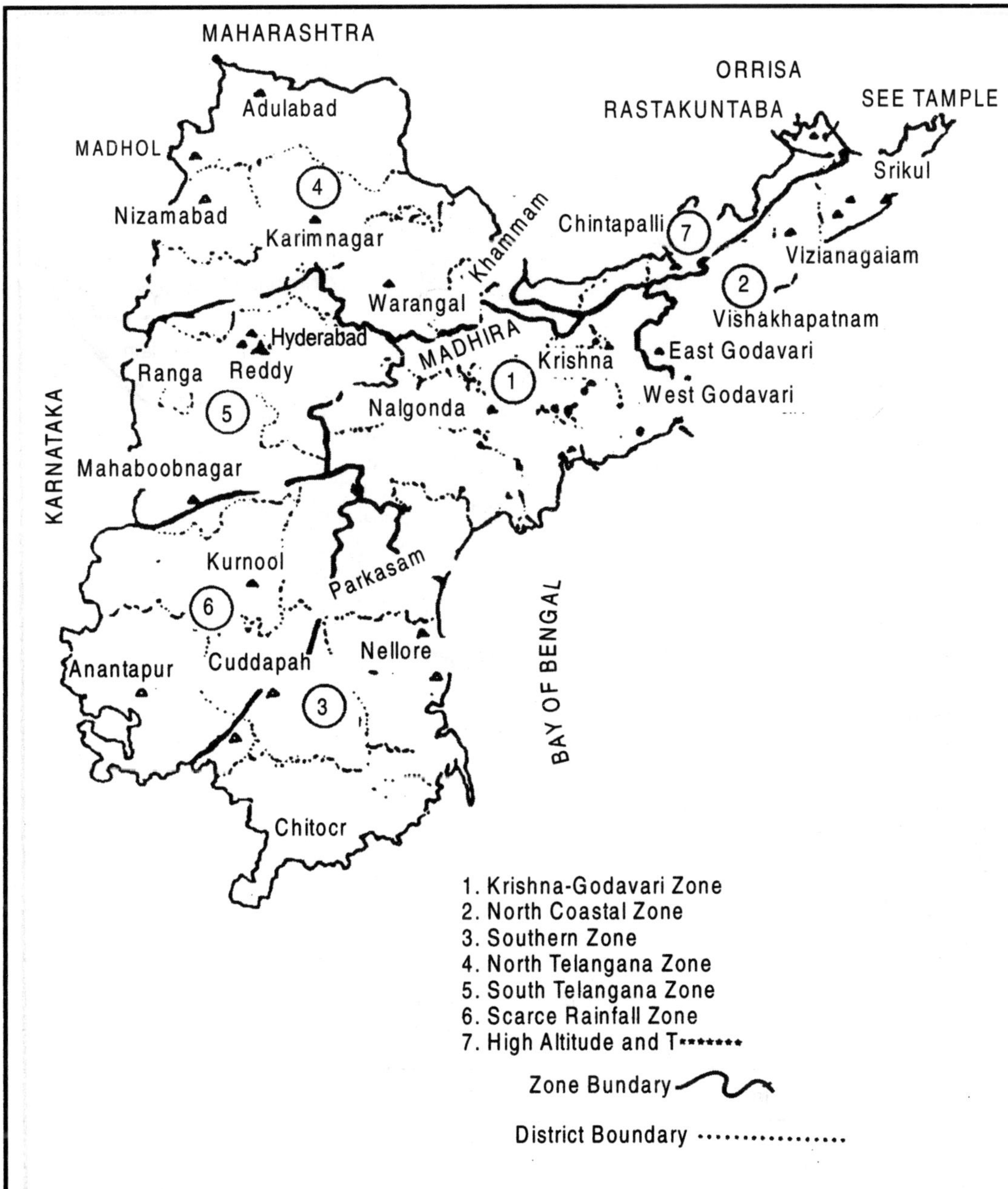

Fig. 2 (ii) Agro-climate Zones of Andhra Pradesh.

CHAPTER 3

ANDAMAN AND NICOBAR ISLANDS

The total area of this union territory is 8,249 square kilometer and Port Blair is the capital. It is situated in Bay of Bengal and comprises of a number (about 200) of small islands. No island is more than 32 km wide. There are hills and valley areas covered with forests. The climate is warm-humid and normal to heavy rains are received throughout the year. There are only two districts viz. Andaman and Nicobar. Agriculture is the main occupation of the people. The main crops grown are rice, rubber, coconut, kahava, chillies, arecanut, annanise, mango, papaya and timber.

TABLE 3.1: Area (ha) and production (t) under vegetables in Andaman & Nicobar

Vegetable	Area (ha)	Production (t)
Assorted Vegetables	2,700	16,200
Total	2,700	16,200

Source : Andaman & Nicobar Administration, Department of Agriculture.

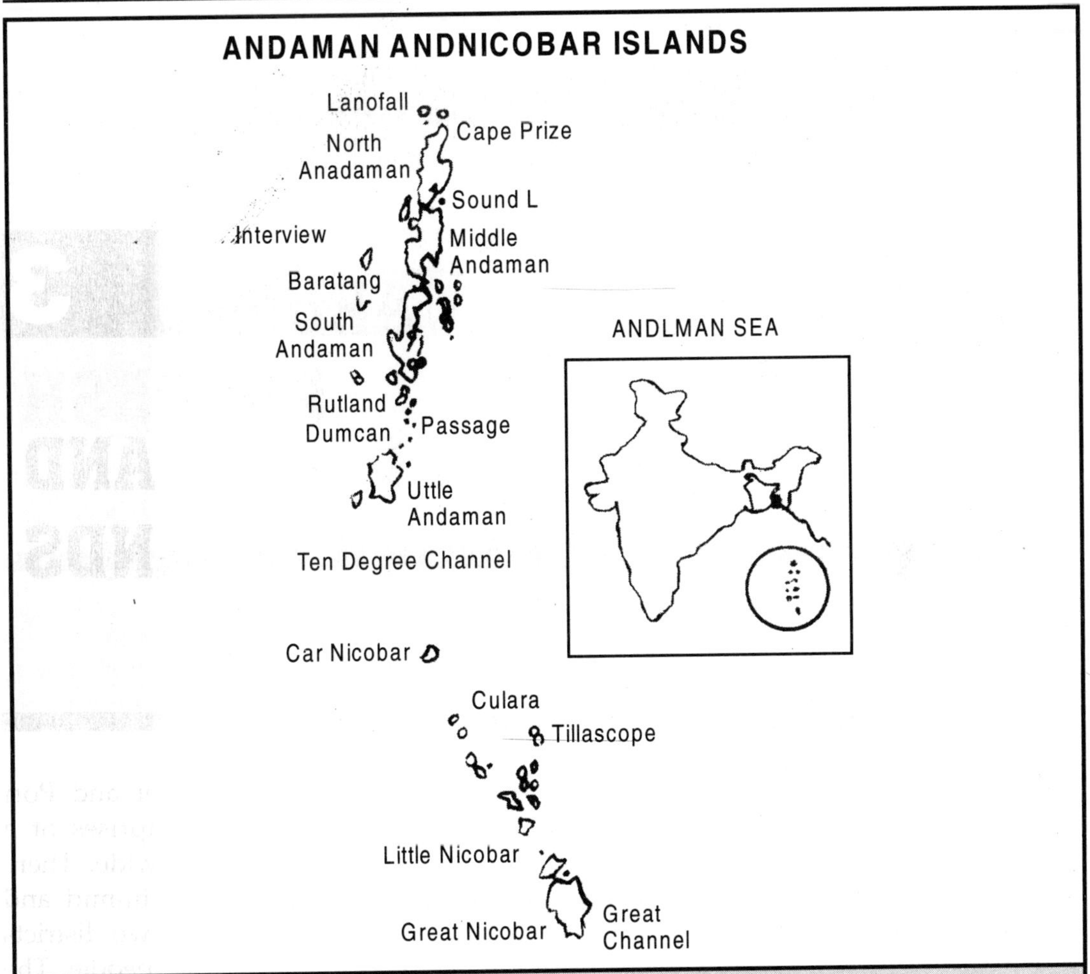

Fig. 3. Location map of Andaman and Nicobar Islands

●●●

CHAPTER 4

ARUNACHAL PRADESH

The total area of the state is 83,743 sq. km. It is the largest state in the north-east foot hills of the Himalayas Itanagar is the state capital. It has been identified as Mayapur, the 14th century historic city of the Jitri dynasty. In 1954 the area became known as the north-east frontier agency.

Geography

The state is stretching from the snow-capped eastern Himalayas, at an altitude of 6000 metres, to the plains of the Brahamputra valley. Arunachal Pradesh lies at the country's north-eastern tip, surrounded by Bhutan China, and Burma. Assam lies to its south.

Rivers

Kamang, Subansiri, Siany (later Brahamputra in Assam), Lohit and Tirap.

Climate

Varies according to altitude, in upper regions, winters are cold and humid, summers are short.

Rainfall

400 cm annually.

Forest cover two-third of the state and are abundant in orchid species some of which are among the world's rarest. Arunachal Pradesh is one of our greenest states with a large part of it covered with forests and have only forest based businesses like timber yards and saw mills, no large manufacturing industry. Nearly 80 per cent of the population is engaged in agriculture. The main crops are rice, maize, millet, pulses and vegetables.

TABLE 4.1: Area (ha) and Production (t) of vegetables in Arunachal Pradesh

	Crop	Area (ha)	Production (t)
1.	Brinjal	110	420
2.	Cabbage	230	1,910
3.	Carrot	40	210
4.	Cauliflower	90	450
5.	Cucumber	130	510
6.	Okra	80	280
7.	Other beans	25,000	63,000
8.	Other vegetables	410	1,650
9.	Radish	130	650
10.	Tomato	802	80
	Total	26,300	69,360

Source : Ministry of Agriculture, Govt. of India.

Fig. 4(i) : Location map of Arunachal Pradesh.

●●●

CHAPTER 5

ASSAM

Assam is the largest and most populated state of the north-eastern states. It derives its name from the Sanskrit world 'asoma' meaning peerless.

Area : Approximately 78,438 sq. km.

Location : Assam is situated south of Arunachal Pradesh. It has international boundaries with Bhutan and Bangladesh. It is geographically divided into two important physical regions. The Barak Valley and the Brahmaputra valley.

Capital : Dispur.

Rivers : The 2900 km long Brahamputra and its 120 tributaries.

Annual Rain Fall: Ranges between 180-305 cm, one of the highest in the world.

TABLE 5.1: Area (ha) and production (t) of vegetables

	Crop	Area (ha)	Production (tonnes)
1.	Ash Gourd	2,197	7,826
2.	Bitter Gourd	3,255	5,798
3.	Bottle Gourd	3,292	11,726
4.	Brinjal	7,789	40,250
5.	Cabbage	125	40,092
6.	Carrot	3,598	4,578
7.	Cauliflower	11,176	34,749
8.	Cow pea	3,912	2,787
9.	Cucumber	4,839	4,335
10.	French bean	1,868	4,578

	Crop	Area (ha)	Production (tonnes)
11.	Luffa	7,373	10,524
12.	Muskmelon	284	1,014
13.	Okra	7,285	16,723
14.	Other Cole crops	774	15,503
15.	Other Gourds	9,606	13,756
16.	Pumpkin	3,518	6,266
17.	Radish	4,642	17,953
18.	Tomato	15,870	16,351
19.	Watermelon	94	338
	Total	91,479	2,55,151

Source : Deptt. of Horticulture, Assam Agricultural University, Jorhat.

Fig. 5 (i) : Location map of Assam

●●●

CHAPTER 6

VEGETABLE GROWING IN BIHAR

Yadav, L.M. and Yadav, R.C.

Geographically Bihar is situated in the East of Indian Union and extends from 21° 58′10" to 21° 31′15" North Latitude and 83° 19′56" to 88° 17′40" East longitude. Total geographical area of the state is 173.3 lakh ha, out of which only 77.25 lakh ha is put under cultivation. In Bihar, vegetable cultivation is done on an area of 84 lakh ha and holds second largest position in the country only next to Uttar Pradesh. The alluvial plains of Bihar, both on the North and South have an elevation ranging between 30-65 meters above m s l. River Ganges serves as the grand main drainage for most part of the two regions. The state of Bihar enjoys four distinct seasons viz. Summer, rainy, post- monsoon and winter. The summer season is at its peak when the average atmospheric temperature ranges between 38°C and 40°C. The monsoon season extending from June 15th to October 15th receives more than 75 per cent of the total annual rainfall. Average annual rainfall of the state is 1272 mm. The state has vast potential for both surface and underground water but presently net area irrigated from all possible sources is only 30 lakh ha which is only 35% of the net area under cultivation.

In Bihar, Onion, Tomato, Chilli, Brinjal, Bhindi, Cauliflower and Cabbage are grown on commercial scale. Although vegetable cultivation is spread over the entire state, but Patna, Nalanda, Champaran, Vaishali, Durnka, Kabhar, Hazaribagh are the major vegetable growing distts of the state. During the year 1998-99 Distt.-wise hecterage under principle vegetables is given in Table 6.1.

TABLE 6.1: District-wise area under different vegetables

District	Cauli flower	Cab-bage	Onion	To-mato	Chilli	Brin-jal	Bhi-ndi	Clim bing	Others	Total
Patna	3290	1960	2205	2075	2500	1740	2810	1445	3430	21475
Nalanda	2615	1360	1790	1775	3710	8545	2620	1380	3710	27505
Bhojpur	825	450	1016	950	510	945	1400	840	1280	8245
Baksar	365	315	710	660	335	560	925	450	780	5100
Rohtas	1195	450	1150	745	520	950	1385	1233	1390	9010
Bhabhua	635	310	710	535	320	640	785	440	800	5175
Gaya	1640	535	1165	860	1335	1510	1720	1785	1935	12585
Tahanabad	640	330	545	1135	480	830	725	405	660	5750
Nawada	1290	675	910	710	850	1190	2225	1050	1415	10315
Aurangabad	1320	650	1010	2585	655	1210	1880	1045	1610	11965
Saran	1870	560	785	1535	1040	1725	2025	1645	1955	13075
Shiwan	1490	900	725	1410	1060	1500	1900	1365	1745	12095
Gopaljang	1760	940	715	1825	945	1305	1780	1270	1595	12135
E.Champaran	1750	1440	2200	1630	1030	1595	2135	2920	2950	17650
W.Champaran	2610	1660	1950	1875	1355	1865	2075	2975	3185	19550
Muzzafarpur	3460	3470	2295	3440	1705	2680	2605	3670	4700	27130
Sita Marhi	1970	1315	1830	2260	1050	1790	1940	2690	2640	17435
Vaishali	4420	2065	1315	3380	1570	2945	3350	4710	4875	28580
Bhagalpur	1220	990	13300	1335	695	1440	1925	2585	2060	13580
Banka	690	540	665	635	435	755	760	1060	835	6475
Munger	585	515	1230	475	1005	845	1215	1555	845	8270
Jamaui	590	285	525	275	775	470	620	765	1040	5345
Khagaria	765	640	785	1075	925	1460	1730	1550	1210	10140
Dumka	4265	960	1045	1420	825	1475	1775	2305	1510	15610
Devghar	775	325	360	600	375	1015	515	385	3855	8215
Godda	800	330	370	545	355	4304	2035	353	410	4013
Shabganj	740	410	470	570	353	330	445	415	410	4143
Darbhanga	3953	1570	950	1385	1480	2310	1915	4885	2415	20863
Madhubani	2485	1445	890	1130	1895	1950	1775	2540	2380	16595
Samastipur	2660	1560	900	1295	950	1950	1695	2460	2740	16220
Begusarai	1585	900	1845	1935	945	2560	2505	2020	2170	17365
Purnea	1750	915	1590	775	1285	930	970	3350	3465	15030
Araria	745	465	1390	685	410	450	715	1400	1065	7325
Kishanganj	790	475	1275	695	490	455	710	1405	1060	7355
Katihara	2595	1695	3890	1285	1745	1615	1670	5715	4460	24670
Sahrasa	1480	700	380	250	485	1175	1095	4075	1340	10985
Madhepura	1520	1520	790	1275	610	1475	1075	5290	2155	15710

District	Cauli flower	Cab- bage	Onion	To- mato	Chilli	Brin- jal	Bhi- ndi	Clim bing	Others	Total
Supaul	500	325	185	460	255	485	705	1035	6551	4605
Ranchi	2210	1900	2090	1765	1840	2690	3565	1680	2255	10545
Gumla	620	410	445	415	500	600	645	580	575	4790
Lohardagga	540	410	445	495	505	920	420	350	353	4620
Palam	570	445	350	795	890	1220	1675	840	1015	8085
Garhwa	360	220	230	430	465	445	800	445	540	3995
E.Singh bhom	715	550	795	1335	790	1250	2365	2185	2015	12040
W.Singh bhoom	600	580	600	835	595	1000	1225	1305	1095	8735
Chatra	430	300	385	520	380	465	625	660	850	4515
Hazaribag	1540	1075	800	1320	785	1400	1690	1830	2050	12540
Giridih	1120	780	845	1750	290	1635	2205	1450	2280	12405
Boikaro	415	340	305	530	330	755	800	710	755	5080
Dhansad	1560	725	853	1215	910	1145	1890	1050	1940	1290
	74780	42635	52395	59395	46435	70185	77425	90375	88015	161640

Based on rainfall, soil type, physiographic features, the state of Bihar is divided into six agro-climatic zones. Figure 1 delineates zonal boundaries in the state

(*i*) North West Alluvial Plains

(*ii*) North East Alluvial Plains

(*iii*) South Bihar Alluvial Plains

(*iv*) Central and North Eastern Plateau

(*v*) Western Plateau

(*vi*) South Eastern Plateau

Zone-wise climatic description, potential areas of vegetable growing, cash crops grown in given hereunder:

(i) North West Alluvial Plains

This zone comprises of 12 districts viz., West Champaran, East Champaran, Gopal Ganj, Siwai, Saran, Sitamarhi, Muzzaffarpur, Vaishali, Madhubani, Darbhanga, Shamastipur and part of Begusarai. The climate is tropical humid to sub-humid monsoon type in Southern portion which changes to sub-tropical humid in the north. Sweet potato, Turmeric, Mangraila and Coriander are important vegetables of this zone. This zone is not important for commercial vegetable growing.

(ii) North East Alluvial Plains

This zone comprises of 6 districts viz., Purna, Katihar, Madepura, Saharsa, Khagaria and part of Bhagalpur district. This zone is also called as Kosi region of Bihar. There is big potential for vegetable and spices in this zones. Agro-climatic conditions are very conductive for growing different types of vegetables.

The Kosi region contributes about a little below 25% to both the state's vegetable area and production. The areas under vegetables within zone are not uniformly distributed but show uneven spread in different districts of the zone. The area under vegetables in different districts are presented in the Table 6.2.

TABLE 6.2: Area under vegetables in different districts and percentage share

Districts	Area (ha)	Percentage of the zone
Saharsa	6141	20.00
Madhepura	3147	10.20
Purnea	14618	47.60
Katihar	4506	14.70
Khagoria	1361	4.50
Naugachhia (Sub. Div.)	917	3.00
	30690	

Only 1.85% of the GCA of the zone is covered by the vegetables (including spices) out of the vegetable area major portion lies in Purnea district (47.6%) and the lowest in Naugachhia sub- division (3.0%) and Khagan district (4.5%). Vegetables and spices growing area in the zone are given in Table 6.3.

TABLE 6.3: Important vegetables and spices growing area in the zone

Locality	District	Crops grown
Farbisganj	Purnea	Ginger, turmeric and gourds
Khagaria	Khagaria	Chillies, bitter gourds, peas, brinjal and tomato
Diara area of the district	Purnea & Saharsa	Parwal, cucumber, melons, gourds, tomato, etc.

So far as spices are concerned, the area is less than 1% of the zone's GCA is covered by them. However, their spread in the zone is fairly high (19.5%) when compared to that in the state. The zone's shares in their state's area under spices is given in Table 6.4.

TABLE 6.4: Area and percentage of state's area in zone under different vegetables

Crops	Area (ha)		Percentage of state's area in zone
	Zone	State	
Ginger	837	1013	82.6
Turmeric	802	4322	30.5
Garlic	744	2708	27.5
Chillies	2177	10874	17.6
Coriander	951	5390	17.6
Onion	2034	14457	14.1
Total	7550	38764	19.5

In the zone, Purnea occupies predominant position in spices acerage (about 60%) and for ginger, turmeric and onion these figures are about 98%, 82% and 84%, respectively. Chillies are extensively grown in Khagaria and coriander's area is almost equally distributed in the district of Purnea, Khagaria and Saharsa (around 30% each).

(iii) South Bihar Alluvial Plains

This zone represents South of river Ganga and spread over seven districts of Bihar, viz., Bhagalpur, Munger, Gaya, Aurangabad, Bhojpur and Rohtas. This is the largest zone in the state. Diara lands in the bank of river Ganga are most suitable for cucurbit cultivation. On higher soils, parwal, bottle gourd, bitter gourd, melons and other cucurbits are extensively grown. Recently, cultivation of tomato as a commercial crop without irrigation has been taken up in the eastern parts of Diara lands.

(iv) Central and North Eastern Plateau zone

This zone represents district Hazaribagh, Giridih, Dhanbad and 1/3 of Ranchi. This zone is characterised by humid to sub-humid tropical monsoon type of climate. In this zone, only 8.2 per cent of the gross cropped area is irrigated. Tanks and large diameter wells are the major source of irrigation. Scope of commercial vegetable growing are limited in this zone.

(v) Western Plateau zone

This zone comprises whole of Palamau, Gumla, Lohardega, Chatra, Hilly Southern part of Gaya, Aurangabad and Rohtas districts. The climate of this zone is sub-humid to sub- tropical with an average annual rainfall of 1324 mm of which 92% is received during April-October. Area under different vegetable crops is given in Table 6.5

TABLE 6.5: Area under different vegetable crops

S.No.	Crop	Area (ha)
1.	Potato	6000
2.	Sweet potato	4108
3.	Onion	839
4.	Garlic	270
5.	Tomato	1290
6.	Brinjal	1370
7.	Bhindi	880

(vi) South Eastern Plateau zone

This zone consists of East and West Singhbhoom district. This zone has a typical humid tropical monsoon type of climate. This zone is characterised by having highest rainfall of 123 mm during summer season. Paddy is the dominant crop which occupies 89% of the cropped area. Vegetables like potatoes, onion and other winter vegetable are grown in paddy based cropping system.

Varietal status, sowing times and major pests of vegetables

Two state Agricultural Universities namely Rajendra Agricultural University and Birsa Agricultural University have initiated several vegetable improvement programmes to boost vegetable production in the state. Comprehensive information regarding varietal recommendations, suitable sowing times and major diseases and pests has been given in Table 6.6.

TABLE 6.6: Varietal status, sowing time and disease and pests of vegetables

Crop	Varieties	Sowing Time	Insect-Disease
Potato	Early-K. Chandermukhi K. Ashoka K. Jyoti Rajendra Aalu-1, Rajendra Aalu-2 K. Sindhuri, K. Lalima	15th Nov.Oct-15	Early & Late blight, Potato virus, Ring disease Tuber moth, Jassids
Brinjal	P.P.L., Mukta,Keshi, Kalyanpur T-3 Rajendra Baigan-1, Rajendra Baigan-2 Pant Rituraj, Arka Shital	Summer-Dec-Jan. T.P. Jan-March	Fruit & shoot borer
Tomato	Pusa Ruby, P.E.D. Marglobe, Sweet 72, HS-101, HS 102, Roma, Hybrid-vaishali Rupali, Rodna Rajani	July-August Early July-Aug., Sept.-Oct. Mid. Sept.-Oct, T.P. Oct.-Nov Summer-Jan.-Feb.	T.M.V., Shoot rot, Damping-off, fruit rot, Fruit borer
Chilli	Sabour Anger, Pusa Jwala, Chanchal, Pant-1, Kalyanpur, Mohini	Feb.-Feb.-March M.C. July-Aug. T.P. Aug-Sept. S.C. Jan.- Feb. T.P. Feb.-March	Thrips, chilli caterpillar
Onion	Pusa Red, Arka Kalyan, N-53, Agri-found Dark Red.	M.C.-Nov.-Dec. T.P. Jan.-Feb. R.C.-July T.P. August	Thrips, onion caterpillar
Pea	Early-Arkal, GC-195, M.C. Bonneville, GC141, Azad Mater	Early-Oct. M.C. Oct.-Nov.	Pod borer, Powdery mildew, leaf blight
Parwal	Nimiya, Rajendra Parwal-1, Rajendra Parwal-2, Swam Rekha, Jhingulla	Upland Sept.-Oct. Low land Oct.-Nov.	Powdery mildew, Red beetle

Crop	Varieties	Sowing Time	Insect-Disease
Cauliflower	Early-Kunwari, Patna Early Katki, Hagipur Mid-Katki, Aghani, Pusa Deepali, P.S.-l, Subhra, Late-Maghi, Snowball-16	Early June-T.P.-July Mid Aug.-T.P. Sept. Oct. Late-Oct. T.P.-Nov.	Black rot, Damping-off Boron Deficiency
Cabbage	Golden Acre, Pride of India, Early drum Head Late-Late Drum Head Hybrid-Pusa Mukta, Quista, Yamuna and Kaberi	Early, Sep. J.P. T.P. Late-Oct-Nov.	Damping-off, Black rot, Mustard saw fly.
Bhindi	Arka Abhay, Arka Anamika, K.S. 312, Parbhani Kranti, Selection-8, Selection-10	S.C. Feb.-March Rainy season June-July	Yellow Vein mosaic virus, powdery mildew
Bottle-gourd	S.C. Pusa Summer Prolific Long, Rajendra Kaddu-b Pusa Naveen, Rainy Season Dholi Safed	S.C. Jan.-March Rainy-July	Red beetles, fruit fly, powdery mildew
Sponge gourd Spinach	Pusa Chikani, Rajendra Nenua-1 Pusa Jyoti, All green, Jobner green, Kalyanpur Smooth	S.C. Jan. -March Rainy-July Sept.-Dec.	Red beetles, Powdery mildew Powdery mildew
Radish	Pusa Rashmi, Pusa Chetaki, Pusa Himani, Pusa Deshi, Japanese Safed	Summer crop-Feb.-May Rainy-July-Aug. Early-Sept Main-crop Oct.-Nov.	
Carrot	Pusa Kesar, Pusa Meghali, Pusa Yamdagni, Nantes, Chanteney	Oct.-Nov.	
Turnip	Golden Ball, Pusa Swarnima, Pusa Kenchan, Pusa Sweti, Pusa Chamdrima, White globe	Mid-Oct. to Jan.	
French bean	Summer-Pusa Komal Pusa Falguni, Pusa Dophali, Selection 2-1, Pusa Rituraj, Rainy season-Pusa Barsati, Selection 2-1, Arka Garima	Summer-Jan.-March Rainy-June-July	

Crop	Varieties	Sowing Time	Insect-Disease
Turmeric	Rajendra Sonia (R.H.-10)	Mid-May to End May	Rhizome rot, Powdery mildew, shoot borer
Ginger	Maran for South Nadia & China for Kachha	Mid-May to End May	Rhizome rot, Powdery mildew, shoot borer
Coriander	Rajendra Swati (R.D. 44) Karan, Pant Dhamia-1	15th Oct to 30th Oct.	
Methi	R.M.-16 Champa & Kasuri	15th Oct to 30th Oct.	Almost free from insects of diseases
Magrinla	Rajendra Shyama	15th Oct to 30th Oct.	Almost free from insects & diseases

Ref. Adhunic Kisan Diary 1998, RAU, Bihar SC - Summer Crop MC -Main season crops. TP — Transplanting

Future strategy to boost vegetable cultivation in Bihar

The following ways and means can go a long way in augmenting the vegetable production in Kosi region. Some of them are monetary (i.e. involving cost) whereas others are non-monetary (non- involving cost).

1. First of all, there is need to create awareness among the people about the importance of vegetables as the "protective food"-in human diet, so that their value is understood not only in commercial but in nutritional terms.
2. As said earlier, utilisation of every possible bit of land for this purpose needs to be done cucurbit for instance, are usually grown near house on thatched roof, usually by low income group of people, during *kharif* season. This area may seem to be insignificant but if the large number of people doing so are taken into account, its contribution towards total production and availability of green vegetables to the low income group of people who otherwise cannot afford to purchase it, may be highly appreciable. The need is to get replaced traditional varieties by improved varieties suited to the local conditions.
3. Kosi region has large area under orchards. The vegetables can be taken in the interspace during early period of orchards establishment.
4. Onion is an important vegetable crop which is grown mainly in *rabi* and spring seasons. But as the experience in other places has shown, the *kharif* onion can be taken in uplands of the region. Likewise other vegetables like tomato and chillies can be profitably cultivated during "traditionally off-seasons. However, research institutes are to take lead in this direction and evolve suitable varieties and agro-techniques for such off-season crops.

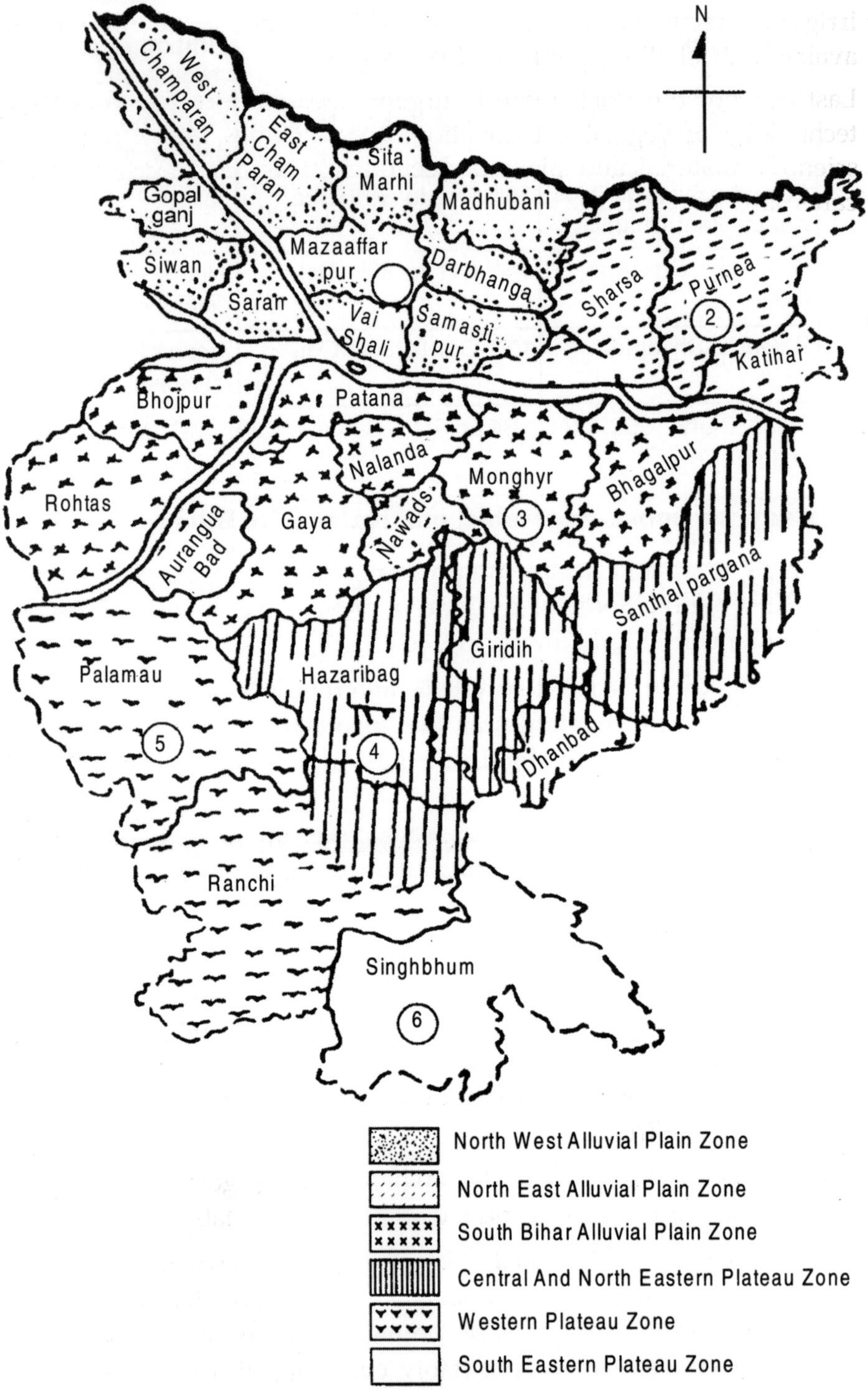

Fig. 6 (i) Agroclimate zones of Bihar

5. Diara lands of main rivers of the state are potential vegetable belts if only irrigation facilities are developed, which is not at all difficult as water available at shallow depth in Kosi region.
6. Last but not the least, there is urgent need for effective transfer of latest technology of vegetable cultivation. This includes use of improved seeds, scientific material and plant protection practices and pre-and post-harvest cares and precautions.

CHAPTER 7

CHANDIGARH

The union territory of Chandigarh is having 114 square kilometre area. It is situated in between the boundaries of Punjab and Haryana states near Ambala. The city is newly established on the modern lines with a excellent landscape at the foot hills of Shiwalik range. Chandigarh is a beautiful city in north India and capital of both Haryana and Punjab states.

TABLE 7.1: Area (ha) and Production (t) of vegetables

Vegetable	Area (ha)	Production (t)
Cabbage	–	700
Cauliflower	–	316
Okra	–	130
Radish	–	230
Tomato	–	450
Brinjal	–	150
Total	–	1970

Source : Chandigarh Administration, Department of Agriculture.

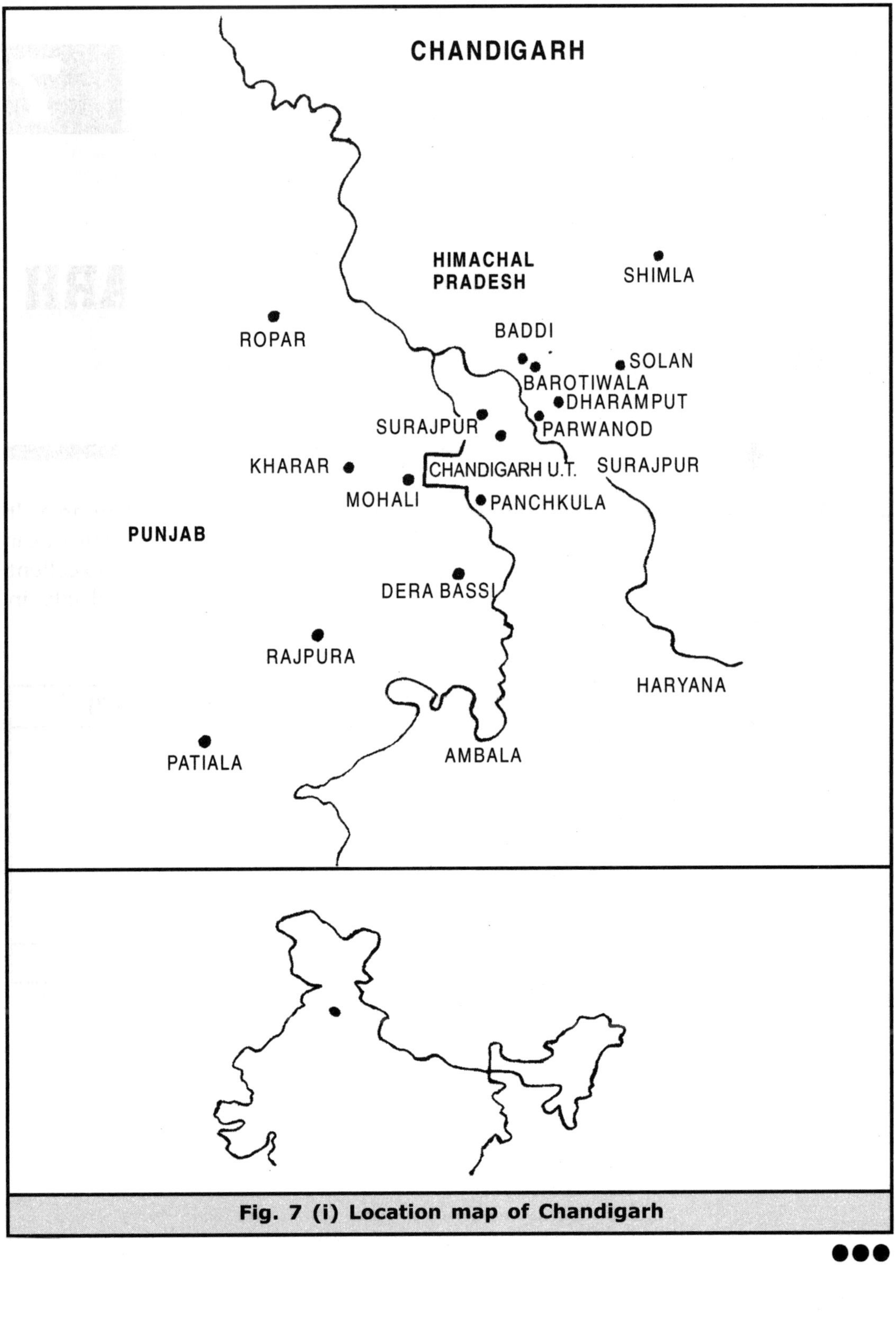

Fig. 7 (i) Location map of Chandigarh

CHAPTER 8

DADRA AND NAGAR HAVELI

The total area of this Island is 491 square kilometer. It is a union territory situated on the south of Gujarat state and northern boundary of Maharashtra, state. Silvassa is the capital of the union territory.

TABLE 8.1: Area (ha) and production (t) of vegetables

Vegetable	Area (ha)	Production (t)
Bottle Gourd	–	20
Brinjal	–	12,500
Cabbage	–	50
Cucumber	–	30
Leafy veg. (Spinach)	–	50
Other beans	–	60
Other vegetables	–	80
Radish	–	120
Turnip	–	400
Okra	–	150
Total	–	13,460

Source : Dadra and Nagar Haveli Administration, Department of Agriculture.

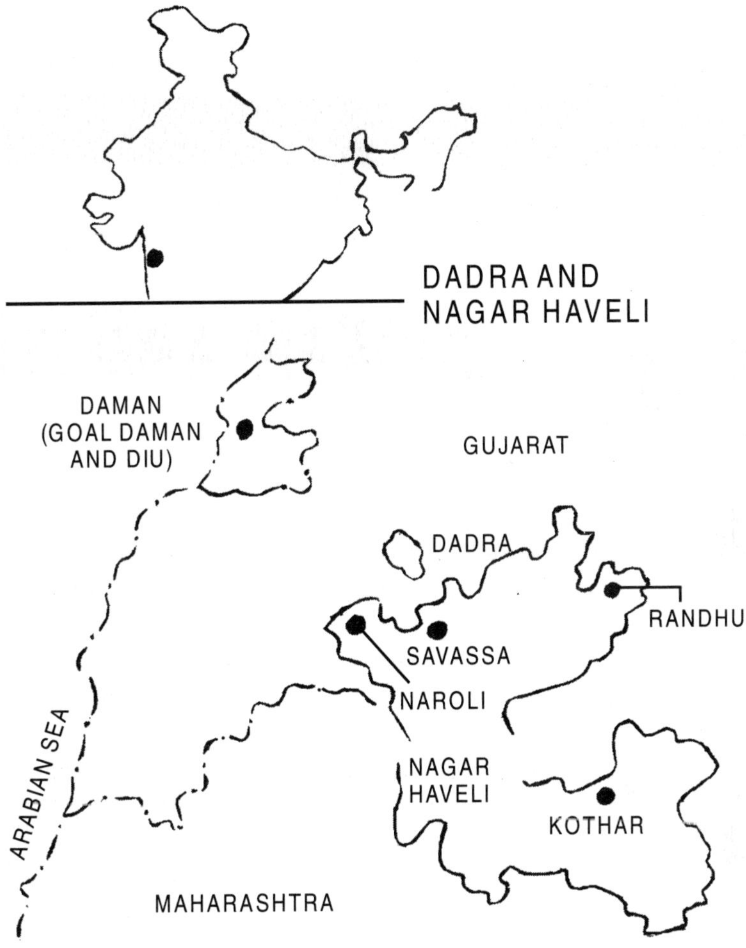

Fig. 8. (i) Location map of Dadra and Nagar Haveli.

CHAPTER 9

DAMAN AND DWEEP

Total area of Daman is 72 square km whereas that of Dweep is 40 square km. It was separated from Goa on 31st May, 1987 and was made an Union Territory. Dweep is a small island close to Saurashtra in the south. Daman is located in the north of Bhagwan river and south of Kalemand in the east and Gujarat state and south Arabian sea.

Fig. 9. (i) Showing location of Daman & Diu islands

CHAPTER 10

DELHI

Delhi is the capital of India located on the bank of river Yamuna in between Haryana and U.P. states. The total area of old and New Delhi is 1483 sq. km However, the length of this region on north-south is 43 km and on east and west the width is 45 km.

The region is divided into four geo-graphical zones.

1. **Khadar zone:** This is comprises of the deltaic river bed area along the Yamuna. The soil is fertile suitable for vegetable cultivation especially during winter.
2. **Bangar zone:** This is located on the North-west part of Delhi and is very fertile. The soils are suitable for vegetable growing on large scale which are supplied to the city.
3. **Dhabar zone:** This comprises of Nafazgarh area and is also low lying zone situated on the South-west Delhi.
4. **Hill zone:** This comprises of South-east Delhi starting from Delhinagar and up to Aravali hills.

Rainfall

The main source of irrigation water is canals from Yamuna river viz. (*i*) West Yamuna canal, (*i*) East Yamuna canal, (*i*) Agra canal which passes through Okhla, (*i*) Hindan canal and Nazafgarh canal (Nallah).

The main crops grown are wheat, maize, sarson, gram, cotton, sugarcane, chillies and all other vegetables because of ease of marketing.

TABLE 10.1: Area (ha) and production (t) under vegetables

Vegetable	Area (ha)	Production (t)
Other vegetables	3,325	2,66,522
Total	3,325	2,66,522

Source : Delhi Administration, Department of Horticulture

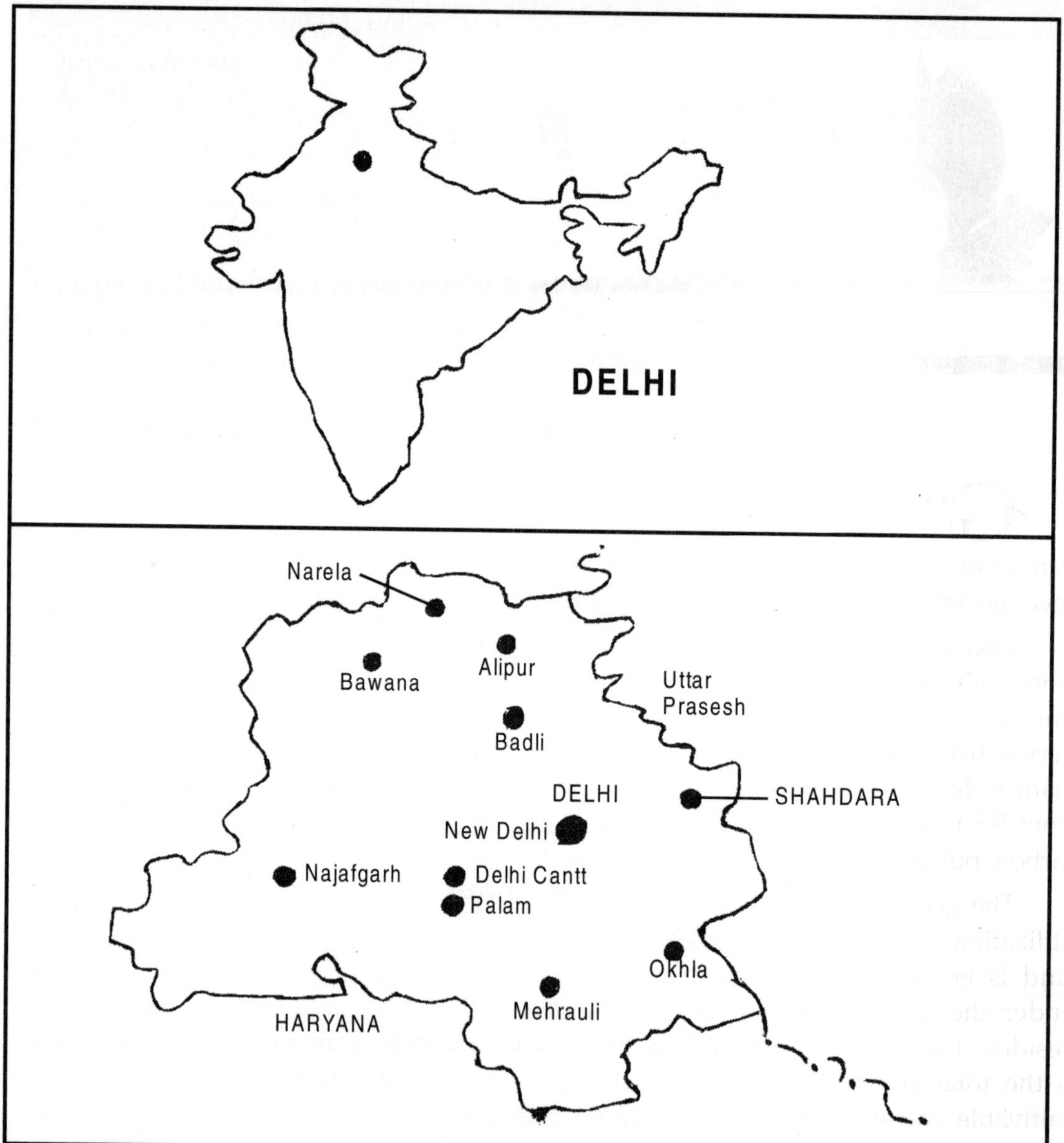

Fig. 10. (i) Location map of Delhi.

CHAPTER 11

STATUS AND PROSPECTUS OF VEGETABLE PRODUCTION IN GOA

D.G. Dhaftdar, V.Y. Gaonkar and S.C. Rana

Goa has two districts — North Goa comprising of Tiswadi,.Bardez, Pernem, Bicholim, Sattari and Ponda talukas; and South Goa which includes Sanguem, Canacona, Quepem, Salcete and Marmugao talukas. There are 402 revenue villages in Goa. In Goa, land elevation ranges from sea level to 1022 m.

Goa experiences warm and humid tropical climate with temperature ranging from 18-35 degree centigrade. Humidity varies from 75% to above 90%. The annual rainfall varies from 2500 to 4000 mm which is mainly received during monsoon period from June to September. The soils are mostly lateritic (81%); whereas sandy loam soils are found in coastal areas. The soils are acidic in nature with ph ranging from 5.5 to 6.5. These soils are deep and porous. Also, soils have moderate organic carbon but are poor in phosphorous and potassium.

The geographical area of Goa is 3701 sq. kms and total reported area for land utilization is 3,61,113 ha. out of this, 1,25,473 ha is under forest cover; 37,137 ha land is not available for cultivation; 1,305 ha is pasture and 580 ha is reported under the miscellaneous tree crops and groves not included in the area sown. Besides, 1,40,935 ha is the net area covered under various crops and 1,69,053 ha is the total cropped area. Significantly, a vast area of 55,683 ha is recorded as cultivable waste land.

The total cropped area in Goa during the year 1997-98 was 1,69,053 ha, of which vegetable crops occupied only 7,550 ha corresponding to 4.46% area. Compared to net cultivated area, the vegetable crops correspond to 5.35% of the land utilization. Cucumber, ridge, gourd, bitter gourd, beans, cowpea, red amaranthus, okra, chilli, brinjal, radish are major vegetables being grown in the state but the local production meets only about 15% demand of the state.

Presently, more than 85% demand of vegetables in the state is met with vegetables supplied from the neighbouring districts of Karnataka and Maharashtra. Among these, Belgaum district alone supply majority of the demands for fresh vegetables. Asparagus, baby corn, Brussels sprout, broccoli, brinjal, bitter gourd, chilli, celery, cucumber, cowpea, cabbage, cauliflower, french bean, cluster bean, amaranthus, tomato, lettuce, knol-kohl, palak, radish, parseley, okra, ridge gourd, water melon etc. can be grown in Konkan region which includes entire Goa state.

Some local varieties of vegetables from Goa have special qualities which otherwise are not found elsewhere in the country. These are chilli, brinjal, red amaranthus, cucumber, ridge gourd, okra etc. which have been observed to have lesser infestation of pests and have special cooking qualities. Local chillis of Goa due to their mild pungency and good colour are much sought after in the European markets. There is need to promote these vegetables by encouraging farmers to grow them on commercial scale. Also, the exotic, salad vegetables have good scope for consumption in hotels. The limiting constraints of marketing these vegetables to fetch remunerative prices if removed will encourage farmers to come forward to grow these exotic as well as local vegetables.

A considerable area of 55,683 ha as cultivable waste land is available in the state. Out of this a major part can be used for cultivation of various vegetable crops either as a sole crop or as a inter crop. Mainly these areas belong to Communidads, Devalayas and Churches. There is a need to motivate these societies to come forward in promoting the vegetable based horticulture development programmes in the state. Goa State Horticultural Corporation Ltd. through farmer's Co-operatives can play an important role in developing these areas on the basis of understanding mutually agreed upon sharing of benefits.

Table 11.1: YEAR-WISE AREA, PRODUCTION AND PRODUCTIVITY OF VEGETABLES IN GOA

S.No.	Year	Area (ha)	Production (t)	Productivity (Kg/ha)
1	1989-90	7250	60,000	8276
2	1990-91	7300	60,000	8219
3	1991-92	7350	60,200	8190
4	1992-93	7400	61,800	8351
5	1993-94	7450	63,300	8497
6	1994-95	7500	65,000	8667
7	1995-96	7500	65,000	8667
8	1996-97	7500	68,000	9067
9	1997-98	7550	69,460	9200

Table 11.2: TALUKA-WISE AREA AND PRODUCTION OF VEGETABLES IN GOA STATE FOR THE YEAR 1997-98

Name of Taluka	Area (ha)	Production (t)
Tiswadi	900	8280
Bardez	2855	26,266
Pernem	810	7452
Bicholim	445	4093
Sattari	90	828
Ponda	500	4600
Sanguem	68	626
Canacona	380	3496
Quepem	80	736
Salcete	1374	12,641
Mormugao	48	442
Total	7550	79460

There are three main seasons of planting vegetables in Goa:

1. **Rainy or kharif season (June-September) :** Cucurbits, beans, okra, brinjal, chilli etc.
2. **Winter or Rabi season (Oct.-Feb) :** Cole crops, root vegetables, onion, amaranthus, beans, chilli, brinjals etc.
3. **Summer season (March to May) :** Cucurbits, bean, okra, chilli, brinjal, amaranthus etc.

The following vegetables are commonly grown in Goa :

Vegetable	Local name	Varieties/Hybrids	Planting time
Bottle Gourd	Konkan Dudhi, keddhu	Local, Pusa Naveen, Pusa Manjari, Pusa Meghdoot, Arka Bahar	June-July
Bitter Gourd	Karathim	Arka Harit, Priya, Pusa Vishesh, Local, Coimbatore Long, Priya, Dapoli-2,	June-July
Snake Gourd	Podolim	CO-1, TA-19, Local, Extra Long	May-July
Ridge Gourd	Ghosalim, Dhodgi	Co-1, Local, Pusa Navbahar, Dapoli-1	June-July
Ash Gourd	Kuwalo	Local, CO-1	June-July
Little Gourd (*Coccinia indica*)	Tendli	Ghodwal local, Alibag Local	June-July
Pumpkin	Bhopla, dudhi	Local, Arka Suryamukhi, Pusa Vishvash, Arka Chandan	June-July

Vegetable	Local name	Varieties/Hybrids	Planting time
Muskmelon	Chibad	Local, Arka Jeet, Arka Rajhans, Hara Madhu, Pusa Madhuras	June-July
Watermelon	Kaling; Kalingad	Sugar Baby, Pusa Bedana. Arka Manik, Ashahi Yamato	Nov.-Jan
Cucumber	Taushim	Local, PoonaKheera, Sh eetal, Japanese Long Green Saharanpur Green Long	June
Cabbage	Cabbage, Cobi	Pusa Drum Head, Golden Acre, Pride of India, September	Rabi
Cauliflower	Flower	Pusa Dipali, Snowball, Himani, Swati	Rabi
Knol-Kohl	Gaddo	White Vienna, Purple Vienna	Rabi
Radish	Mulo	Local, Japanese White, Arka Nishant	Rabi
Sweet Potato	Kandga	Pusa Lai, Pusa Saffaid, Pusa Sunheri	Rabi
Elephant Foot	Suran	Local	June-July
Yam	Chirco, Kate Kandga	Local	June-July
Colocasia	Alu	Local	Kharif, Rabi
Brinjal	Vayingim	Talicgao Local (round) Agaisaim Local, Pusa Purple Cluster, Arka sheel, West Coast Purple	All the year
Chilli	Mir sang, mirchi	Aldona Black & Kholla Red (Local), Pusa Jawala, Byadgi, Konkan Kirti	All the year
Red Amaranthus	Tambdi bhaji	Canara local. Agaisaim Local, CO_1, CO_2	Oct.-March
French Bean	Farasbi, Wai Papadi, Shraw an Ghewda	Pusa Parvati, Arka Komal, Contender, Giant Stringless	Nov.-March
Cluster Bean	Guar, Chidki-Midki	Pusa Sadabahar, Pusa Mousami, Pusa Naubahar	Summer, Kharif
Onion	Kando, Piao	Pusa Red, Pusa Ratnar, Arka Kalyan, Arka Pargati, Arka Niketan	Oct.-Nov.
Okra	Bhendi	Local (Long), Pusa Sawani, Parbhani Kranti	Kharif, Summer

MAJOR PESTS AND DISEASES

COLE CROPS

Pests-Mustard saw fly, Mustard aphid, cabbage butter fly

Diseases-damping off, black rot, leaf spot and blight

CUCURBITS

Pests-red pumpkin beetle, fruit fly, aphids, epilachna beetle

Diseases-fusarium root rot, powdery mildew, downy, mildew

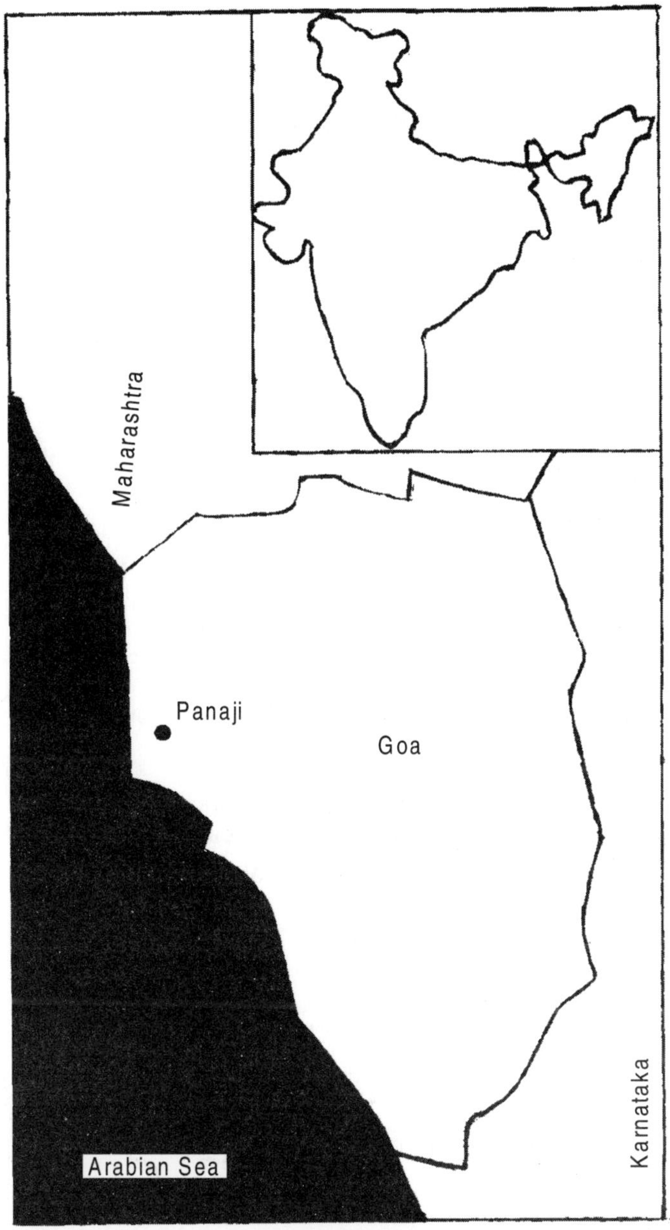

Fig. 11. (i) : Location map of Goa.

SOLANACEOUS VEGETABLES

Pests-white fly, aphids, thrips, shoot & fruit borer

Diseases-blossom end rot, bacterial wilt, leaf curl, anthracnose, leaf spot, early blight

ROOT CROPS

Pests-aphids, semi loopers

Diseases-none

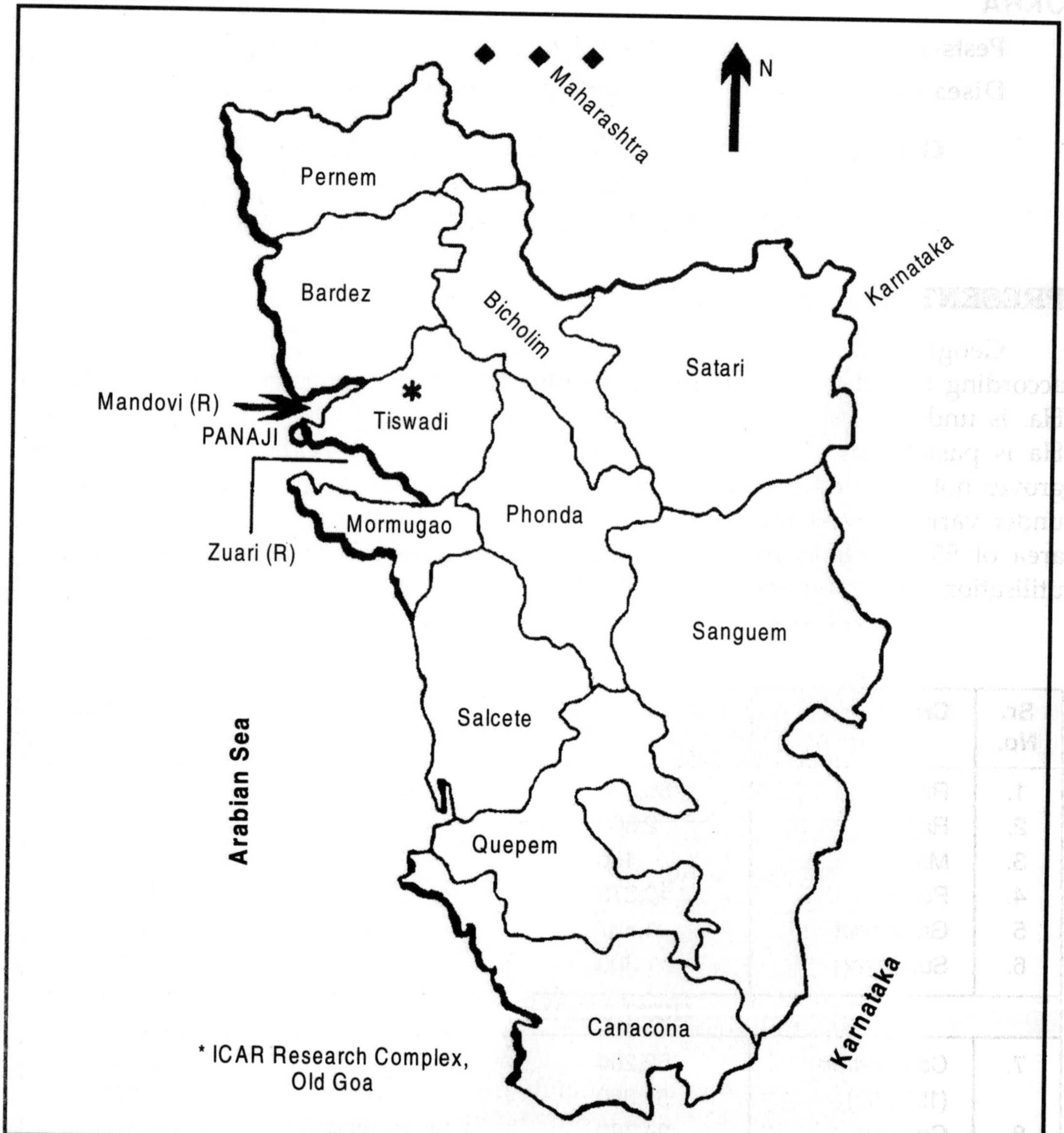

Fig. 11 (ii) : Goa at a Glance.

BEANS

Pests-aphids, thrips, beetle, pod borer

Diseases-blight, sooty mould, leaf curl

ONION

Pests-thrips, maggots

Diseases-downy mildew, smut, fusarium & bacterial rot

OKRA

Pests-aphids, jassid, shoot & pod borer

Diseases-yellow vein mosaic, powdery mildew

GOA STATE HORTICULTURAL CORPORATION LTD. PROPOSED PERSPECTIVE PLAN FOR THE DEVELOPMENT OF HORTICULTURE IN GOA

PRESENT STATUS IN GOA

Geographical area of Goa State is 3701 sq. kms and total reported area according to Village records for land utilisation is 3,61,113 Ha. Out of this 1,25,473 Ha. is under forest cover, 37,173 Ha of land is not available for cultivation, 1305 Ha is pasture and 580 Ha is reported under the miscellaneous tree crops' and groves not included in the area sown. Besides, 1,40,935 Ha is the net area covered under various crops and 1,69,053 Ha is the total cropped area. Significantly a vast area of 55,683 Ha is reported as cultivable waste land (Figure are as per land utilisation report for the year 1997-98 issued by the Directorate of Agriculture).

Table 11.3: Areas covered under various crops alongwith production are given below.

Sr. No.	Crops	Area in (Ha)	Productivily Kg/Ha	Production in Tons
1.	Rice	55,534	2,656	1,47,503
2.	Ragi	2,800	899	2,476
3.	Maize	150	4,000	600
4.	Pulses	10,275	759	7,799
5.	Groundnut	1,437	1,776	2,552
6.	Sugarcane	1,300	48,000	62,400
	HORTICULTURAL CROPS			
7.	Cashewnuts	52,204	100*	5,220
	(1996-97)	51,360	299	15,357
8.	Coconut	24,780	4,841 (Nut/Ha) (Million Nuts)	120

Sr. No.	Crops	Area in (Ha)	Productivily Kg/Ha	Production in Tons
9.	Arecanut	1,450	1,241	1,800
10.	Mango	3,990	1,000	3,990
11.	Banana	1,875	5,680	10,650
12.	Pineapple	300	15,000	4,500
13.	Vegetable	7,550	9,200	69,460
14.	Other Fruits	5,400	12,153	65,628
	Total of Horticultural	97,549		

* In the year 1997-98 productivity of cashewnut was low due to unusual adverse climatic conditions.

The total cropped area in Goa during the year 1997-98 was 1,69,053 Ha of which Horticultural crops occupy 97,549 Ha corresponding to 57.7%. Compared to net cultivated area the Horticultural crops correspond to 69% of the land utilisation. Over and above, the areas under floriculture and nurseries, though small in size but definitely not insignificant, have not been accounted for in the land utilisation.

A considerable area of 55,683 Ha cultivable waste land is available in the state. Out of this a major part can be used for cultivation of various Horticultural crops. Mainly these areas belong to communidads, Devalyas and churches. There is a need to motivate these societies to come forward in promoting Horticultural Development programme in the state. Goa State Horticultural Corporation Ltd. can play, important roll in developing these areas, on the basis of understanding mutually agreed upon sharing of benefits.

CLIMATE AND SOILS :

Goa has a tropical climate, with temperature varying from 16° C to 18° C minimum and 30° C to 34° C maximum. Humidity ranges between 75% to above 90%. The average rainfall is about 2700 mm which is mainly received during monsoon period from June to September with sporadic shower during December to February. The soils are mostly lateritic, whereas sandy loam soils are found in coastal areas. The soils of Goa State are acidic in nature ranging the pH from 4.5 to 6.5. Also soils are deep and porous. The climatic conditions and soils are very much suited for various Horticultural crops.

IMPORTANCE OF HORTICULTURE

Intensive cultivation is required for Horticultural crops to have optimum productivity. Horticultural crops have wider agro- climatic adaptability. It is very

Table 11.4: DIRECTORATE OF AGRICULTURE GOA STATE PATTERN OF LAND UTILIZATION FOR THE YEAR 1997-98. (Area in Ha.)

State/ District/ Taluka	Total reported area according to village papers for land utilization	Forest			Land not available for cultivation	Permanent pastures & other grazing land	Land under miscellaneous tree crops & groves not included in the area sown	Cultivable waste land (including fallow land)	Fallow land		Net area sown	Area sown more than once	Total cropped area
		Govt.	Private	Total					Fallow land other than current fallow	Current fallow			
1	2	3	4	5	6	7	8	9	10	11	12	13	14
Goa State	361113	105473	20000	125473	37137	1305	580	55683	N.A.S.	N.A.S.	140935	28118	169053
North Goa District	167436	29396	5646	35042	20519	629	570	25215	N.A.S.	N.A.S.	85,461	21,305	106766
Tiswasi	16611	178	178	–	3394	–	143	94	N.A.S.	N.A.S.	12,802	3,144	15,946
Bardez	26480	–	10	10	6100	–	29	3116	N.A.S.	N.A.S.	17,225	7,190	24,415
Pernem	24200	1319.	450	1769	2188	–	–	5144	N.A.S.	N.A.S.	15,099	3,307	18,406
Bicholim	23633	716	380	1096	4200	153	45	4206	N.A.S.	N.A.S.	13,933	2,498	16,431
Sattari	51284	24252	4606	28858	2238	233	4	4859	N.A.S,	N.A.S.	15,092	2,254	17,346
Ponda	25228	2931	200	3131	2399	243	349	7796	N.A.S.	N.A.S.	11,310	2,912	14,222
SOUTH GOA DISTRICT	193677	76077	14354	90431	16618	676	10	30468	N.A.S.	N.A.S.	55,474	6,813	62,287
Sanguem	88660	50070	6410	56480	4540	99	10	13428	N.A.S.	N.A.S.	14,103	1,977	16,080
Cana-cona	34736	14328	5721	20049	1383	–	–	2811	N.A.S.	N.A.S.	10,493	805	11,298
Quepem	34731	11679	2218	13897	756	577	–	9144	N.A.S.	N.A.S.	10,357	932	11,289
Salcete	27719	5	5	–	5261	–	–	4269	N.A.S.	N.A.S.	18,184	2,713	20,897
Mormugao	7831	–	–	–	4678	–	–	816	N.A.S.	N.A.S.	2,337	386	2,723

N.B. Estimated Figures Directorate of Agriculture N.A.S. Not available separately. Panaji–Goa.

important to diversify Horticultural activities to generate gainful employment, since produces require pre and post harvest management, processing, preservation and marketing etc. The need to diversify Horticultural activities is mainly on account of the following.

1. Cultivation of Horticultural crops need 600-800 man-days/Ha i.e. four time more than field crops.
2. By and large tenfold more productivity and income is generated from Horticultural crop compared to field crops.
3. Fruit crops, in particular, can be grown on a wider range of soils.
4. Cultivable waste land having moisture stress, saline land and lands subjected to erosion can be developed and used to cultivate Horticultural crops.

●●●

CHAPTER 12

VEGETABLES IN GUJARAT

S.P. SINGH[26]

1. Name of state : Gujarat
2. Total Geographical area : 110 lakh ha
3. Area under cultivation : 97 lakh ha
4. Irrigated area in Gujarat : 24.6%
5. Area under vegetable crops : 1.68 lakh ha
6. Production of vegetables : 20.89 lakh MT
7. Future prospects : Future of vegetable is bright because its area are in increasing order
8. Important information on major vegetable crops. (Statement No. 1)

(1) Tomato
(2) Brinjal
(3) Chillies
(4) Okra
(5) Onion
(6) Garlic
(7) Potato
(8) Cabbage
(9) Cauliflower
(10) Musk melon
(11) Bitter gourd
(12) Cucumber
(13) Bottle gourd
(14) Pointed gourd
(15) Indian bean
(16) Cluster bean
(17) Cow pea

9. Export potential

(*a*) Domestic market. Disposal of vegetables is through co-operative societies. Direct sale in the market. Direct auction in the field.

(*b*) Abroad : Vegetables like Tomato, Chillies, Onion, Garlic have better potential.

10. Major production constraints

(1) Insufficient irrigation facilities.

(2) Salinity tolerant varieties are not available.

(3) Lack of multiple resistant varieties against pests and diseases.

(4) Insufficient co-operative societies for vegetables.

(5) Lack of cold storage.

(6) Lack of standardized post harvest technologies.

(7) Insufficient availability of seeds of high yielding varieties.

(8) Lack of crop insurance.

(9) Lack of processing units.

(10) Frequent occurrence of natural calamities (cyclones and droughts).

11. Major area of production

South Gujarat : Pointed gourd, little gourd, tomato, brinjal, chillies, sweet potato, Indian bean, suran, bottle gourd, sponge & ridge gourd, cabbage (not for seed production).

Middle Gujarat : Tomato, brinjal, chillies, bottle gourd, sweet potato, suran, pointed gourd, little gourd, potato, radish, carrot, cabbage (not for seed production), cauliflower, methi, palak, karela.

North Gujarat: Potato, cluster bean, Indian bean, tomato, okra, radish, carrot, cabbage, cauliflower, methi, palak, bottle gourd.

Saurashtra : Chillies, tomato, brinjal, okra, sweet potato, cluster bean, Indian bean, onion, garlic, radish, carrot, karela, bottle gourds, cabbage (not for seed production), cauliflower, methi, palak.

12. Any other information :

There is an urgent need to initiate protected cultivation of value based vegetables in Gujarat state that will enhance export potential thereby improve economic status of cultivators and state's economy.

13. Important seed vegetable are

Tomato, brinjal, chillies, okra, radish, carrot, onion, garlic, potato, Indian bean, cluster, cluster bean, cucurbits.

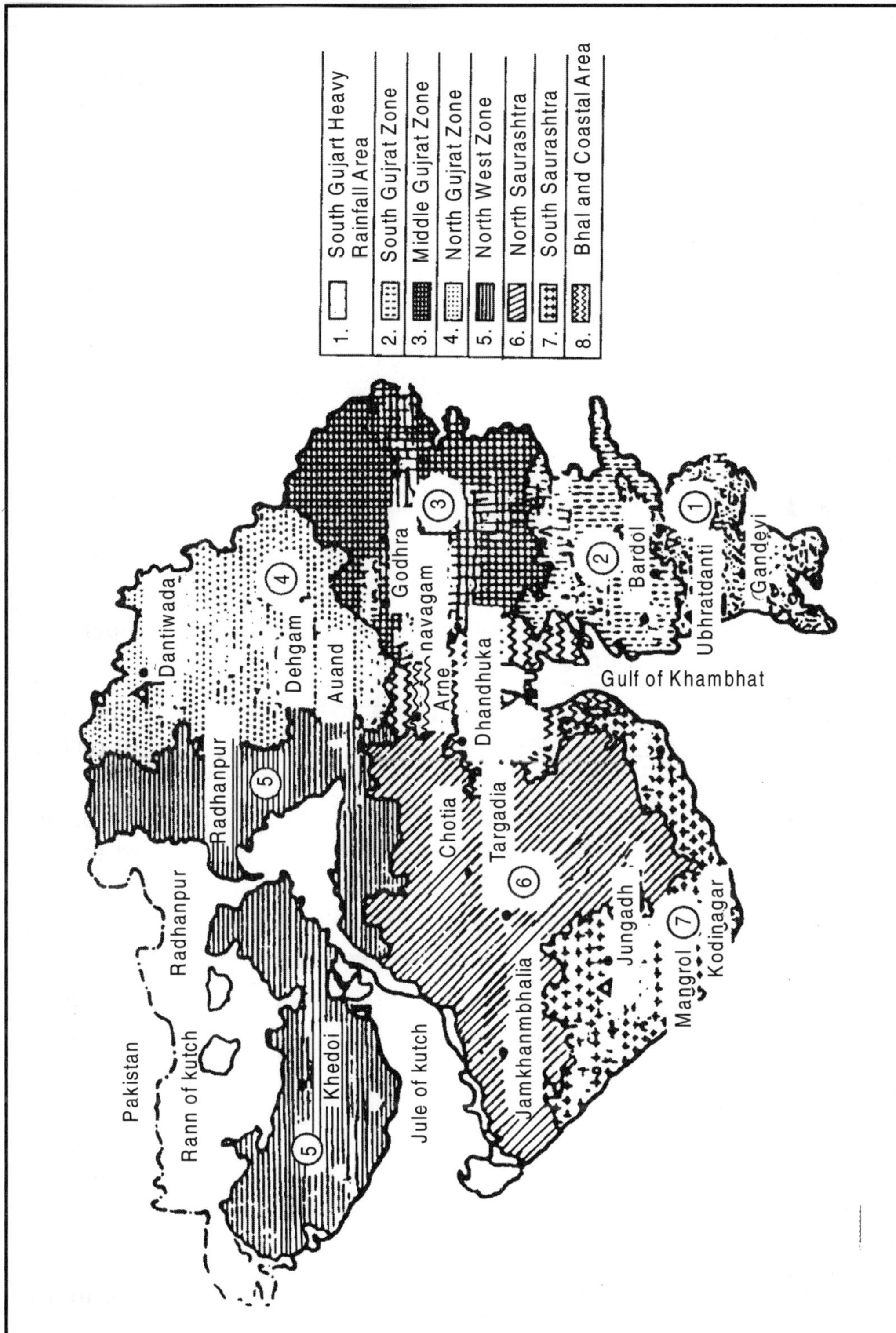

Fig. 12 (*i*) Agro-climate Zones of Gujarat.

TABLE 12.1: Important varieties of commercial vegetables, their manurial requirement, planting time, availability and pests and diseases

Crop	Varieties	Fertilizer (kg/ha) N : P : K	Manure (t/ha) FYM	Planting time		Availability	Pests	Diseases
1	2	3	4	5		6	7	8
Tomato	Junagadh Ruby Pusa Hybrid-1 Pusa Hybrid-4 Pusa Ruby	100 : 100 : 100 50 : — : — 150 : 100 : 100	20	S	Sept.-Oct. Dec-Jan.	Dec.-Jan. Mar. - Apr. (60 to 70 days after trans-planting)	–Fruit borer –Jassids –White	–Leaf curl virus –Mosaic disease fly Damping off –Early blight –Late blight
Brinjal	Junagadh Long P.L.R.–I K.S.–224. Pusa Purple Long Surti Gota	50 : 50 : 50 50 : — : — 100 : 50 : 50	20	R W S	June-July Nov. -Dec. Mar.-Apr.	Sept.-Oct. Feb.-March June-July (After 80 to 85 days of transplanting)	–Shoot and fruit borers –Jassids –Red mite –Epilachana beetle –Leaf eating caterpillar	–Damping off –Phomopsis –Fusarium wilt –Bacterial wilt –Little leaf –Leaf blight
Chillies	Jwala Reshma Patta Gujarati Chilli-1 S - 49, Dholar Sindhur, Pant C-I Pant C-2	50 : 50 : 50 25 : — : — 25 : — : — 100 : 50 : 50	20 -25	W S	Aug-Sept. Jan-Feb.	Dec.-March May-June	-Thrips -Fruit borer -Aphid -Mites	-Damping off -Anthracnose -Wilt -Fruit rot -Blight -Bacterial leaf spot -Mosaic -Leaf curl
Okra	Parbhani kranti Gujarat Hybrid-1	50 : 50 : 50 50 : — : — 100 : 50 : 50	10-12	R S	June-July Feb-Mar.	Aug.-Sept. Apr.-May	-Jassids -Shoot and fruit borer -Red spider mite	-Yellow vein mosaic -Damping off -Leaf blight

1	2	3	4	5		6	7	8
	Gujarat Bhinda-2 Pusa Sawani Punjab Padmini Vaishali						-White fly	-Powdery mildew
Onion	Junagadh Local Talaja Local Agrifound Lightred	37.5 : 50 : 50 37.5 : — : — 75 : 50 : 50	20—25	R W	July-Aug Oct.-Nov.	Dec.-Jan. Mar.-Apr.	-Thrips -Borer -Onion maggot	-Downy mildew -Onion smut -Purple blotch -Onion Smudge
	Pusa White Flat -131 Nasik-53						-Mites	-Bacterial soft rot
Garlic	Gujarat Lasan-1 G-10 GG-2 GG-3 Jamnagar Local	25 : 50 : 50 25 : — : — 50 : 50 : 50	20-25	W	Oct.-Nov.	Feb.-March	-Aphid -Mites -Thrips	-Damping off -Rust -Black spot -Yellowing of leaves
Potato	Khufri Badshah Khufri Pukharaj Khufri Bahar (Khufri Jawahar) Khufri Chandramukhi Khufri Jyoti Khufri Lavkar Khufri Sinduri Khufri Ashok Khufri Alankar	100 : 100 : 200 100 : — : — 200 : 100 : 200	25-30	W	Oct-Nov.	Jan-Feb.	-Cutworms -Epilachna beetle -Leaf eating caterpillar -Aphids -Jassids -Tuber moth	-Early blight -Late blight -Black scarf -Scab -Bacterial brown rot -Charcoal rot -Leaf roll -Mosaic disease

1	2	3	4	5		6	7	8
Cabbage	Golden Acre Pride of India Early drum Head Pusa Drum Head	60 : 60 : 80 40 : — : — 100 : 60 : 80	15-20	E M L	July-Aug. September Oct-Nov.	Sept.-Oct. Nov.- Dec. Jan.-Feb.	-Cabbage white fly -Cabbage root fly	-Black rot -Club rot -Blackleg -Cabbage yellow
Cauli-flower	Early Kuari Pusa Kartiki Pusa Deepali Pusa Synthetic Pusa Subra Pusa Snowball	100 : 75 : 37.5 100 : — : — 200 : 75 : 37.5	15-20	E M	July-Aug. Oct.-Nov.	Nov-Dec. Jan.-Feb.	-Aphid -Diamond back moth -Bihar hairy caterpillar -Cut worm	-Damping off -Black rot -Leaf spot & blight - Phytophthora-root rot
Musk melon	Pusa Madhuras Punjab Sunhari Punjab Sankar G. MM -1 G. MM -2 Hara Madhu	50 : 50 : 50 50 : — : — 100 : 50 : 50	10-12		Jan.-Feb.	Apr-May	-Fruit fly -Aphids	- Powdery mildew -Anthracnose
Bitter gourd	Pusa Do Mausami Pusa Vishesh, Priya, Coimbatore long, Arka Harit, Pride of Surat, Pride of Gujarat	30 : 60 : 60 30 : — : — 60 : 60 : 60	10	R S	June-July Feb. -Mar.	Sept-Nov. Apr. - May	-Frurt fly	-Downy mildew
Cucum-ber	Japanese Long Green Straight Pusa Sanyog	25 : 30 : 40 25 : — : — 50 : 30 : 40		S R	Feb.-Mar. June-July	Apr.-May Aug-Sept	-Red pumpkin beethe -Aphid -Cut worm -Fruit fly	-Wilt -Anthracnose -Powdery mildew

1	2	3	4	5		6	7	8
Bottle gourd	Pusa Summer, Prolific long, Pusa Naveen, Arka Bahar, Punjab long, Junagadh, Tender Long Punjab Kamal	25 : 50 : 50 25 : — : — 50 : 50 : 50	25 S	R	June-July Feb. -Mar.	Aug-Sept. Apr.- May	-Aphid -Fruit fly	-Powdery gourd mildew -Downy mildew
Pointed gourd	Local Pattawala (patles) Oblong Dark Green Long	30 : 40 : 0 30 : — : — 30 : — : — 90 : 40 : 0	25		July-Sept.	Oct-Dec	-Mealybugs -Caterpillar	-Powdery mildew
Indian bean	Gujarat Wal 1 Pusa Early Prolific TDL 37 Kalyanpur T1 Valor Virpur.	20 : 50 : 40 10 : — : — 10 : — : — 40 : 50 : 40	10-15		Oct.-Nov.	Dec-Jan.	-Aphid -Jassids -White flies -Maygots -Pod borer	-Cercospera leaf spot
Cluster bean	Pusa Sadabahar Pusa Navabahar Guwar Gujarat —1 IC - 11388	25 : 37.5 : 37.5	10-12	R S	July Feb.	September April	-Aphids -Jassids -Thrips -Galerucid beetle -Mites	-Powdery mildew -Bacterial blight
Cow Pea	Pusa Phalguni Pusa Barasti Pusa Rituraj	20 : 50 : 40 10 : — : — 30 : 50 : 40		R W S	June-July Dec.-Jan Apr-May	Aug-Sept. Feb-March June-July	-Aphids -Jassids -White flies -Pod borer-	-Cercospora leaf spots -Stem rot -Bacterial blight

R-Rainy season; S-Summer season; W-Winter; E-Early; M-Mid; L–Late

N B. : Application of nitrogen is done in mainly two splits except in pointed gourd and Indian bean alongwith whole dose of phosphorus and potassium. The second half dose of nitrogen is top dressed after 3 weeks of planting/sowing.

●●●

CHAPTER 13

VEGETABLE PRODUCTION IN HARYANA

Suresh K. Malhotra

1. Name of state. — Haryana
2. Total geographical area (ha) — 4374000 ha
3. Area under cultivation (ha) — 3790400 ha
4. Irrigation area (ha) net — 1353000 ha
5. Area under Vegetables (ha) (1996-97) — 98000 ha
6. Production (t) — 1455000 Metric Tons
7. Productivity (t) — 14.8 t/ha
8. Anticipated in 2000 AD-Area — 120000 ha
9. Production — 1600000 Metric tonnes

TABLE 13.1: Area, production and productivity of different vegetables

Crop Area (ha)	Production (M/t)		Productivity (t/h)		
	1996-97	2000 AD	1996-97	2000 AD	1996-97
Potato	15300	17000	229900	250000	15.03
Onion	6400	9000	109500	130000	17.11
Cabbage	3800	4500	62000	67000	16.32
Cauliflower	7000	8200	129600	50000	18.51
Tomato	8800	12000	153500	62000	17.44
Okra	6600	7000	75400	82000	11.42
Peas	7500	8300	94600	10000	12.61
Radish/Turnip	6900	7000	109000	20000	15.80

Crop Area (ha)	Production (M/t)		Productivity (t/h)		
	1996-97	2000 AD	1996-97	2000 AD	1996-97
Carrot	4800	5500	88700	93000	18.48
Chillies	5300	6500	50100	58000	9.45
Brinjal	4200	5000	69900	72000	16.64
Cucurbit	10300	13000	111100	25000	10.80
Leafy vegetables	2900	5000	36400	39000	11.93
Others	8900	12000	138900	142000	15.63
Total	98000	120000	1455000	1600000	–

TABLE 13.2: Crop-wise recommended varieties/hybrids, planting times, availability period, major pests and diseases.

Crop	Varieties/ hybrids	Planting time	Availability	Major	
				Insects	Diseases
Tomato	Hisar Arun, Hisar Lalit & Hisar Lalima	June-July, Nov-Dec.	Sept-Nov., March-May	White-fly, fruit borer	Early blight, Leaf curl virus, Nematodes.
Brinjal	BR-112, Hisar Shymal, & Hisar Pragti	June- July, Oct-Nov., March	Sept-Nov., March-May, June-Aug.	Jassids, White fly, fruit and shot borer, mites.	Fruit rot, little leaf, mosaic, nematode.
Chilli	NP-46A, Pusa Jawala & Pant C-l	May-June, Oct-Nov	Sept-Nov, March-May	Termites thrips & mites	Leaf curl virus, fruit rot & die back.
Bhindi	Pusa Sawani, Varsha Uphar & Hisar Unnat	Feb- March, June-July	April-July, Aug-Nov.	Jassids, white fly, fruit borer, mites	YVMV, root rot and Nematodes.
Cauliflower	Pusa Katki (early), Hisar-1 (Mid) Snowball-16 (late)	May-June, July-Aug., March-April	Aug-Oct., Oct-Nov., March-April	Diamond back moth, tobacco caterpillar & aphids	Black rot, downy mildew and Alternaria blight.
Cabbage	Pride of India, Golden Acre & Large Late Drum Head	Sept- Nov.	March-April	-do-	-do-
Knol-khol	Early White Vienna	Sept-Nov.	March-April	-do-	-do-
Radish	Pusa Chetki, Pb. Safed, Japanese White & White Icicle	Aug-Sept. & Oct.-Nov	Oct.-Dec. & Dec.-Feb.	Aphids	Alternaria blight

Crop	Varieties/ hybrids	Planting time	Availability	Major	
				Insects	Diseases
Turnip	White-4 & PTWG	Aug.-Sept. & Oct.-Nov	-do-	-do-	-do-
Carrot	Pusa Kesar, Hisar Garic & Nantes	-do-	-do-	-do-	-do-
Peas	Arka Hisar, Hark & Bonneville	Mid-Sept-Oct. & Oct.-mid-Nov.	Dec-April	Thrips, leaf minor aphids & fruit borer	Powdery mildew, ro ot rot & rust.
Onion	Rabi-Hisar-2, Pusa Red, Kharif-N-53 & ADR	Oct.-Nov. & June	April-May & Oct.-Nov.	Thrips	Purple Blotch
Garlic	G-1	Sep.-Oct.	April-May	-do-	-do-
Muskmelon	Punjab Sunehari, Hara Madhu, Hisar Paras & Hisar Madhu	Mid-Feb- Mid-March	May-July	Red Pumpkin Beetle, Jassids, Aphids, mites & fruit fly.	—
Watermelon	Charleston Grey & Sugar baby	-do-	-do-	-do-	Powdery mildew anthracnose, gummy collar rot, downy mildew & mosaic.
Bottle gourd	PSPL PSPR	Feb.-March & June-July	May-Aug. & Sep.-Nov.	-do-	-do-
Bitter gourd	Coimbator · Long & Pusa mausmi	-do-	-do-	-do-	-do-
Long melon	Lucknow Early & Karnal Selection	Feb.-March & June July	May-June & Sep.-Nov.	-do-	-do-
Round melon	Hisar Selection & Bikaneri Green	-do-	-do-	-do-	-do-
Pumpkin	Pusa Vishwas & Arka Charidan	-do-	-do-	-do-	-do-
Cucumber	Japanese Long & KH-3	-do-	-do-	-do-	-do-

Crop	Varieties/ hybrids	Planting time	Availability	Major	
				Insects	Diseases
Ridge/ Smooth Gourd	Fusa Nasdar & Pusa Chikni	-do-	-do-	-do-	-do-
Summer Squash	Hisar Selection & Pusa Alankar	Nov.-Dec.	Jan.-April	-do-	-do-
Dolichos Bean	HD-1 & HD-18	July	Sep.-Oct.	Aphids & White fly pod borer	Anthracnose & mosaic
Cluster Bean	Pusa Barsati & Pusa Dofasli	Feb.-March & July-June	May-July & Aug.-Nov.	-do-	-do-

Export Potential

Horticulture is a sun rise area attracting farmers entrepreneurs, small investors, traders and specialists. There has been significant increase in the horticultural crops particularly vegetable crops in terms of area and production during the last few years Farmers are taking up vegetable crops as a separate viable economic activity. Among vegetable crops the bulk of export is in onion and potato mainly centered to Delhi and the neighboring states. Other vegetables which are being exported to Delhi Azadpur market in smaller quantities are okra, brinjal, tomato, chillies and cucurbits. There is no specific data available on the export of vegetable crops from Haryana. Though there is tremendous scope of export of onion, chillies cucurbits and tomato from Haryana due to its close proximity to New Delhi.

Major Production Constraints

The productivity and quality of several vegetable crops have continued to remain much below the potential demonstrated. Our yields are much below the world average except in potato. Poor management practices and post-harvest handling system contribute to the low quality of final produce. Some of the major biotic and abiotic production constraints are listed below.

(*a*) Biotic

(*i*) Several chronic production problems due to attack of insect-pests particularly fruit borer, white flies, aphids, jassids, mites and diseases., mainly leaf curl virus, mosaic, blights and rots become impediment in the successful production of vegetable crops.

(*ii*) Shortage of manpower for post-harvest handling, processing and marketing of fresh vegetable crops.

(b) Abiotic

(i) Highly inadequate availability of vegetable seed of high yielding varieties and hybrids.

(ii) Acute shortage of infrastructure for post-harvest handling of vegetable crops.

(iii) Un-organized marketing system.

(iv) Non-availability of credit facilities,

(v) Week data base.

Topographic regions and potential pockets for commercial production by depicting in the map of the state. The state has been divided into two distinct zones from climatic point.of view, which are as recommended as under:

TABLE 13.3 : Different zones and the vegetables recommended in Haryana

Zone	Vegetables Recommended
(A) Eastern Zone	
(i) **Shivalik Hilly regions** (Sub-humid with high rainfall) -Kalka), Naraingarh, Chhechhranli, Jagadhari, Karnal, Panipat, Ladwa and Indri.	Tomato, Brinjal, Chillies, Cole crops, Root Crops, Peas, European Vegetables, Bhindi, Onion, Garlic, and cucurbits.
(ii) **Alluvial Plain** (Sem-arid with medium rainfall) Faridabad, Palwal, Ballabhgarh, Gurgaon, Nuh, Patandi, Sonipat, Karnal, Panipat, Kurukshetra, Kaithal, Guhla, Pehowa, Parts of Rohtak and Jind districts.	Tomato, Brinjal, Chillies, Cole Crops, Root Crops, Peas, Bhindi, Onion, Garlic and cucurbits.
(B) Western Zone	
(i) **Alluvial plain** (Semi-arid with medium to low rainfall) Parts of Hisar, Rohtak, Bhiwani, and whole of Mahendergarh.	Tomato, Brinjal, Chillies, Cluster bean, Dolichos bean, Peas, Palak, Beet root, Carrot and Cucurbitaceous Vegetables.
(ii) **Sandy dunes** (Arid zone/rainfed with low rainfall) Western and South western parts of state adjoining to Rajasthan i.e. Sirsa, Bhiwani and Rewari.	Cluster bean and Cucurbit vegetables.

The potential pockets for commercial vegetables production are depicted in the Haryana Map (Fig. 13.1).

Any other information : Nil

Vegetable Seed Production

The seeds of open-pollinated varieties of tomato, brinjal, Chillies root vegetables (Asiatic) cauliflower (early and mid), onion, bhindi, peas and other cucurbitaceous

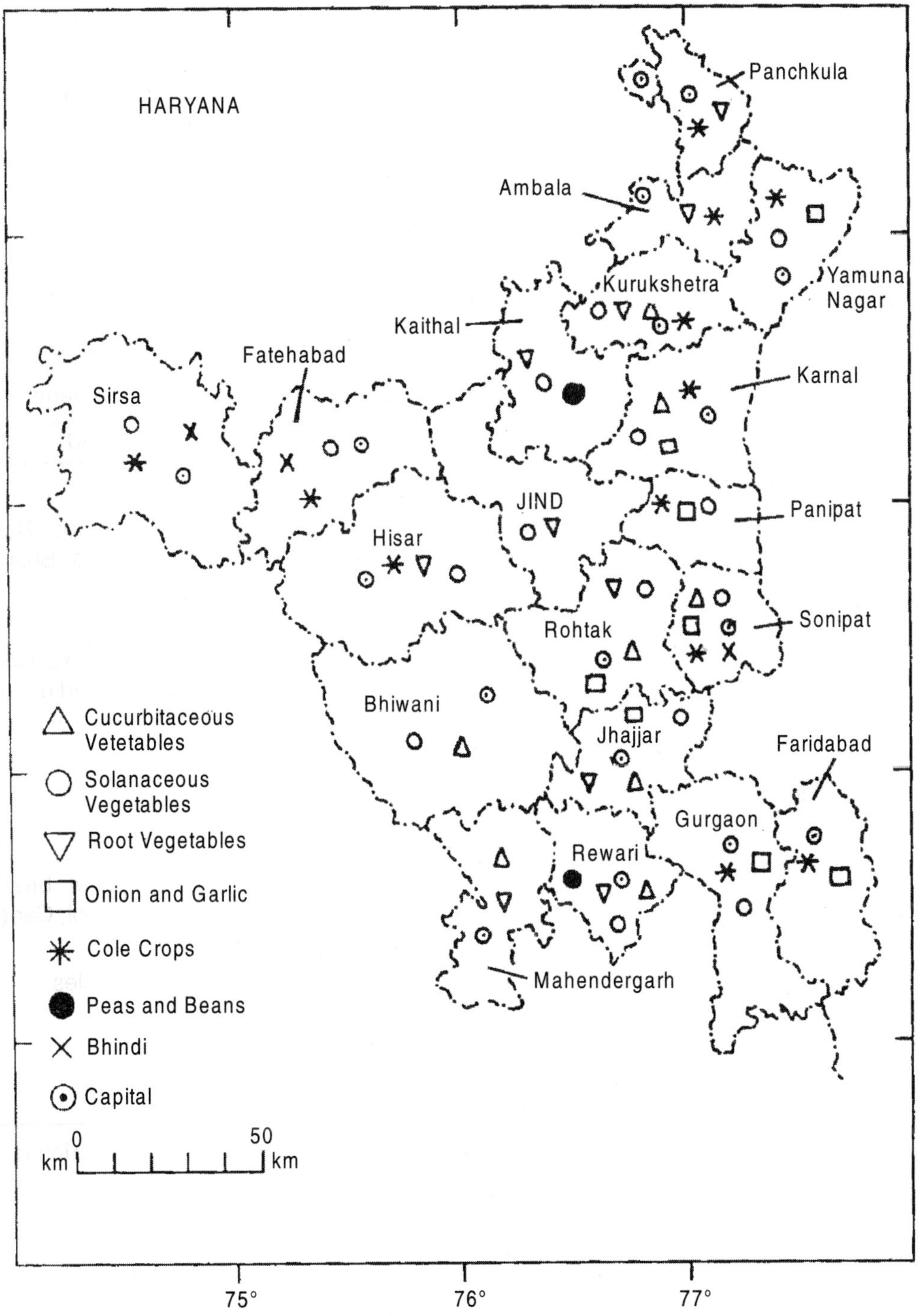

Fig. 13. (i) Potential pockets for commercial vegetable crops of Haryana.

vegetables are being produced in Haryana. At present, seed multiplication programme of recommended varieties of above crops is being taken up mainly by NSC, SFCI. Haryana State Seed Corporation (HSDC), at State Department of Horticulture farms and SAU. The total requirement of certified seed on the basis of replacement rate, crop-wise is given here under in Table 13.4.

TABLE 13.4: Area, total requirement, replacement rate and requirement of certified seed of different vegetables in Haryana.

S.No.	Crops	Area under cultivation (h)	Total seed requirement (q)	Replacement rate (%)	Requirement of certified seed (q.)
1.	Peas	7500	7500.0	7.5	560.00
2.		5800	2900	3.0	8.70
3.	Carrot	5000	500.0	3.0	15.00
4.	Bhindi	6500	1300.0	15.0	195.00
5.	Muskmelon	3200	80.0	7.5	6.00
6.	Tomato Desi	7200	9.0	7.5	0.70
	Hybrid	NA	10.8	100.0	10.80
7.	Cucumber	700	17.5	100.0	17.50
8.	Brinjal Desi	5000	12.5	7.5	0.95
	Hybrid	NA	6.3	100.00	6.30
9.	Onion	6000	600.0	7.5	45.00
10.	Cauliflower	6000	28.8	7.5	45.00
	Desi				
	Hybrid	NA	12.0	100.0	120.00
11.	Chillies	5500	55.0	7.5	4.10

Source: Directorate of Horticulture, Chandigarh

CHAPTER 14

VEGETABLE GROWING IN HIMACHAL PRADESH

Sant Parkash and Arya PS.

Himachal Pradesh, a state of small and marginal farmers, though spread over a large geographical area of 5.57 million hectares has small cultivated area of only 0.63 million hectares. The area under irrigation is only 1.0 lakh ha, thus leading major part of the cultivated area as rainfed. On the other hand agro-climatic variations are quite large, dividing the state into following four district zones on the basis of elevation, temperature, soil type and cropping sequence.

(*a*) **Sub-montane and low-hill subtropical zone :** This zone comprises Una, Bilaspur, Hamirpur districts and parts of Sirmour, Chamba, Solan and Kangra districts. The area in this zone, lies between 350 to 914 m above mean sea level. Soils are shallow, light textured and low in fertility. Average rainfall is 110 cm of which 80 per cent is received during July-September, Brinjal, cucumber, okra, peas, cauliflower, potato, ginger, turmeric and colocasia are the major vegetables/spices of this zone.

(*b*) **Sub-temperate sub-humid mid hill zone :** This zone represents parts of Kangra, Mandi, Kullu, Solan, Sirmour, Shimla, Bilaspur and Chamba districts with an elevation ranging from 915 m, to 1523 m above mean sea level. Average rainfall of this zone is 280 cm. Cultivation of cash crops like ginger and offseason vegetables viz., tomato, French bean, capsicum, cabbage, cucumber, peas and cauliflower is done on commercial scale.

(*c*) **Wet temperate high-hill zone :** This zone includes major parts of Shimla and Chamba districts and some parts of Kangra, Mandi, Kullu, Solan and Sirmour districts. This high-hill moist zone lies in between 1524-2472 m above mean sea level and receive moderate to heavy monsoon rains of about 100-200 cm annually. Snow is usual feature during winters thus preventing crop growth from November-March. The important vegetable crops of the zone are peas, cauliflower, cabbage, root and leafy vegetables which are grown during summer months as an off-season vegetables.

(*d*) **Dry temperate high-hill zone:** It comprises the districts Kinnaur, Lahual and Spiti and parts of Chamba and Kangra Districts. The elevation of this zone extends beyond 2472 m above mean sea level and the cultivation of the crops is restricted from April-October. This zone is ideally suited for the production of temperate vegetable and their quality seed production. Average rainfall is very low (25-40 cm) and the zone remains covered with snow from November to March.

Due to small and fragmented holdings coupled with rapid population increase, the state has been experiencing heavy pressure on land and natural resources.

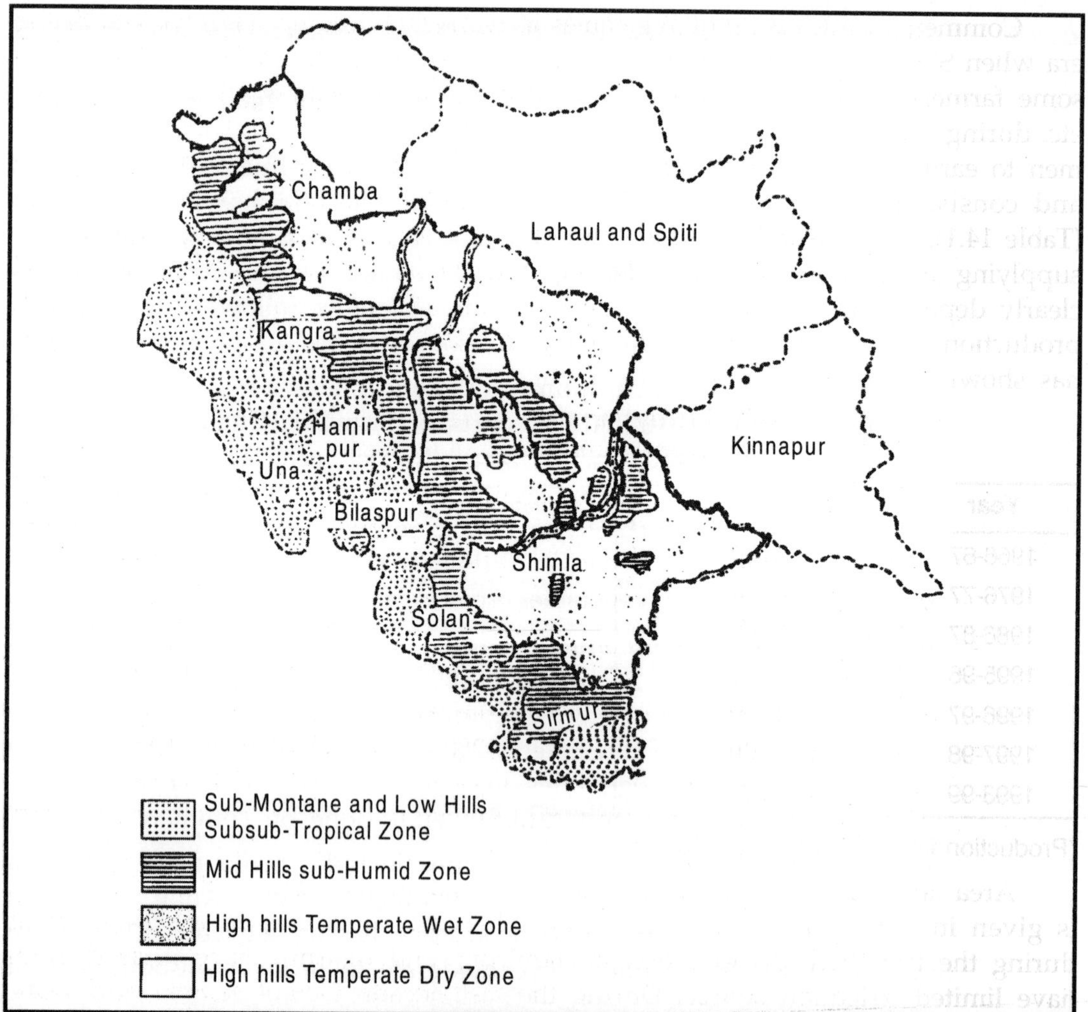

Fig. 14. (i) Agro-climatic Zones of Himachal Pradesh

After attaining self sufficiency in food grain production, there is an urgent need to adopt crop diversification by switching over to cash crops. Doubtlessly, the state has already achieved a metric rise in area and production of vegetable crops by recording an annual production of more than 5.0 lakh. M tonnes, a bulk of which is marketed as an off-season vegetable to the neighbouring state. The hills provide conducive conditions and serve as a natural green house for producing of vegetables particularly, peas, tomato, cabbage, beans, cauliflower, capsicum, cucumber, at such a time when their availability is almost over in plains due to un-favorable agro-climatic conditions. This offers ready market for these crops. Thus, the state has immense scope to further increase the area and production of vegetable crops for the overall socio-economic upliftment of the hill farmers.

Area and Production

Commercial cultivation of vegetables in Himachal Pradesh dates back to British era when Shimla used to be the summer capital of the country. During those days some farmers around Shimla grew few vegetables like cauliflower, cabbage, pea, etc. during summer months as an off-season and sold them to Britishers and Army men to earn some income. Thereafter, the Pradesh has been witnessing a regular and consistent increase in area and production of different vegetables crops (Table 14.1). At present, Himachal Pradesh has emerged as a leading hilly state in supplying array of vegetables to the adjoining states as an off- season. Table 14.1 clearly depicts that Himachal Pradesh has attained a quantum jump in vegetable production over the years. As compared to 1966-67 the present area and production has shown an increase of more than three and fifteen times, respectively.

TABLE 14.1: Increasing trend in Area and Production of vegetable in Himachal Pradesh.

Year	Area (000 ha)	Production (000 M.T.)	Productivity (t/ha)
1966-67	8.00	30.00	3.75
1976-77	14.14	84.00	5.94
1986-87	17.00	2760.00	15.88
1995-96	25.00	425.00	17.00
1996-97	25.50	440.00	17.25
1997-98	27.50	475.00	17.27
1998-99	29.00	500.00	17.24

*Production figures exclude potato

Area and production under different vegetables recorded in the year 1995-96 is given in Table 14.2. Area under vegetables has increased in all the districts during the last three decades except Hamirpur and Bilaspur since these districts have limited irrigation source. During the last decade Lahaul & Spiti and Kullu districts recorded the highest increase in area, production and productivity of vegetables. However, the principal constituent districts are Shimla, Solan and Mandi.

TABLE 14.2: Area and Production and productivity under different vegetables in Himachal Pradesh during 1996-97.

S.No.	Name of crop	Area (ha)	Production (MT)	Productivity (q/ha)
1.	Potato	16200	140000	864.1
2.	Peas (Green)	7270	72773	100.1
3.	Tomato	2570	79057	307.6
4.	Beans	2080	20853	100.3
5.	Onion and Garlic	1500	29535	196.9
6.	Cabbage	1640	42656	260.1
7.	Cauliflower	690	13800	20.00
8.	Ginger	2500	—	—
9.	Radish, Turnip and Carrot	845	18421	21.80
10.	Bhindi	390	4875	12.50
11.	Cucurbit	2630	83897	31.90
12.	Capsicum & chillies	1045	10241	9.80
13.	Brinjal	265	4532	17.10
14.	Spinach and other leafy vegetables	2850	28557	10.02
15.	Other minor vegetables	1225	15803	12.90

Source : Directorate of Agriculture, Himachal Pradesh, Shimla-5.

Potential pockets and commercial vegetables crops

Himachal Pradesh has been endowed with varied agro-climatic conditions. This wide range of agro-climates provides immense scope for hill farmers having small and scattered holdings to grow commercial vegetables at one elevation or the other throughout the year. Attempts have been made identify zone-wise potential pockets and vis-a-vis commercial crops which can be grown with high profitability. District-wise potential pockets and distribution of important vegetables and vegetable seed crops in different agro-economical sub-regions (Zone I to IV) have been given in (Table-14.3).

TABLE 14.3: District-wise potential pockets of important different agro-economical commercial vegetables in sub- regions of Himachal Pradesh.

Agro-eco.l sub.regions	Distt.	Pockets	Commercial fresh vegetables	Potential Seed Crops
Zone-1: Sub-mountain, low-hill sub-tropical zone				
–	Hamirpur	Naduan, Rangas, Nalti, Nara, Bhareri, Kanga, Mundkhar, Jahu Dugha and Phahal	Tomato, Onion, Cucumber, Beans, Cauliflower, Radish, Brinjal, Colocasia Turnip & Bitter gourd	Radish & Bhindi

Agro-eco.l sub.regions	Distt.	Pockets	Commercial fresh vegetables	Potential Seed Crops
–	Bilaspur	Daslehra, Ghumarwin	Cauliflower, Chilli, Radish, Bhindi	Peas, Radish & Onion.
–	Una	Swan river beds, Santokh garh area, Akrot & Amb	Early cucumber, Long melon, Bottle gourd, Watermelon, Muskmelon, Cauli-flower, Beans Colocasia, Tomato	Early cauliflower, onion & bhindi
–	Kangra	Nurpur, Kandrori, Indora, Chinour, Raja Ka Talab, Jawali Dehra Lambagaon, Ichhi Jaisinghpur, Jama-nabad, Sunehar, Samloti, Thanpuri, & Dada Shiba	Cucumber, Bhindi, Brinjal, Bottle Gourd, Radish, Turnip, Biter gourd, Onion, Garlic & Rainfed Tomato	Bhindi, early cauli-flower, onion & ginger.
–	Chamba	Sinhunta & Chowari	Tomato, Brinjal, Bhindi, Radish, Turnip & Beans	—
–	Mandi	Sandhol, Nagwai, Bachhwar & Belh	Colocasia, Beans, Onion & Garlic	Peas, Bhindi, French Bean & Radish
–	Solan	Nalagarh, Sproon, Darlaghat, Shogi & Kandaghat	Tomato, Bhindi, Beans & Onion	Onion, Late cauli-flower, French Bean, Radish (Pusa Himani)
–	Sirmour	Paonta, Majra, Bikram Ka Bagh, Shivpur Bhugrani.	Tomato, Brinjal, Carrot, Bhindi & Beans	Radish, Carrot, Onion Turnip & Early Cauliflower
Zone-II : Mid-hill zone Sub-humid sub temperate				
	Bilaspur	Panjgain, Namhol, Jukh ala Swarghat	Ginger, rainfed Tomto & Peas	Peas
	Kangra	Nagrota, Pathiar, Paprola & Chobin	Spring potato, cucumber, beans, bottle gourd, cauli-flower (mid group) & brinjal	Peas, Radish & Bhindi
	Chamba	Udaipur, Sarola, Sahu & Baniknet	Cabbage, Cauli-flower, Tomato, Beans	Cauliflower, Radish & Palak.

Agro-eco.l sub.regions	Distt.	Pockets	Commercial fresh vegetables	Potential Seed Crops
	Mandi	Nagwain, Panarsa, Mandi sadar, Sarang, Sihan, Rajgarh & Lohara	Tomato, Beans, Cabbage, Brinjal Cauliflower (early mid & late group), Summer Squash & Cucumber	Cauliflower, Radish, Brinjal, Tomato, Beans, Palak & Turnip
	Solan	Kumihar, Basal, Saproon, Kanda-ghat, Dharampur & Oachghat	Tomato, Beans, Capsicum, Colo-casia, Chilli, Cabbage & Peas.	Late Cauliflower, Palk and Radish
	Kullu	Hurla, Kalehli, Thrash, Mohal, Bhuntar, Lag Valley & Fozal	Tomato, Cabbage, Capsicum, Beans, Peas, Cauliflower, (all groups) Euro-pean vegetables, Radish, Cucumber & Summer squash	Cauliflower, Pea, Radish, Brinjal, Tomato & Turnip.
	Sirmour	Dadahu, Narag, Pachhad, Rajgarh, Shilai, Andheri & Sarahan	Ginger, Tomato, Peas, Cabbage, Beans and Chilli	Cauliflower
	Shimla	Shogi, Tatapani, Duttnagar, Snni & Ramnur	Tomato, Beans, Cabbage, Radish & Turnip	—
Zone-III : Wet temperature High hills.				
	Kangra	Chhota Bangal	Peas, Cabbage, Potato (Seed crop) & Cauliflower	—
	Chamba	Deoga, Salooni, Kutlar, Bandal, Tissa & Alha	Potato, Peas & Cauliflower	—
	Mandi	Janjehli, Karsaog, Chailch owk, Barot & Chuhar Valley	Potato, Peas, Cabbage & Cauliflower	—
	Kullu	Sairaj, Dujar, Bahu Mohni, Gada, Gsaini, Nagar, Katrain, Sarasai & Baragaon	Peas, Cauliflower, Cabbage, Carrot & Tomato	Cabbage, Carrot, Turnip, Radish and Beans
	Solan	Chail	Peas & Cabbage	—
	Sirmour	Haripurdhar, Puhul-bahal, Rohnat & Dhamla	Cabbage, Peas & Cauliflower	Cabbage and Potato

Agro-eco.l sub.regions	Distt.	Pockets	Commercial fresh vegetables	Potential Seed Crops
	Shimla	Theog, Cheog, Shilaroo, Matiana, Narkanda, Kufri, Sandhol, Kotkhai, Baghi, Kotgarh and Rohru	Peas, Cabbage, Red Cabbage, Broccoli, Potato, Cauliflower, Carrot, Radish, Turnip & Leaf Vegetables	Seed Potato, Turnip, Carrot & Cabbage
Zone-IV : Temperature Dry high hill zone				
	Kangra	Bara Bangal	Peas & Cabbage	Potato & French bean
	Chamba	Pangi, Bharmour & Holi	Peas & Cabbage	Potato, Peas, Cabbage & French bean
	Kinnaur	Kalpa Pooh, Ribba, Samdho, Chango, Sangla, Chini, Leo & Rarang.	Peas, Cabbage & Hops	Peas, potato, temperate varieties of Cabbage, Car rot, Turnip, Radish, Sugar beet & chicory
	Lahaul and Spiti	Koksar, Tandi, Shishoo, Goshal, Tholong, Jahlama, Thirot, Udipur, Miar Valley, Spiti, Lari, Tabo, Kaza, Kibbar & Trilokinath	Peas, Cabbage & Hops	Potato, French bean, Temperate varieties of Cabbage, Red Cabbage, radish, carrot & Turnip

Varietal status, planting times, availability period and major pests/ diseases

The varietal agro-climatic conditions of the Pradesh favour off- season production of many vegetables,which are commercially grown and find ready market in the northern plains at lucrative prices. However, as many as 40-50 vegetables are grown in one or the other parts of the State but efforts have been made to give information regarding varietal status zone wise, planting time, availability period of major crops only (Table 14.4). Due to mild weather conditions in the state, there is no severe incidence of diseases and pests unlike plains, however, the most serious diseases and pests prevailing on different vegetables have been mentioned in Table 14.4.

Vegetable Seed Industry in Himachal Pradesh

Quality seed is the basic input in vegetable production. Most vegetable crops are propagated by seed. A seed is a ripened ovule used for multiplication. According to Manu "Good seed on good land yields abundant produce" The use of good

TABLE 14.4: Varietal status, planting time, availability periods, major diseases, insect-pests of different vegetables in Himachal Pradesh.

S.No.	Crop.	Popular Varieties/ Hybrids	Plantingtime (Zone wise)				Availability	Major diseases	Important pests
			ZI	II	III	IV			
1	2	3	4	5	6	7	8	9	10
1.	Peas	Lincoln, Azad Pea, Palam Priya, Arkel* Solan Nirog	Oct-Nov.	Sep-Nov.	Oct-Nov.	Mar-April, June-July	Mar-Nov.	Powdery mildew, Ascochyta blight & Bacterial blight	Pea leaf minor & pea pod borer
2.	Tomato	Solan Gola, Roma, Solan Bajar, Rupali & Naveen (Fl).	Nov-Feb	Feb-June	April	–	June-Oct.	Early & late blight buckeye, fruit rot & bacterial wilt	Fruit Fly
3.	French bean	Contender, Lakashmi & SVM-1	Feb-Aug., Sep	Feb-Aug	April-May	May-July	April-Nov	Angular leaf spot	Anthracnose web blight
4.	Cabbage	Golden Acre, Pride of India, Hybrid- Bahar, Bajrang Quisto	Oct-Nov	Sept-Oct	Mar.-May	May-June	Mar.-Nov.	Black rot	–
5.	Capsicum	Cauliflower, Yolo winder Bharath (Fl)	Nov-Feb	Feb-April	April	–	May-Sep.	Bacterial wilt	–
6.	Chilli	Solan Yellow & Surajmukh	Nov.	Feb., May	Mar.-May	April May	–	Bacterial wilt	–
7.	Potato	Kufri Jyoti & kufri Chancjermukhi	Sep-Oct	Jan-Feb.	Mar.-April	April-May	May-June	Early blight	Potato tuber moth
8.	Onion	Nasik Red	Patna Red, Agri found dark red & N-53	Oct-Nov.	Oct-Nov.	—	—	May	Doweny Red, mildew & Purple block

1	2	3	4	5	6	7	8	9	10
9.	Garlic	Large Segmented & GHC-1	Oct-Nov.	Sep-Oct.	—	—	May	-do-	-do-
10.	Cauliflower	Early Kuari, Pusa Deepali, Aghani, Possi & Early Snow ball	—	May June	—	—	July-Aug	Black rot .	Cabbage catter piller
11.	Sprouting Broccoli	Palam Samridhi	Sep	Sep-Oct	Mar.	—	Dec-Feb., June-July	—	—
12.	Ginger	Himgiri Local vars	June	May	—	—	Oct- Nov	Ginger yellow & rhizome root complex	
13.	Brinjal	PPC	Pusa Purple Long	Arka Keshav & Arka Keshav	Nov-Feb., Mar	Feb.- April	June-Sep.	Phomopsis rot & Bacterial wilt	Fruit and shoot borer
14.	Turmeric	Local vars	May-June	—	—	Nov-Dec.	—	—	—
15.	Bhindi	Parbhani karnat	P-7 & Local vars	Feb-Mar., June	Mar.- April, June	—	—	May-Octi	YV mosciac virus blister beetle
16.	Radish	Pusa Chetaki, Chinese Pink, Mino Early White, Japa-nese White Local vars.	Jan.-Nov	Jan. Nov	Mar. May	April-June	All the year	—	—
17.	Turnip	Purple Top White Globe	Sept. Oct.	Aug.- Sept.	Mar.- May	May-June, April	-do-	—	—
18.	Carrot	Pusa Yandagini	Nantes & Pusa Keshav	Sept.-Oct	Aug	March	May	Feb.-Aug.	—

1	2	3	4	5	6	7	8	9	10
19.	Cucumber	Local Var. & Poinsett	Green Long	Feb.-Mar., June	Mar.-June	May	—	June-Oct.	Powdery Mildew Downy Mildew Fruit Fly & Red Pumpkin Beetle
20.	Pumpkin	Solan Badami & Local Var	June	June	May	—	Sept.-Oct.	-do-	-do-
21.	Chowchow	Local Var.	May-June	Mar.-June	—	—	Sept.-Oct.	-do-	-do-
22.	Sponge Gourd	Local Var.	Feb.-June	Mar.-June	—	—	June-Oct.	-do-	-do-
23.	Spinach beet	Pusa Harit & Local Var.	Sept.-Oct., Feb.	Aug.-Oct., Feb.-Mar.	Mar.-April	—	Year round	—	—
24.	Colocasia	Local Var.	May-June	May	—	—	Nov.-Dec.	—	—
25.	Coriander	Indescripher & Local Var.	Sept.-Oct	Aug.-Oct.	Mar.	—	Year round	—	—
26.	Methi	Pusa Kasuri & Local Var.	Sept.-Oct.	Aug.-Oct.	Mar.	—	Nov.- Jan., May-July	—	—
27.	Bitter Gourd	Solan Hara, Solan Safaid & Local Var	Feb.-Mar., June	Feb.-Mar., April	—	—	June-Sept.	-do-	-do-
28.	Summer Squash	Pusa Alankar (Fl)& Australian Green	Feb.	Mar.	April	May	May-Aug.	-do-	-do-

quality seed is indispensable for the successful production of any vegetable crop. The cost of seed is a small fraction of the total cost of inputs involved in raising the crop to maturity. All efforts go waste if poor quality seed is used what are known as the seeds of hope may turn into seeds of frustration (Sen, 1974). Quality seed should be true to type or name (genetic aspect), viable (physiological aspect) free from seed borne diseases and insect-pests (galls) pathological and entomological aspects, free from weed seeds, foreign matter (dust and inert) or mixture (physical aspect) fairly priced from the stand point of both sellers and buyer (marketing aspect), bold and uniform is size (graded) of the desired type, better longevity of seeds, good appearance, good yielding ability and wider adaptability.

Most parts in the country, particularly dry temperate areas are ideal for the production of quality seeds of many temperate vegetable varieties. National Seeds Corporation and many other organizations including many reputed seed companies have already made a remarkable progress in vegetable seed trade. High value of vegetable seeds and increasing problems related to the packing and transportation of perishable horticultural and fresh produce from the hills are attracting more and more growers to take up vegetable seed production. To sustain and encourage further expansion of vegetable seed industry in the country, it is quite necessary to strengthen systematic research on production, processing and storage of vegetable seeds. The technology for maintenance and development of parental lines of hybrid varieties shall have to be made available to the seed producing agencies. Seed production technology, therefore, has to play an increasing important role in enhancing the income of farmers engaged in various vegetable seed production and in saving the precious foreign exchange of the country.

Main Functions of seed Industry

Vegetable seed industry covers all aspect from the development of a variety/hybrid, its multiplication, post-harvest management, transport, marketing, proper and timely distribution among the farmers and the ultimate sale at reasonable price. The main functions are :

(*i*) Vegetable breeding and research on all related aspects.

(*ii*) Cultivar/hybrid assessment.

(*iii*) Multiplication,

(*iv*) Post-harvest handling.

(*v*) Processing including drying, packaging labeling etc.

(*vi*) Storage

(*vii*) Transportation and marketing.

(*viii*) Control-including legislation, notification, seed law enforcement and certification.

(*ix*) Quarantine.

(*x*) Extension.

At present, the private sector is not involved fully (except in few cases) in vegetable breeding, research, cultivar assessment and quarantine. It is dependent upon Government Research Institutes and Agri./Hort. universities.

Conditions favourable for quality seed production in Himachal Pradesh :

1. Soils mostly are fertile, rich in organic matter and well drained.
2. Availability of congenial agro-climatic conditions.
3. Over-wintering of seed crops is done easily and naturally.
4. Pockets and valleys are suitable and conveniently considered for raising seeds of different vegetable varieties.
5. Isolation distance, the hill tops, forest areas and river catchment area, provides natural barriers between the valleys pockets or seed producing areas for getting genetically pure high quality seed yields.
6. Pollinating agents especially bees flora-honey bees, and other types of bees butterflies and other pollinators are available in plenty naturally.
7. Natural sources of irrigation viz. perennial rivers, nallahs, springs etc. are available.
8. Identification of vegetables/varieties should be done, keeping in view the economics of seed production and its requirement in other parts of the state, country and world.
9. Provision of foundation and certified seed need to be done timely and should be given to the registered farmers under a legal agreement.
10. Imparting of proper technical know-how about seed production technology to the farmers well in advance through personal contact, by organising training, camps, literature, newspaper (locally), radios, television, etc.
11. Strict supervision in a well planned manner by the well trained staff.
12. Proper post-harvest handling of vegetable seed crops.

Future strategies

The suitable strategy of state and central governments and non-government organisations through various agencies-state Deptt. of Agri./Horticulture Universities, Institutes, NSC and others, now need to put more emphasis on cash crops and to increase the income of the hill farmers. However, vegetable seed production can help to a great extent in this direction. In view of the disturbed situation in Jammu and Kashmir, Himachal Pradesh has to step up the production of seeds of temperate vegetables. Future strategies are :

1. Exploitation of new seed production pockets.
2. Notification of seed production zones and enactment of seed laws.
3. Mapping of suitable seed production areas for different vegetables, varieties and hybrids.

4. Precautions required for sustaining seed production for long time without deterioration in productivity and quality.
5. Zonalization of areas for specific varieties to avoid isolation problem.
6. Sufficient pollinators.
7. To develop a code of conduct to eliminate the menace of poaching.
8. Seed demand survey and its publication for-indigenous requirement and export.
9. Breeding varieties for export markets.
10. Development of marketing infrastructure.
11. Establishment of State Seed Corporation.
12. Short term courses.
13. Encouraging production of hybrid seeds.
14. Increasing production of breeder seed.
15. Creation of an authority/forum for settling disputes.
16. Putting more area under vegetable seed crops.

TABLE 14.5: List of Varieties/Hybrids released and likely to be released by HPKV[1] Palampur and UHF[2] Solan in Himachal Pradesh

S.No.	Vegetable	Varieties/Hybrids
1.	Tomato	Yahswant (A-2), Solan Gola, Solan Surkha, Solan Vazar, BL-342-1, (Palam Pink), EC-151936 (Palam Pride) and Solan Shogun
2.	Capsicum	Solan Hybrid No. 1
3.	French Bean	Lakshmi and SVM-1
4.	Peas	Solan Nirog, Palam Priya, DPP-9411, DPP-9414
5.	Chillies	Surajmukhi, Pachhad Yellow
6.	Pumpkin	Solan Badami
7.	Cucumber	Kheera-75, Kheera-90
8.	Cauliflower	DNKL-1
9.	Cabbage	KGAT-III
10.	Garlic 1	Solan Selection, GHC-1
11.	Chinese Cabbage	Palampur Grewn
12.	Sprouting Brocccolt	Palam Samridhi, DPGB-12 (Late green), DPPB-1 (Purple heading), DPYgB-1 (Yellow heading)
13.	Radish	DPR-1
14.	Knol-Khol	DPKK-1
15.	Leek	DPL-1
16.	Bitter Gourd	Solan Hara, Solan Safaid

1. Himachal Pradesh Krishi Vishvavidyalaya, Palampur-176 062, District Kangra, (H.P.) INDIA.
2. Dr. Y.S. Parmer University of Horticulture and Forestry, Nauni-173 230, District Solan, (H.P.) INDIA.

At least seed production of those vegetables/varieties/hybrids should be taken up on priority basis which are recently developed and recommended for commercial production and have seed potential.

At present, vegetable seed growers are obtaining vegetable seeds from Department of Agriculture, Agricultural/Horticultural Universities and National Seeds Corporation, only 10 per cent of the requirement of Vegetable growers is met by the different government and semi government agencies.

I. **Cultural practices :** The seed production technology developed has been helpful to produce high quality vegetable seeds under conditions of good field and crop standards. The standardization of seed production techniques in late cauliflower is a notable example. Timely sowing and transplanting particularly in cole and root crops, better management of fertilizer and water are very helpful in increasing the seed yield.

II. **Plant Protection:** Efficient disease and insect control is an important factor in raising healthy seed crops. The quality of seeds obtained from diseases and insect damaged vegetable crop is very poor. Use appropriate chemical at the right time for the control of diseases and insects. Removal of diseased plants from time to time is helpful in checking the further spread of diseases.

III. **Precautions during post-harvest handling:** The time and stage of harvesting is the most important from the point of view of seed yield and its quality. The optimum time of harvest should be determined very carefully to have maximum quantity of fully mature seed with the least damage depending on the nature of crop and the prevailing climatic conditions. Proper curing of the harvested crops particularly of cruciferous helps to attain good colour and size of seeds. The crop should be dried before threshing which is best done on cemented or tarpaulin covered floor. Avoid threshing injury to seeds of garden pea and French bean on beating with a stick. Always do beating gently. Before grading and storing of seeds, it must be dried in order to maintain seeds viability and vigour. The seed should be stored in moisture proof bags or containers.

IV. **Isolation :** Isolation of a seed crop from the fields of other varieties of the same crop or the same variety not conforming to varietal purity requirement under certification or between different kinds of crops crossable to each other is a must to avoid genetic contamination.

V. **Managing pollinators :** In areas where natural pollinators arc not available it will be necessary for making arrangement of bee colonies for brining colonies @ 2-3 bee hives per hectare area. These need to be managed properly and effectively viz. may need to be fed with sugar during slack season or in areas receiving heavy snowfall during winter, area required to be shifted to safer places in the plain areas where the conditions are favourable,

Table 14.6: Seed Companies and other. Agencies operating in Himachal Pradesh

Seed Company	Vegetable seed Crops	Area (ha)	Areas of production	Gross return (Lakhs)
NSC	Late cauliflower, Radish, Sugarbeet	150	Arki, Namohl, Rajgarh, Kinnaur Nalagarh, Sproon	40
-Century seeds	Late cauliflower, Cabbage, Radish	60	Rajgarh, Pulwahal, Noradhar	12
-Sun-Grow	Late Cauliflower, Cabbage, Radish	40	Solan, Sirmour	8
-Sutton's	Late Cauliflower	—	—	—
-Mahyco	Cabbage	140	Solan, Sirmour	40
-Durga Seeds	Radish		Bilaspur	
-Dhanoka seedsand others	—	—	—	—
-State Deptt. of Agriculture	—	—	—	—
-Universities (Agriculture/Horticulture)	—	—	—	—
-IARI* Regional, Station, Katrain	—	—	—	—
-CPRI*, Shimla	Potato	—	—	—

*Only supply breeder and foundation seeds.

TABLE 14.7: Projected Vegetable Seed Production in H.P. During 8th Plan (Quantity of seeds produced during 8 years)

Crop	(Weight in quintals)							
	92-93	93-94	94-95	95-96	96-97	97-98	98-99	99-2000
Peas	4350	4750	5125	5425	5700	6050	6200	7000
Cabbage	12.5	13.0	13.3	14.0	14.3	14.5	14.8	15.0
Cauliflower	175	180	190	200	205	210	215	220
Bhindi	278	300	313	330	339	352	364	375
Turnip	5.5	5.8	6.0	7.0	7.4	7.5	7.8	8.0
Carrot	12.4	12.5	12.9	13.0	13.5	13.8	14.0	15.0
Radish	18.8	22.5	25.3	27.0	29.8	30.0	32.5	35.0
Capsicum*	70.0	80.0	85.0	90.0	95.0	100.0	105.0	110.0
Brinjal*	64.0	80.0	100.0	115.0	124.0	135.0	141.0	150.0
Tomato*	48.0	50.0	60.0	65.0	68.0	70.0	72.0	75.0
Methi	55.0	70.0	75.0	80.0	90.0	95.0	100.0	110.0
Spinach	3.1	3.3	4.0	4.6	4.9	5.2	5.6	5.9
Beans	27.0	33.5	37.0	42.0	46.3	57.5	69.5	101.0

Note: *Weight in Kg.

TABLE 14.8: Registration of Vegetable Crops for Seed Production in H.P.

Crop	Area (ha)	Approximate production (q)
Potato	2000	20000
Ginger	20	2000
Garden Pea	350	3500
Bhindi	25	150
Tomato	2	4
Brinjal	1	1.5
Capsicum	1	1.5
Radish	56	340
Turnip	2	10
Cabbage	10	60
Cauliflower	10	50
Sugar beet	8	56
Beans	1	8
Methi	1	5
Spinach	2	1

Future Prospectus and strategies

Although the seed improvement programme, National Seed Project and Private Seed Industry Sector has developed rapidly during the last two decades, the state is producing only 50% requirements of the certified seeds of the country and the seed replacement rate is very low, therefore, more efforts are needed to increase seed replacement in the country. The breeder, foundation, and certified seed claim is also very weak. Many times adequate quantities of foundation seed are not produced from breeder seed. Foundation seed is also not utilized for certified seed production. The ICAR has made sincere efforts to streamline breeder seed production and its proper utilization. Since ICAR is handling the breeder seed production of a large number of varieties of different vegetables and different season at a number of locations. To consolidate and simplify the breeder seed production it is desirable that the ICAR should take up varieties of national importance and production is arranged on regional centers which have all facilities available.

1. **Hybrid varieties :** India in general and hilly areas (H.P.) in particular should cause for low productivity in the absence of hybrid varieties whose yields are very high as compared to open- pollinated varieties. The area in H.P. under hybrid tomato and cabbage is 15,000 to 20,000 ha and around 6000-8000 ha, respectively. Most of the hybrid seed is imported. Only a few private seeds man have organised commercial hybrid seed production especially in tomato in the country.

2. **Major import of vegetable seeds :** Import of Vegetable hybrids can serve as a catalyst for development of indigenous hybrid seed production technology. So far a few seed companies have the technological competence and commercial hybrid seed production facilities and the import component in hybrid seed production is a major share in the cost of hybrid seeds being produced and marketed at present. Because of varied agro- climatic conditions available the Ft hybrids would be preferred in selected pockets and in high value vegetables such as tomato, cabbage, capsicum and cauliflower etc.

3. **Seed Quality control :** Vegetable seed production system in hills especially H.P. State can be improved by stream lining the seed multiplication claim, augmentation of seed production, processing, storage and marketing will produce quick results. However, quality of seeds alone can bring about a significant increase in the productivity levels at least by 25-30% seed quality control measures will have to be reviewed and enforced better with proper and efficient testing and inspection facilities, research efforts should improve the seed yield per hectare especially in the context of incidence of pests and diseases in seed crops of cabbage, cauliflower, onion and garden peas.

4. **Vegetable Seed Policy :** A state/zone seed policy has to be formulated and implemented without any delay for successful, economic and dependable regular supply of vegetable seeds. For this production statistics of current status of vegetable seed and crop production should be organised, and a hill/state vegetable seed committee need to be set up to over seed the formulation and execution of the composite seed production and marketing programme. These should identify sector-wise responsibilities, commercial production management, quality control and its evaluation breeding and research efforts, processing and storage facilities, pricing and marketing policies, extension and training, system and also funding mechanism. Lack of efficient seed processing, testing and storage facilities is hindering the seed production programme especially when the seed industry is monopolised by the big companies who possess such facilities.

   With all this in view, Govt. of India evolved a new policy on seed development which is being implemented from 2nd October, 1988. This seed policy puts special emphasis on : —

   (*a*) Import of high quality seeds.

   (*b*) A time bound programme to strengthen/modernise plant quarantine facilities.

   (*c*) Effective observance of procedure for quarantine and post entry quarantine (PEQ) and

   (*d*) Incentives to encourage the domestic seed industry including areas.

5. **Middle men's share** : There is need to create alternative marketing channels by establishing co-operative growers organisation to collect, store, grades and marketing the seed at right remunerative price on the pattern of potato seed growers association in Kashmir Valley, only then the middlemen can be eliminated.
6. **Post-harvest handling of the seed** : The seed being living organisms need to be handled properly after drying and curing. Efforts should be made to formulate a plan of loss reduction through better varieties, better handling techniques and packaging. Production and marketing system have to be integrated to reduce post harvest losses. The implementation of a seed production plan should be adequately funded to provide an efficient infrastructure for well coordinated research and development efforts. A national vegetable seed policy and plan for prevention of post-harvesting losses should form the strategy in stepping up vegetable production and consumption
7. **Improving of means of communication** : Lack of proper communications hampers the efficient seed development programme. As more far-flung areas are being brought under vegetable seed production, they need to be provided with timely inputs which is possible if they are properly accessible. The state which has already taken lead in temperate vegetable seed production programme, needs the intensification of research can seed production of temperate, tropical and sub-tropical vegetable varieties and also breeders seed production programme.
8. **Vegetable seed improvement training** : There is urgent need for imparting training on vegetable seed production of all kinds of vegetables to bring improvement regarding seed improvement, seed production techniques, mechanism of quality control i.e. seed certification, seed testing, seed processing and storage, seed marketing and a promotion to equip the trainees with the working knowledge on the above said subject by NSC, Deptt. of Agriculture/Horticulture, Agricultural/Horticultural Universities and other Institutions.
9. **Non-government organisations :** There are a number of private vegetable seed growers, estimated to be around 4 to 5 thousand, in the entire country. There are about 500 seed traders, in the country but only about 25 of them are involved in the supply of good quality seeds after packaging them nicely with printed and beautiful labels in paper packs or tin containers and some of them export vegetable seeds to other countries also after obtaining permission for such trade from the concerned Ministry, Government of India.

Future strategies

The suitable strategy of state and central governments and non-government organisations through various agencies-state Deptt. of Agri./ Hort. Universities, Institutes, NSC and others, now need to put more emphasis on cash crops and to increase the income of the hill farmers. However, vegetable seed production can help to a great extent in this direction. In view of the disturbed situation in Jammu and Kashmir, Himachal Pradesh has to step up the production of seeds of temperate vegetables. Future strategies are :

1. **Exploitation of new seed production pockets** : There are many area? in the hill zone especially H.P. which have suitable agro-ecological conditions congenial for quality seed production of vegetable varieties/hybrids which need to be exploited thereby bringing more area under seed production. This should be done as early as possible.

2. **Notification of seed production zones and enactment of seed laws :** The State Department of Agriculture/Horticulture, State Seed certification Agency and others like NSC used to notify zones during early seventies to different seed organisation for late cauliflower seed production under Essential Commodities Act, 1966 but this did ont work. Proper Seed Laws have to be enacted and implemented.

3. **Mapping of suitable seed production areas for different vegetables/ varieties/hybrids** : The suitable areas in the hills should be located and identified for each vegetable/variety or hybrid depending on their agro-ecological requirements and the quantum of seed need to be produced. However, other factors also need to be kept in mind viz. transportation system, closeness to the road, socio-economic status of the farmers and their acceptability to the seed production programme.

4. **Precautions required for sustaining seed production for long time without deterioration in productivity and quality**: Every care should be taken in the seed production programme right from seed sowing to seed harvesting viz. careful and timely cultural operations, curing, post-harvesting handling pest infestation etc.

5. **Zonalization of areas for specific varieties to avoid isolation problem :** Every effort should be armed to select a independent pocket or zone for each vegetable variety or hybrid to have natural barrier viz. hills, river or forest area between two zones where varietal genetic purity is maintained.

6. **Sufficient pollinators** : There should be sufficient pollinators population or bee flora to carry cross-pollination in the seed crop as 'most of the vegetable crops are highly-cross- pollinated and in some vegetable varieties self-incompatibility exists and services of suitable and efficient pollinators are required to improve quality of seed and increase seed productivity.

7. **To develop a code of conduct to eliminate the menace of poaching** : To safe guard the interest of seed producers and the seed agency a proper code of conduct should be maintained enabling them to trust each other fully. There should be a legal agreement prepared on a judicial paper in which an agreement mentioning there in neither the seed producer refuses to sell the seed to the concerned agency or the seed agency can not refuse to procure/purchase the seed. However the price is always prefixed per kg or quintal agreeable to both parties.
8. **Seed demand survey and its publication for-indigenous requirement and export** : A proper and detail survey should be made through various sources/agencies through out the country, out side in foreign countries and local, specific demand for each vegetable variety that how much need is required. The same should be clearly published in leading papers, reports, pamphlets, folders etc. This will help to assess the quantum of seed to be produced **for** indigenous and export.
9. **Breeding varieties for export markets** : Emphasis should be given to breed varieties and produce their seed which have export potential and possess the acceptable characteristics in the international market.
10. **Development of marketing infrastructure** : Setting up of vegetable seed growers co-operative marketing societies like Lahaul Potato Grower's Marketing Society, which is efficiently handling huge quantities of potato seed produced in the Lahaul Valley, will prove useful.
11. **Establishment of State Seed Corporation:** The corporation may cover the whole hill zone in each state and give competition to the private companies which are taking up seed production programmes at convenient places.
12. **Short term courses** : Starting short term courses for vegetable seed producers and a selected few be also trained for seed production of hybrids.
13. **Encouraging production of hybrid seeds** : Production of hybrid seeds of vegetables is required to be encouraged by providing parental lines and technical knowhow. Possibilities of selling the rights of parental lines of superior hybrids to seed companies need to be explored.
14. **Increasing production of breeder** seed : With increase in area under vegetables, the demand for breeder seeds is likely to be doubled by 2000 A.D. More funds shall have to be provided to cope up with additional demand of vegetable seeds.
15. **Creation of an authority/forum for settling disputes** : A specific authority or form may be organised or constituted at the district and state level under the chairmanship of Director of Agriculture with Official and non-official members of various organisations/agencies directly or indirectly

dealing with vegetable seed production. The main aim of the forum should be to settle the disputes arising at any stage of vegetable seed (industry) production programme.

Conclusion

Dry temperate climate of hilly areas particularly Himachal Pradesh is quite ideal for the production of quality seeds of many temperate, sub-tropical and tropical vegetable/varieties National Seeds Corporation and many reputed seed companies have already made a land mark in Vegetable Seed Trade in the state/ hills with a gross turn over of more than two crores of rupees. Small size holdings, improved irrigation facilities, high value of seeds of temperate vegetables and increasing problems related to packaging and transportation of perishable horticultural produce and fresh vegetable produce are attracting more and more growers to take up vegetable seed production. To sustain and encourage further expansion of vegetable seed industry in the hills/state it is necessary to strengthen research on production, post-harvest handling-processing and storage of vegetable seeds. The technology for maintenance and development of parental lines of hybrid varieties shall have to be made available to the seed producing agencies. Seed technology, therefore, has to play an increasingly important role in enhancing the income of farmers of hills/Himachal Pradesh and in saving the precious foreign exchange of the country.

CHAPTER 15

VEGETABLE GROWING IN JAMMU & KASHMIR

Arun Kumar Gupta

State of Jammu and Kashmir comprising extreme western sector of the Himalayas occupies almost a central position in the continent of Asia. It lies in the north of the Indian Union and extends from 32° -17' to 37° -50' N Lat. from 72° -40' to 80° -30' E longitude. The geographical area of the state is 222236 sq. kms. which includes 115669 sq. kms under illegal occupation of Pakistan and China. The area under cultivation is 818000 ha. It has high mountains with many snow covered peaks. The altitude ranges between 215-7012 metres above ms 1.

The state forms a transitional region of diverse physical features between the week monsoon zone of Punjab and cold arid dry zone of Tibet. On the basis of altitude and climate state may be-divided into four zones i.e. Sub-tropical, Intermediate, Temperate and Arid zone.

Sub-tropical zone

The outer plains and outer hills of Jammu province (Jammu Kathua and part of Udhampur districts) are grouped in this zone. The altitude ranges from 215-360 metres. The normal precipitation of the zone is 1000 mm. The area under this region represents fringle of level lands in continuation with the Punjab plains and touches the Jammu hills. There are broad longitudinal valley in this region.

Broadly two groups of soils are observed in this zone :

(*i*) Shiwalik soils

(*ii*) Lower belt soils

(*i*) **Shiwalik soils** : These are found in the foot hills of Shiwalik range extending from Madhopur to Udhampur and beyond. The topography of the area is undulating with ravines and gullies spread in it. Pebbles, gravels and rockout crops are observed over the surface and are also encountered in the profiles at varying depths, thus the soils are shallow to deep. These are moderately slopy to steep slopy with severe erosion. Most of the area is under sparsely forest vegetation. These are mostly unirrigated soils and dry land farming is practiced in this region. These are moderately coarse textured soils and have been formed from weathered sand stone's and clay stone. These are well drained soils with rapid permeability. The predominant soils observed in the region are Orthents and Ochrepts.

(*ii*) **Lower belt soils** : These are observed on the top slopes of Shiwalik range and border Gurdaspur and Pakistan. These are alluvial in nature and are moderately fine textured soils. These are found on plain topography, with moderate erosion and are moderately drained to poorly drained. The ground water is usually observed at a depth of 50 cms and higher in the border areas. These are irrigated soils but net work of canals has contributed to the formation of waterlogged and saline soils in the area where adequate drainage facilities have not been provided. Ochrepts and Udalfs are the common soils observed in this zone.

Intermediate zone

These are sub-mountainous soils and comprises parts of Doda, Udhampur, Poonch and Rajouri districts of the state. The average altitude is about 750 metres and snowfalls on higher reaches during winter. The mountains in this zone are cut by ravines and valleys. The area experiences rugged terrain, steep slopes, lofty hills with little area available for cultivation. These are severely eroded soils and are shallow to moderately deep. These are mostly used for maize. Orthents, Ochrepts and Udalfs are mostly observed in this area.

Temperature zone

This zone comprises whole of Kashmir valley and higher reaches of Doda and Poonch district. The area has a marked variation in temperature and precipitation. The altitude of this zone varies between 1500-2500 metres above m s 1 The normal precipitation is 650 mm, mostly received during March-April. There are broadly 3 group of soils in this zone : (*i*) High altitude, (*ii*) Valley basin, (*iii*) Karewa soils.

High altitude soils :

These are located within a altitude of 1800-2500 metres stretching from kerawas and bordering forests on the other. These are heavy textured soils. The area is mostly rainfed and maize is predominant crop These are moderately sloping lands with moderate severed erosion which has resulted in the formation of gullies.

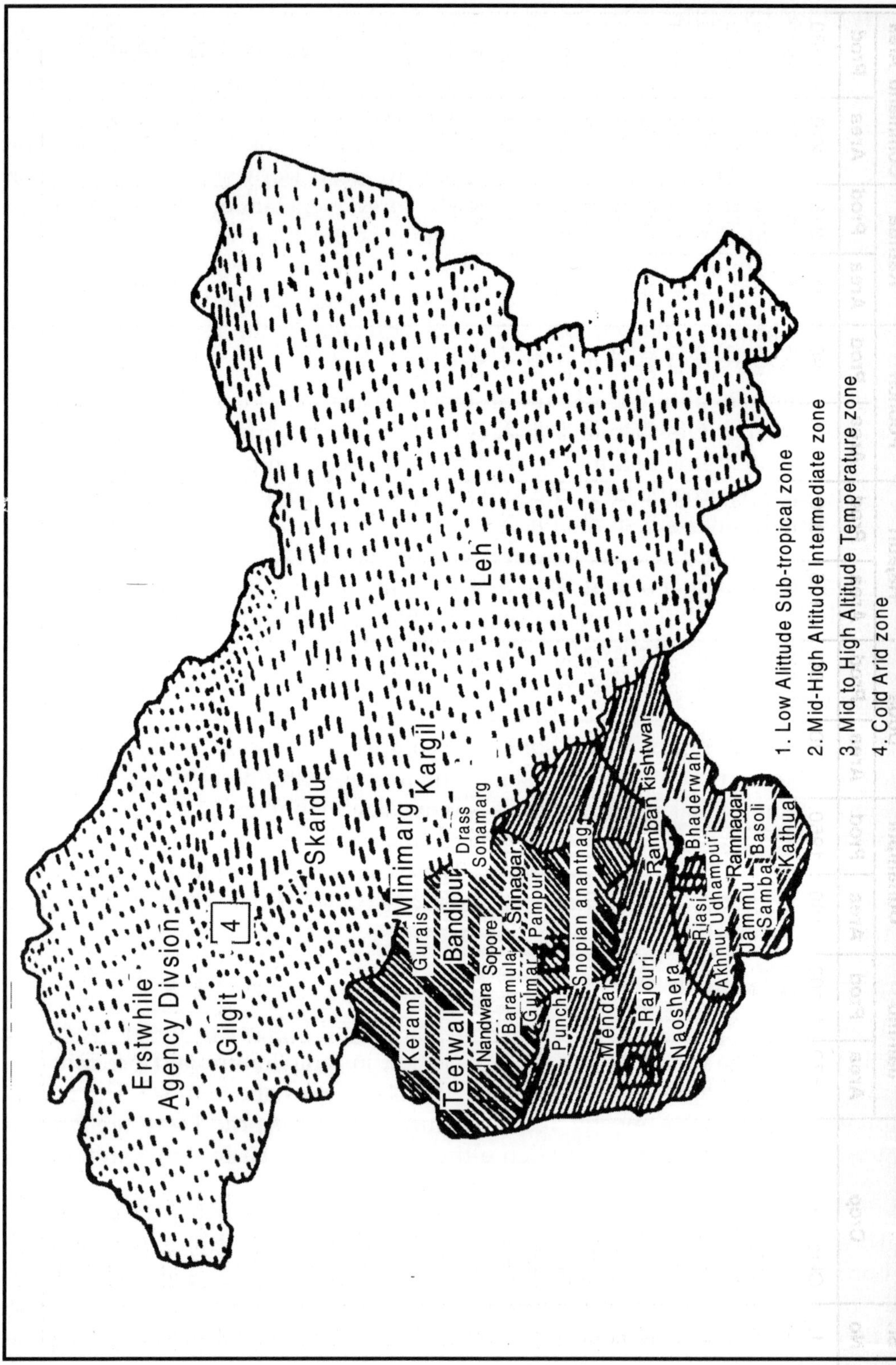

Fig 15. (i) : Agro-climatic Zone of Jammu and Kashmir

TABLE 15.1: District wise area (ha) and production (MT) of vegetable crops in Jammu Division.

Sr. No	Crop	Jammu Area	Jammu Prod	Udhampur Area	Udhampur Prod	Doda Area	Doda Prod	Rajauri Area	Rajauri Prod	Poonch Area	Poonch Prod	Kathua Area	Kathua Prod	Command Area Area	Command Area Prod
1.	Okra	570	17100	180	1950	20	100	105	1330	15	90	45	315	210	1580
2.	Tomato	88	3450	87	1566	30	180	42	245	15	95	6	30	58	1210
3.	Brinjal	165	8178	45	540	110	1320	28	250	15	105	10	100	95	1330
4.	Cauliflower	940	40801	60	1440	50	720	28	198	2	16	10	100	140	2520
5.	Cabbage	260	13220	25	575	60	720	2	20	2	16	10	120	105	1680
6.	Knol-khol	290	10820	895	1945	110	580	40	528	30	300	40	360	116	1624
7.	Radish	585	14900	125	300	50	600	41	533	24	288	40	400	160	2400
8.	Carrot	65	1825	20	200	10	100	10	50	5	50	8	96	106	1590
9.	Turnip	330	7935	40	800	50	350	66	924	38	494	16	153	48	720
10.	Onion	94	1410	40	960	76	912	52	520	45	510	24	210	231	1016
11.	Garlic	30	270	40	400	–	–	25	200	43	300	4	32	12	108
12.	Potato	2821	15786	405	4887	170	1360	110	1647	36	44	15	215	513	10260
13.	Chillies (g)	100	3000	41	350	100	300	87	96	31	243	7	42	20	120
14.	Peas (g)	340	8765	85	765	130	1850	72	615	6	29	11	71	45	450
15.	Beans (g)	127	3127	75	900	83	906	7	63	12	120	5	40	8	96
16.	Capsicum	30	560	8	72	10	90	50	30	2	10	5	30	12	72
17.	Hak Sag*	4	12	3	9	4	16	1	2	1	3	1	2	–	–
18.	Methi	6	1220	3	12	2	8	4	12	6	24	2	6	10	50
19.	Spinach	90	2700	4	24	30	240	22	154	5	35	10	100	36	208
20.	Colocasia	18	290	–	–	–	–	–	–	–	–	–	–	–	–
21.	Tinda	130	3750	–	–	–	–	–	–	–	–	–	–	–	–
22.	Muskmelon	670	9196	–	–	–	–	–	–	–	–	5	50	53	742
23.	Watermelon	1090	17440	2	12	–	–	–	–	–	–	–	–	105	1680
24.	Bitter Gourd	100	2500	42	252	3	13	8	55	2	12	4	28	10	80
25.	Bottle Gourd	498	6474	22	320	50	600	5	45	16	144	5	60	12	144
26.	Cucumber	190	3920	30	270	245	2450	15	105	16	144	5	30	15	105
27.	Pumpkin	20	240	5	60	532	14250	2	16	8	24	5	50	8	80
28.	Other Cucurbit	–	–	–	–	–	–	–	–	–	–	–	–	–	–

g = green, * = Kale

These are deep soils and are excessively drained. The predominant soils in the area are Udlfs, Udolls and Orthents.

Valley basin soils :

These have resulted from alluvium deposited by their river Jehlum and its tributaries. These lie at an altitude of 1500-1600 metres above ms 1. These are poorly drained soils but the soils on terraced topography are well drained. These are irrigated soils and are put under the cultivation of paddy. Soil in the area are moderately eroded. Aqualfs, Aquepts and Udalfs are predominant soils observed in the area.

Karewa soils :

These are pleistocene and post-pleistocene deposits commonly known as Karewa (table land) occupy nearly half of the valley. These consists of fine grain bluish and buff coloured sandy clay partly compacted conglomerates and embedded more rains. These are severely eroded to moderately eroded soils and are located within an altitude of 1650-1800 metres above ms 1. These are gently sloping uplands and have undulating topography. Udalfs and Ochrepts are the major soils observed in the area.

Arid zone :

Ladakh, the cold arid belt in Indus valley region inter woven with a complex net work of nude Himalayan ranges is the loftiest in inhabited region of the world. It is a mountainous country mostly a desert of bare crags and granite dust with vast arid table land of high elevation. The climate of Ladakh is characterised by great extreme of heat and cold and excessive dryness. The soils are sandy derived from weathered debris of the rocks and are subject to the great diurnal as well as seasonal alternation of temperature, topographical variation of the region has accelerated the sheet and gully erosion. The soils are coarse textured and sand content usually shows an increasing trend from Drass to Leh. Orthents and Ochrepts are dominant soils in the area.

●●●

CHAPTER 16

VEGETABLE PRODUCTION POTENTIAL IN LADAKH

Brahma Singh & Sanjai K. Dwivedi

Ladakh, as a whole constitute almost 2/3 of geographical area of J & K state and is comprised of Leh and Kargil districts is located at an altitude between 2900-5900 m above msl. Leh alone is extended over an 45,110 sq km but only a little area of about 11,000 hectares are presently under the cultivation of various agricultural crops. This area is characterised by uneven land, barren mountains, arctic desert and extremely cold weather for 7 months of the year. Minimum winter temperature of — 30°C (Leh) and — 40°C (Changthang) make any cultivation in the period just about impossible. Normal agricultural practices are restricted to the summer months from May till September. Very low annual precipitation (9 to 23.9 cm) and relative humidity (31- 64%) form further impediments to the practice of successful agriculture (Chaurasia and Singh, 1996).

Agriculture is the main source of livelihood in Ladakh. The major agronomical crops include grim and wheat while, vegetables are playing major role in supplementing the income to the farmers and hence assured great importance in Ladakh in recent years. Despite local population, armed forces deployed at China and Pakistan border of Ladakh has enhanced the vegetables demand manifold in the region.

Summer Vegetable Production

The area under vegetables has increased to about 400% and the production rose upto 8400 MT during the year 1998. Out of which vegetable worth ₹ 1.5 crores

* Director, DFAS, Room No. 326, 'B' Wing, Sena Bhawan, New Delhi-11

** Scientist 'C Field Research Laboratory, C/O 56 APO

has been supplied to Defence forces besides 400-500 MT surplus and requiring export market. Local vegetables supplied to army during 1998 includes potato (465 mt), onion dry (29 mt) and other vegetables (235 mt). Anticipated production of vegetables during the year 1999 is 9000 MT in Leh district. Crop-wise vegetable cultivation area, production and surplus quantity have been presented in Table 16.1. (Bhat, 1998). Open vegetable cultivation in summer is restricted from May to September only. Traditionally vegetable cultivation was restricted to growing of local radish, turnip, swede and potato. With the screening of other vegetables suitable for cultivation in this region over 45 new types viz, broccoli, brussels sprout, tomato, cabbage, cauliflower, peas etc. have been introduced and their cultural practices standardized (Table-16.2) (Singh, 1995). This has given a boost to the production of vegetables in this area. Fresh vegetables like cabbage, cauliflower, knoll-khol, pea, carrot, radish, onion, potato etc. are available in plenty during July-September when other part of the nation experience acute crisis of fresh vegetables due to monsoon season and this can be exploited by developing marketing net work.

TABLE 16.1: Cross-wise Vegetable Cultivation Area Production and Surplus Quantities During 1998 in Leh District

Crop	Area (HA)	Prod (MT)	Surplus (Q)
Potato	370	3000	2000
Cabbage	125	1500	400
Cauliflower	80	800	300
Radish/Turnip	50	500	100
Carrot	50	400	100
Peas	130	1300	500
Tomato	15	150	200
Leafy vegetables	20	140	400
Brinjal & Other fruit vegetables	05	175	over
Onion	25	125	–
Total	870	8090	

Rare Vegetable Cultivation

Tropical vegetable crops like cucurbits, capsicum, brinjal, okra, chily etc are rare for Ladakh since they are susceptible to low temperature and thus can not be grown in normal conditions of this temperate climate. However, certain technologies have been developed which enable raising of nursery in mid April to early May under cover (Singh, 1995).Seeds of cucurbits are generally grown in polytube under cover. The seedlings at 5-6 leaf stage can be planted either in green house or in the open by adopting black polyethylene mulch. Recommended varieties and other tips for cultivation are given in Table-16.2.

TABLE 16.2: Cross-wise Recommended Varieties/Hybrids, Planting Time, Availability Period, Major Pests and Diseases

Crop	Variety	Planting Time	Availability Period	Major pests/ Diseases
Crop crops				
Cabbage	Golden Acre, Early Drum Head	March-April	July-Sept.	Aphids
Cauliflower	Pusa Snow Ball & 1, K-l	March-April	July- Sept.	
Knolkhol	White Vieana, Purple Vieana	March-June	Aug.-Sept.	
Broccoli	Packaman, Pyrett	April-May	Aug.-Sept.	
Root crops				
Radish	Pusa Himani, Local	Mar.-Oct.	June-Nov.	Aphids
Turnip	Purple Top White Globe,	-do-	Feb.-Oct.	
	Golden Ball	-do-	Feb.-Nov.	
Carrot	Nantes Local	-do-	Mar.-Nov.	
Beet Root	Detroit Dark red	-do-	Mar.- Nov.	
Swede	Local			
Leafy Vegetables				
Beet leaf	K.Raya, FRL Sel	Mar.-Oct.	Throughout year	Aphids
Spinach	Prickly Seeded	-do-	-do-	
Mustard	ARU Black	-do-	Feb.-Nov.	
Fenugreek	Kasuri Pusa Early Bunching	-do-	-do-	
Karam Sag	Kashmiri	-do-	Mar.-Oct.	
Orich (Ustakh)	Kashmiri	-do-	-do-	
Coriander	PD-1, Pand Haritima	-do-	Feb.-Nov.	
Leguminous crops				
Pea	Bonneville Arkel	April-May	July-Aug.	Nil
French Beans	Contender	April-June	-do-	
Broad Bean	Local	April-June	-do-	
Bulb crops				
Onion	Local White, Pusa Red	April-May	Aug.-Sept.	Nil
Tuber crops				
Potato	Kufari Chandar Mukhi, Kufri Jyoti	April-May	September	Aphid, Potato tuber moth
Solanaceous fruit crops				
Tomato	Rupali, Pusa Hybrid-1	May-June	Aug.-Sept.	Fruit borer

Crop	Variety	Planting Time	Availability Period	Major pests/ Diseases
Brinjal	Pusa Purple Round, PPL	-do-	-do-	Jassids
Capsicum	California Wonder, Bharat	-do-	-do-	
	Jwala			
Chilli	Varsh, Prabhani Kranti	-do-	-do-	
Okra		-do-	-do-	
Cucurbits				
Pumpkin	Pusa Vishwas	May-June	Aug.-Sept.	Fruit Fly
Summer				and
Squash	Australian Green	-do-	July-Sept.	Powdery
Bottle Gourd	Pusa Naveen, Pusa	-do-	- do-	Mildew
Ridge	Gourd Sandesh	-do-	-do-	
Sponge Gourd	Pusa Nasdar	-do-	-do-	
Long Melon	Pusa Chikni	-do-	-do-	
Cucumber	Green Long	-do-	-do-	
Musk Melon	Poinsette, Pusa Sanyog	-do-	-do-	
Water Melon	Hara Madhu Sugar Baby	-do-	Aug.-Sept.	

Mulching

Scarcity of water, low night temperature and excessive weed population has necessitated the adoption of mulch technique in vegetable cultivation in Ladakh. Findings on this aspects clearly indicate that mulching with black polyethylene has several advantages. A favourable response for earliness (16-20 days) and higher productivity (89-189 qt per ha) have been observed in cabbage, cauliflower and tomato (Singh *et al,* 1998). Weed population was also negligible and thus no weeding was required. The technology is gaining popularity especially for growing of rare vegetables in Ladakh.

Vegetable Seed Production

Long day length, high light intensity and low atmospheric humidity coupled with lack of disease and pest incidence throughout the growing season provide an ideal condition for production of quality seed of temperate vegetables. Suitable cultural practices have been standardized for seed production in crops like Cabbage (Singh *et al.* 1997 a), beet root (Singh *et al.* 1997 b) carrot, onion, knoll-khol, radish spinach and true potato seed.

It has been proved that the area has a vast potential for vegetable seed production. Development of vegetable seed industry in the region will not only improve the economic status of the tribal farmers but also overcome the need for import of vegetable seeds like cabbage beetroot, etc from abroad.

Organic Farming

Dependence on synthetic chemical materials such as fertilizers, insecticides/ pesticides, fungicides, weedicides or growth regulators is necessitated because of their quick response in over all crop production. These chemicals play an important role in vegetable production. But besides damaging soil structure and environment these chemicals are a potential health hazard to human health. Organic farming of vegetable makes a positive contribution for the protection of soil, environment and human health. It is dependent upon maintaining ecological balance and developing biological processes to the optimum.

Ladakh is following the traditional method of organic farming. Use" of fertilizers is mostly avoided in vegetable production. Use of pesticides and growth regulators is either nil or negligible since incidence of pests/diseases are very little due climatic factors. Animal manure, night soil and kitchen waste etc is used for enriching the soil. This condition makes Ladakh ideal for organic vegetable cultivation which has vast market abroad and thus can be developed commercially for export purposes.

Winter Vegetable Production

Ladakh remains cut-off from rest of the nation from November to June every year due to heavy snowfall which causes blockage of roads. Subzero temperature prevails from December to February throughout Ladakh whereas, zero degree is experienced during the rest of the winter months. Under such circumstances, it is not possible to grow vegetables in the open field and transportation of fresh vegetable is also problem. Landing cost of vegetables by air adds about ₹ 20 per kg which necessitates the need of vegetable cultivation in the region (Singh *et al;* 1999).

Protected cultivation is the only alternative for cultivation of vegetables in winter. Various greenhouse structures viz glasshouse, polyhouse, Ladakhi polyhouse, trench and tunnel for cultivation were studied. Of these, the trench has been found to be the most suitable and economic structure for the region followed by Ladakhi Polyhouse (Table-16.3 & 16.4) (Singh *et al;* 1998). This is because it

TABLE 16.3: Performance of Beetleaf (Var. all Green) in Greenhouse During Peak Winter (Nov.-March)

Strcutre	Av. Plant height (Cm)	Av. yield (kg/m^2 /cutting)	Total* yield (kg)
Glasshouse	21.8	1.1	3.3
Ladakhi Polyhouse	22.0	1.8	5.4
Polyhouse	19.3	0.9	2.7
Trench	26.8	2.1	6.3
Tunnel	17.0	1.1	3.3
Unit Polyhouse	21.4	1.5	4.5

* Total of three cuttings taken on 30 Dec, 30 Jan and 20 Feb.

retains the increased day temperatures even during night. The trench, as proposed by the laboratory is an underground structure. It may be of convenient variable dimensions covered with UV stabilized transparent polyethylene (400 gauge). At night another covering of black polyethylene is given to harness the soil temperature which has increased during the day and to minimise the heat loss (Singh, 1995).

TABLE 16.4: Production Economics of Beet Leaf (per m^2) in Various Greenhouses

Structure	Total Cost	Life Span (Yr)	Area (m^2) Year	Cost (₹) (m^2/year)	Produce (kg/m^2) 15/kg	Cost @	Profit (₹)
Glasshouse	115200	10	40	288	3.3	49.5	–238.5
Ladakhi Polyhouse	5240	3	50	35	5.4	81.0	46.0
Polyhouse	52000	2	70	125	2.7	40.5	–84.5
Trench	1960	6	24	14	6.3	94.5	80.5
Tunnel	6240	2	140	22	2.2	33.0	11.0
Unit Polyhouse	5300	2	70	38	4.5	67.5	29.5

Studies carried out at Field Research Laboratory-Leh during 1996- 1999 indicates that leafy vegetables like lettuce, vegetable mustard, coriander, fenugreek and beetleaf etc can be successfully grown under protected structures (Table-16.5) (Singh *et al;* 1998).

TABLE 16.5: Performance of Various Leafy Vegetables Grown Under Polyhouse During Peak Winter (Nov.-March)

Crop/Variety	Av. Plant height (cm)	Yield/m^2 (kg)
Beet Leaf (All Green)	21.36	1.25
Beet leaf (Mongol)	34.44	2.50
Coriander (Local)	39.8	2.25
Fenugreek	39.92	2.50
Lettuce (Great Lake)	23.84	4.50
Veg Mustard (ARU Black)	46.56	4.50

TABLE 16.6: Blockwise Status of Greenhouse in Leh District Dec. 1997

Block	No. of families	No. of greenhouse	No. of greenhouse required
Durbuk	870	552	318
Khalsi	3390	2831	559
Leh	9659	4449	5210
Nubra	3260	1471	1789
Nyoma	1853	1471	1412
Total	19032	9744	9288

Districtwise Status of Greenhouse in Cold Arid Region (Ladakh) Till March 1999

Distt.	No. of families	No. of greenhouse	No. of greenhouse required
Leh	19032	14,500	4532
Kargil	21700	7000*	14700

* Project figure

Though studies carried by the Field Research Laboratory-Leh recommends trench type of greenhouse for Ladakh however, the region is predominated by Ladakhi polyhouse. It is similar to normal polyhouse but the only difference is its surrounding mud brick wall in place of polyethylene sheet which not only cut down the installation cost but also reduce the adverse affects of strong winds and increase temperature retention and thus ultimately net profit get increased. This is generally lean type have three sides made of mud bricks. The back wall is 8 ft in height while front has no wall. The length is 32 ft-with a width of 16 ft. The polyethylene is supported on wooden poles and side walls.. The two side walls are descending towards the front. J & K State Deptt of Agriculture/Horticulture provides cash subsidy of ₹ 3,000/- besides a 32 X 16 ft free polyethylene sheet. This has brought boost to the greenhouse revolution in Ladakh. Status of greenhouse in Ladakh has been shown in Table-6.

Potential areas for Ladakh

(*i*) Supply of off-season vegetables like peas, Tomato, Cabbage, Cauliflower, Carrot etc to plain area during peak rainy season.

(*ii*) Production of exotic vegetables like Broccoli, Brussels Spout, Parsley, Celery etc.

(*iii*) Establishment of vegetable seed industry for the precious crops like Cabbage, beet root, Onion etc. to cut down the import of seeds.

(*iv*) Organic vegetable farming has unlimited scope to exploit vegetable market in advanced countries.

(*v*) Processing industry establishments for surplus and organically produced vegetables.

Limitations

(*i*) Non-availability of quality seeds to interior region of Ladakh.

(*ii*) Lack of proper extension of new technology and potential areas.

(*iii*) Crisis of inputs like fertilizer, irrigation water, power etc.

(*iv*) Storage and transportation of vegetables is mega hurdle.

(*v*) Lack market net work and communication means.

REFERENCES

1. **Bhat, G.H. (1998).** Status of agriculture and strategy for future development in district Leh. Chief Agriculture Office Report, Leh.
2. **Chaurasia, O.P. and Singh, B. (1996).** Cold Desert Plants. Vol-I. DESIDOC-Delhi.
3. **Singh, B (1995 a).** Vegetable Production Ladakh. Field Research Laboratory, C/O 56 APO.
4. **Singh, B. (1995 b).** Green House Development in Leh. Paper Presented in National Workshop on Commercialization of tissue culture and greenhouse technology, Bangalore, India 5-6 May 1995.
5. **Singh, B.; Jadhva, K.L. and Paljor, Eli (1997 a).** Potentials of cabbage seed production in Leh valley. Indian Horticulture. 41 (4) : 36-37.
6. **Singh, N.; Singh, B. and Sareen, S.K. (1997).** High altitude cold desert beet seed production. Indian Horticulture. 41 (4) : 57-58.
7. **Singh, B.; Dwivedi, S.K.; Singh, N. and Paljor, Eli (1998).** Sustainable Horticulture Practices for cold arid areas. Paper presently in International Symposium on sustainable agriculture in hill areas. 29-31 Oct. 1998. HPKW-Palampur. Abstract, pp 35-36.
8. **Singh, N.; Dwivedi, S.K. and Paljor Eli (1999).** Protected vegetable cultivation in Ladakh (In Hindi) Field Research Laboratory-Leh (Ladakh).

CHAPTER 17

STATUS AND PROSPECTS OF VEGETABLE PRODUCTION IN KARNATAKA

L.B. Naik

Karnataka is one of the leading states in the scientific and technological developments in the country today. However, the state has lagged behind in agricultural production which has been reflected in the lower per capita income in comparison with that of the average, national income. Besides, although Karnataka being the first state in India to have a full fledged department of horticulture, the production of vegetables has not received the required attention. This is inspite of the fact that the state is endowed with rich and abundant natural resources for the production of varieties of vegetable crops. The moderate climate throughout the year, well distributed rainfall during the rainy season, availability of different soil ranging from well drained sandy loam soils in southern Karnataka to very rich black cotton soils of northern parts of the state, etc. provide a very good potential for growing most of the vegetable crops which can fetch considerably higher income than any other agricultural crop. Yet the expansion of the area under vegetable crops as well as overall development of vegetable industry in the state is not as rapid as could have been.

The rise in the income of middle class population and the rapid increase in the population of urban areas especially cities like Bangalore has given a big boost to the demand for vegetables. Besides the availability of good quality seed especially hybrid varieties through the entry of multinational companies has given greater impetus to the vegetable production in recent years.

Status of Vegetable Production

The state of Karnataka has a total geographical area of 19.18 million hectares. The area under cultivation is 12.01 million hectares. This includes a net area sown of 10.42 million hectares and sown more than once 1.59 million hectares according to 1995-96 figures. Therefore, the net area sown is about 54.7% of the total geographical area.

The net irrigated area is 2.30 million hectares while the gross irrigated area is 2.84 million hectares. The combined irrigated area under fruits and vegetables is 1.22 lakh hectares which works out a paltry 4.3 per cent of all the crops.

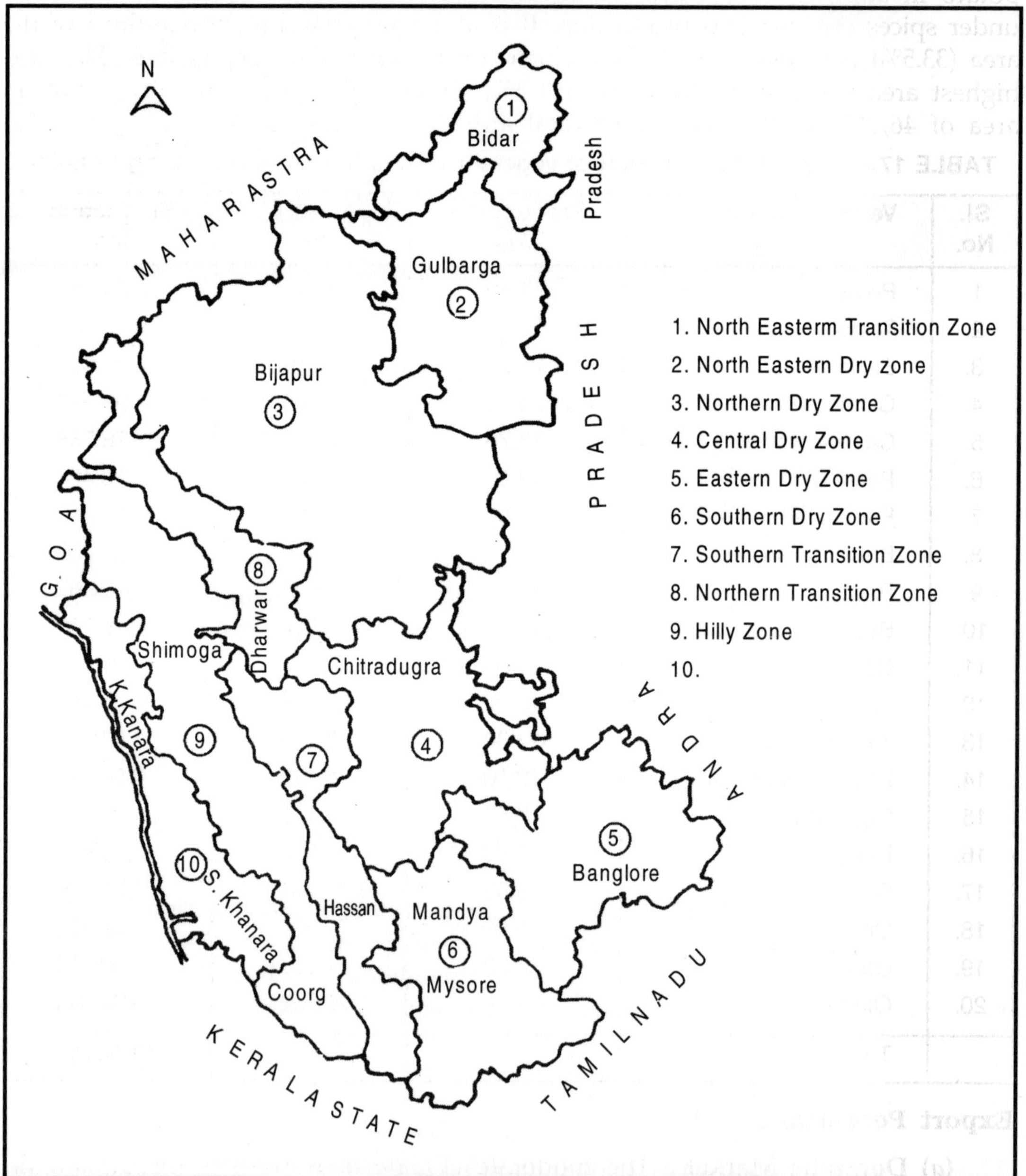

Fig. 17. (i) Agro-climatic Zones of Karnataka

According to 1995-96 figures, vegetable crops occupy an area of 4,46,948 hectares with a production of 61.10 lakh tonnes in Karnataka. The productivity works out about 13.70 tons per hectare. The anticipated area and production of vegetables in the year 2000 AD would be 4,80,469 hectares and 65.68 lakh tonnes respectively.

The area and production of various vegetable crops during 1995-96 is presented in the Table-17.1. It is pertinent to note that the area and production includes potato in addition to chillies, onion and garlic which are sometimes included under spices for area and production. It is also noted that nearly one third of the area (33.5%) is covered by chillies which consists of mainly dry chillies. The next highest area is occupied by onion (11.3%). Potato takes the third place with an area of 46,115 hectares (10.3% of total area).

TABLE 17.1: Area and production of vegetable crops in Karnataka during 1995-96.

Sl. No.	Vegetable crop	Productivity t/ha	Area ha.	Production ton
1.	Potato	17.90	46,115	8,25,459
2.	Tomato	25.00	36,516	9,12,900
3.	Brinjal	27.00	26,050	7,03,350
4.	Cabbage	24.00	8,263	1,98,317
5.	Cauliflower	18.70	4,208	78,768
6.	Peas	12.50	2,227	28,463
7.	French bean	22.50	18,383	4,13,618
8.	Bhindi (Okra)	8.75	14,368	1,25,720
9.	Radish	43.50	8,482	3,68,967
10.	Beet root	18.75	2,652	49,725
11.	Carrot	20.00	4,584	91;680
12.	Tapioca	15.00	2,411	36,165
13.	Sweet potato	14.00	10,768	1,50,752
14.	Leafy vegetables	12.50	20,482	2,56,025
15.	Capsicum	6.80	3,428	23,310
16.	Pumpkin	40.00	7,992	3,19,680
17.	Chillies (dry)	2.50	1,49,734	3,74,335
18.	Onion	15.00	50,490	7,57,350
19.	Garlic	7.50	4,077	30,578
20.	Others	–	25,668	3,64,913
	Total		4,46,948	61,10,055

Export Potential :

(*a*) **Domestic Market :** The moderate climate of Karnataka throughout the year has made it possible to produce large number of vegetable crops throughout the year. The availability of hybrid vegetables in cauliflower and cabbage tolerant to moderately higher temperature has made it possible to produce even such vegetables for most parts of the year in the state. Most of the states located in the northern part of the country experience shortage of vegetables in summer as well as winter seasons of such vegetables which do not tolerant to extreme higher or lower temperatures. The prices of such vegetables rules very high during the off period. A great deal of potential exists in Karnataka especially the irrigated areas of north Karnataka to produce such vegetables and supply to the northern parts of the country. Introduction of special trains on the line of 'Milk Specials presently running from Gujarat to Calcutta, shall go a long way in fetching better prices for vegetables in southern parts of the country besides alleviating the hardships of consumers in northern India.

(*b*) **Export to Other Countries :** The favorable climate of Karnataka for vegetable production has also encouraged several entrepreneurs located here as well as abroad in contract production of vegetable in Karnataka and export to other countries. Gherkins (pickling cucumbers) are being produced and exported to West European and North American countries. Some vegetables including broccoli are being produced on contract and exported to Australia and some east Asian Countries. Potential also exist for export of vegetables to West Asian and Arab Countries.

Major Production Constraints

The vegetable production in Karnataka is beset with several problems which may be biotic or abiotic. The major bottlenecks are outlined here.

1. Majority of the vegetable growers in the state are small holders and economically weak. Hence they cannot afford for higher investment required for vegetable production.
2. Non-availability of good quality seeds of required varieties/hybrids of various crops at required time and place.
3. Weak transport facilities in vegetable production centres located away from cities face severe problems of transport facilities which includes absence of roads as well as vehicles.
4. Poor marketing facilities : The marketing costs are very high. Malpractices are very common. In fact marketing is the most serious problem in vegetable production.
5. Besides, inadequate knowledge of vegetable production, inexperience in the field of vegetable growing and lack of proper attention needed to the crop greatly limit the vegetable production.
6. Lack of labour availability in irrigated areas in sufficient number at reasonable wages.
7. Lack of machanization in vegetable production.

Vegetable Seed Production

Vegetable seed production activity in Karnataka is quite well advanced in comparison to other states in the country. In fact large number of national and multinational companies have established their seed production and processing centres in the state. Karnataka is emerging as a major research, development production and processing centre for many hybrid vegetable seeds (Raghavan, 1991). There are various reasons for the state's growing prominence in this field.

1. **Climate :** In many parts of Karnataka, including Bangalore, temperature, rainfall and humidity are never extreme making it conductive for research as well as production of seeds of several vegetable crops. In plant bio-tech research, in particular expenditure on energy for climate control is far less as national temperatures are moderate.
2. **Infrastructure :** Reliable technological inputs and facilities are available close at hand from institutions such as Indian Institute of Horticultural Research, Indian Institute of Science, University of Agricultural Sciences (Dharwar and Bangalore) and from private seed companies such as Indo-American Hybrid Seeds.
3. **Production base :** Karnataka is a production centre for various vegetable seeds such as tomato, brinjal, watermelon etc. Major seed production areas are Haveri, Ranebennur, Bellary and Raichur, Ranebennur is such an important R and D centre that over 50 seed companies have officers or representatives.
4. **Market:** Because of the moderate climate large number of vegetables are cultivated throughout the year in different parts of the state, giving a good market for the vegetable seeds.
5. **Labour :** In areas cited above farm labour is comparatively cheap and that makes cost of seed production competitive, especially in the areas like Ranebennur, Harappanahalli, Haveri, Kundagol, Byadgi, Kotur etc. which have become the nucleus of seed production activity in the country mainly because of the following reasons.
    1. **Skilled Labour :** Many of the farmers are well trained in the various specialized activities of seed production including hybrids like pollen collection, emasculation, crossing, fermentation of the fruits and seed extraction, seed drying etc.
    2. **The absence of canal irrigation :** Bio urban areas and industries in many of these areas has greatly eased the problem of labour availability in these areas.
    3. **Fertile soil** : The fertile, well drained medium black cotton soils of north Karnataka and medium sandy loam soils of south Karnataka are ideal for seed production.

TABLE 17.2: Recommended varieties/hybrids, planting time, availability, pests and diseases in vegetables

S. No.	Crop	Recommended Varieties/hydbrids	Planting	Availability	Insect-pests	Diseases
(1)	(2)	(3)	(4)	(5)	(6)	(7)
1.	Potato	1. Kufri Chandramukhi 2. Kufri Badshah 3. Kufri Jyoti 4. Kufri Sindhuri 5. Kufri Kuber 6. Upto Date	1. May-June 2. Oct.-Nov.	Aug.-Nov.	Aphids, leaf hpper, Epilachna beetle, Cut worm, Tuber worm, Root grub.	Early blight, Bacterial brown roll, Leaf roll, Mosaic, root knot mematode.
2.	Tomato	1. Arka Vikas 2. Arka Sourab 3. Arka Ahuti 4. Arka Ashish 5. Arka Meghali 6. Arka Abhijit (FI) 7. Arka Vardan (FI) fruit 8. Pusa Ruby mildew. 9. Megha 10. NDTR-1 Roma	1. June-July 2. Oct-Nov. 3. Jan.-Feb.	Dec-June	Jassid fruit borer, Root grub, white fly.	Damping off Leaf curl, leaf sp. Leaf blight Bacterial wilt, Fusarium wilt, root knot nematode rot & powdery
3.	Bringal	1. Arka Sheel 2. Arka Shirish 3. Arka Kusumakar 4. Arka Navneet (FI) 5. Arka Neelkant 6. Erenger 7. Kengeri 8. Malapurall	1. June- July 2. Oct.-Nov. 3. Jan.-Feb.	Throughout the year	Epilacna beetle, Jassid, stem borer, shoot & fruit, borer apfeid, mealy bug, mite, root grug weevil grub.	Damping-off leaf curl, leaf sp. Leaf blight, Bacterial wilt, root knot nematode, fruit rot & powdery mildew.

(1)	(2)	(3)	(4)	(5)	(6)	(7)
		9. Mattigua 10. West Coast Round 11. Pusa Kranti 12. Composite 1 & 2				
4.	Chilli	1. Byadgi 2. Sankeshwar 3. Chincholli 4. Mysore 5. Gowribidanur 6. Np-46A 7. G-3 8. Pusa Jwala 9. Arka Lohit	1. May-June 2. Oct.-Nov. 3. Jan.-Feb.	Mar.-Apr.	Thrips fruit borer, Aphid, mite white fly	Damping-off Anthracnose, leaf sp. Leaf curl, powdery mildew. Fusarium wilt, root knot mematode fruit rot & powdery, mildew.
5.	Capsic	1. California Wonder 2. Arka Gaurav 3. Arka Mohini 4. Arka Basant 5. Bharat (Fl) 6. Dharwar local (Tarihal) 7. Yolo Wonder	1. July-Aug. 2. Oct.-Nov.	Dec- Mar.	Thrips fruit borer, Aphids mites, white fly.	Damping-off, urn Anthracnose, Bacterial wilt, Cercospora leaf spot, leaf curl, powder mildew, root knot nematode, fruit rot & powdery
6.	Cabbage	1. Pride of India (Early) 2. Golden Acre (Early) 3. Early Drumhead (Early) 4. Late Drumhead (late) 5. Danish Ball Head (late)	1. June-July 2. Oct.-Nov.	Jan-March Aug-Nov.	Aphids leaf webber, Semi looper, Diamond back moth, head borer, cabbage bug.	Bacterial black rot, Collar rot, blight, white rust.
7.	Cauli-flower	1. Early Snowball (Early) 2. Snow ball (medium) 3. Late Snow ball (late)	1. Aug.-Sept. (early & med.) 2. Oct.-Nov. (late)	Dec-March	Aphids leaf webber, Semi looper, Diamond back moths,	Black rot, collar rot, blight, downy mildew.

(1)	(2)	(3)	(4)	(5)	(6)	(7)
8.	Knolkhol	1. White Vienna 2. Purple Vienna 3. Jan.-Feb.	1. June- July 2. Oct-Nov.		Aphids, leaf webber, semi lopper Diamond back moths	Damping-off collar rot, blight downy mildew.
9.	Okra	1. Arka Anamika 2. Arka abhay 3. Pusa Sawani 4. White Velvet	1. June-July 2. Jan.-Feb. 3. Jan-Feb.	June- Sept.	Jassid, Red cotton bug fruit borer, spider mite, blister beetle	Yellow vein mosaic, anthracnose powdery mildew, Cercsospora leaf spot.
10.	French Bean	1. Arka kormal (Bush) 2. Contender (Bush) 3. Bangalore local (Bush) 4. Kentucky Wonder (pole)	1. June-July 2. Jan.-Feb.	Oct.-April	Agromyzid fly, aphid, mites, pod borer.	Yellow vein mosaic, anthracnose, phytophthora pod rot, rust, Angular leaf spot, Rhizoctonia root rot.
11.	Peas	1. Bonneville 2. Arkel 3. Perfection New Line 4. Early Badger 5. Arka Ajit 6. Magadi	1. June-July 2. Oct.- Nov.	Nov.-March	Aphids, pod borer Root grub. white fly	Powdery mildew, stem rot, rust.
12.	Cowpea	1. Arka Suman 2. Pusa Phalguni 3. Pusa Barsati 4. Pusa Dofasli 5. 5-288	1. May-July 2. Dec-Jan.	Oct.-May	Pod borer, Aphids, Plant hopper	Powdery mildew, Phytophthora pod rot, rust. Fusarium wilt,
13.	Cluster	1. Pusa Sadabahar 2. Pusa Mousami 3. Pusa Naubahar	1. June-July 2. Feb.-Mar.	Oct.-May	Bean weevil, Bean aphids, pod borer.	

(1)	(2)	(3)	(4)	(5)	(6)	(7)
14.	Water-melon	1. Arka Manik 2. Arka Jyoti 3. Asahi Yamato 4. Sugar Baby.	1. Nov.-Jan.	Jan.-May	Aphid, pumpkin beetle, fruitfly.	Wilt, anthracnose, downy mildew, Powdery mildew, fusarium wilt.
15.	Muskm	1. Arka Rajhans 2. Arka Jeet 3. Pusa Sharabati 4. Hara Madhu	1. Jan.-Feb.		Pumpkin beetle, Aphid, fruitfly.	Downy mildewelon powdery mildew, Anthracnose.
16.	Cucu-mber	1. Japanese Long Green 2. Straight 3. China 4. Local types (a) North Karnataka type (*b*) South Karnataka type (c) West Coast type	1. June-July 2. Jan.-Feb.	Throughout the year	Red Pumpkin beetle, cut worm, fruitfly Root knot nematode	Bacterial wilt, Anthracnose, Powdery mildew.
17.	Pumpkin & Squash	1. Arka Suryamukhi 2. Arka Chandan 3. Co-1 4. Hybrid squash	1. June-July 2. Jan.- Feb.	Oct.-May	Pumpkin beetle, aphid, fruitfly.	Anthracnose
18.	Ash Gourd	1. Co-1	1. June-July 2. Sept.-Oct. 3. Feb.- Mar.	Oct.-May	Red pumpkin beetle, Aphids	Anthracnose, powdery mildew, Sclerotial wilt.
19.	Bottle gourd	1. Arka Bahar 2. Pusa Summer Prolific Long 3. Pusa Summer Prolific Round 4. Pusa Meghdoot 5. Pusa Manjari	1. June-July 2. Oct.-Nov. 3. Feb- Mar.	Oct.-May	Aphids, pod borer, Root grub, white fly.	Powdery mildew, stem rot, rust.

(1)	(2)	(3)	(4)	(5)	(6)	(7)
20.	Bitter gourd	1. Arka Harit 2. Coimbatore Long	1. June- July 2. Jan.-Feb.		Red pumpkin beetle, fruitflies.	Anthracnose, Powdery mildew.
21.	Chow-Chow	Green fruited and White fruited types	1. April-May 2. Oct.-Nov.		Pumpkin beetle, Aphid, fruitflies.	Anthracnose, Powder mildew.
22.	Tonde (Coccinia)	Sweet and bitter types	1. June-July	Oct.-May	-do-	-do-
23.	Ridgeg ourd	1. Arka Sujat 2. Arka Summet 3. Pusa Naar 4. Co-1 5. Selection 4-12	1. June-July 2. Jan.-Feb.	Oct.- May	Fruitfly, aphids.	Powdery mildew, Downy mildew, rust.
24.	Radish	1. Arka Nishant 2. Japanese White 3. White Icicle	1. June-July 2. OctT-Nov.	Oct-April	Aphids, sawfly semi-looper	Downy mildew.
25.	Beetroot	1. Crimson Globe 2. Detroit Dark Red	1. June- July 2. Oct.-Nov.	Oct.-April	Aphids.	Leaf spot.
26.	Turnip	1. Snowball 2. Golden Ball 3. Early Million 4. Pusa Kanchan	1. June-July 2. Oct.-Nov.		Aphids, sawfly semilooper.	Downy mildew.
27.	Carrot	1. Pusa Kesar 2. Nante half Long 3. Giant Chanteney 4. Asiatic local	1. June-July 2. Oct.-Nov. 3. Jan.-Feb.	Dec-March	Leaf hopper, weevil Aphids.	Leaf spot, blight, Powdery mildew
28.	Onion	1. Arka Kalyan 2. Arka Niketan 3. Arka Pragati	1. June-July 2. Sept.-Oct.	Aug.-Jan.	Thrips.	Smut, purple blotch, Alternaria.

(1)	(2)	(3)	(4)	(5)	(6)	(7)
		4. Bellary Red 5. Pusa Red 6. Dhulia or Bombay 7. N-53 8. Tellagi whited & Tellagi Red 9. Arka Pitarnber 10. Arka Lalima 11. Arka Kirthiman				
29.	Sweet Potato	1. V-6 2. V-12 3. H-41 and H-42 4. Vikram (C-I-853-4)	1. June-July 2. Sept.-Oct.	Oct.-April	Sweet potato weevil	No major diseases
30.	Amorpho-phalles (Elephant foot, yam)	Local types	1. Mar- April	—	—	Leaf blight.
31.	Dioscor	Local types	1. April-May		No severe pests and diseasesea	
32.	Tapioca (Cassava)	1. Shri Rashmi 2. Shri Pallavi	1. June-July	Red mites, scale		Cassava mosaic, cercospora leaf spot
33.	Methi	1. Pusa Early bunching 2. Kasuri Selection	1. Aug.-Nov.	Oct.-Jan.	Aphids, leaf eating caterpillar	Leaf spot, downy mildew.
34.	Amaran-thus	1. Choti Chaulai 2. Badi Chaulai 3. Pusa Chaulai	1. March-Sept. 2. Oct.-Nov.	Jan.-Dec.	-do-	White rust.
35.	Palak	1. Pusa Jyoti 2. All Green rust.	1. Sept.-Nov.	Jan.- March	-do-	Cercopora leaf spot,

As a result Karnataka is now seen as an ideal base for seed production and processing in the country.

Important Seed Vegetables

Since the temperature conditions are moderate in the state throughout the year, production of seeds is taken up only in such vegetables which do not need cold stimulus for flower initiation and seed set. The important vegetable crops where seed production is undertaken in Karnataka are :

Tomato, Brinjal, Chilli, Capsicum, Okra, Onion, Watermelon, Muskmelon, Cucumber, Amaranthus, Beans, Dolichos, Cowpea, Ridge gourd, Pumpkin and Bottle gourd.

CHAPTER 18

VEGETABLE PRODUCTION IN KERALA

V.S.Devadus

Kerala state nests in the South-West corner of India between 8° 18' and 12° 48' North Latitudes and 74° 52' and 77° 22' East longitude as a long narrow strip of land between the Western Ghats in the East and Arabian sea in the West. The state has a total geographical area of 38863 km with total cropped area of 45 million ha. The state is divided into five agro-climatic zones. Brief description of each agro-climatic zone is as under.

Northern Zone

Northern zone of Kerala is a long normal strip consisting of 4 distts. namely Malla puram, Kozhileele, Cannanore and Kasargode. The mean annual maximum temperature is 33°C and minimum 24°C. This zone experiences heavy rainfall during June-August leading to waterlogging and flooding. Pepper, Tapioca, Turmeric, Ginger, Cardamom and other seasonal vegetables are grown on an area of about one lakh ha. Cucumber, Pumpkin, Guards and Watermelons are generally grown in rice- fallows rotation. There is a regular increase in area under vegetables due to remunerative returns per unit area.

Central zone

This zone represents three districts. namely Palghat, Trichur and Ernakulam. Vegetables are grown in rice and Banana based production system.

High Attitude zone

This zone is a part of Western ghat with an elevation of about 750 metres above m. s. 1. Pepper, cardamom, tapioca, drum-stick are the main vegetables grown in this zone.

Problem area zone

This special zone comprises of districts Alleppey, Kettayam, Ernakulam, Trichur and Malappuram covering an area of 5254 km^2. This zone is prone to floods in *Kharif* and drought during both periods of rabi seasons. Yam, Tapioca are inter-cropped in coconut crop.

Southern zone

This zone comprises the districts of Trivendrum, Guilon, Pathanamthitta, Alleppey and Kottayam. This zone has a tropical humid climatic conditions. The hot season from March to May is followed by South West monsoon from June to September. Tapioca, Pepper Ginger, Turmeric, Yam are the main vegetables grown in this zone.

Area and Production under vegetgables

Kerala with its unique warm tropic climate provides an ideal condition for cultivation of 12 major and 23 minor vegetables. Despite the favourable growing conditions of such a large number of vegetables, the consumption per capita is hardly 50 g which is lowest in the country. Total area under vegetable crops is estimated to be 27814 ha with an annual production 2.5 lakh tonnes (except tuber crops). In Kerala, gap between present day consumption to the tune of 12.0 lakh ton annually. To overcome this alarming situation in the state many strategies are being formulated to make vegetable cultivation a remunerative activity in the state Distt.-wise production of different vegetables for the year 1998-99 under Intensive vegetable development programme has been shown in Table 18.1.

Kerala Agricultural University has released several varieties of different vegetables for boosting vegetable production in the state. Complete list of improved varieties along with their important charadteristics has been given in Table 18.2. In order to take the serious problem of bacterial wilt in saponaceous vegetables particularly tomato, brinjal, and chillies. The University has also evolved disease resistant varieties in all the crop, List of such varieties along with varietal characters is given in Table 18.3.

Vegetables are important components of daily diet because they contain large quantities of vitamins, minerals and many other essential nutrients and they protect us from various diseases; hence vegetables are considered as protective food. They are alkaline in nature, contain fibre and improves digestion. The ICMR recommends a daily intake of 300 g vegetables.

In India, about 50 kinds of various vegetables are grown. India is the second largest producer of vegetables in the World, next to China. Certain statistics related to vegetable production and consumption in our country are given below :

Total cropped area	: 45 million ha
Area in vegetables (excluding Potato & Tubers)	: 4.0 million ha

KERALA

TABLE 18.1: District-wise production of Vegetables under Intensive Vegetable Development Programme 1998-99

(Production in MT)

	TVM	KLM	PTA	ALP	EKM	KTM	IDK	TCR	PKD	MPM	KZD	KNR	WYD	KSD	Total
	1	2	3	4	5	6	7	8	9	10	11	12	13	14	15
Bittergourd	1924	802	878	3005	3473	950	1780	3180	4525	1143	851	3060	260	118	**25949**
Snakegourd	615	728	720	3120	1888	1561	615	6023	3258	750	3818	2820	612	1032	**27864**
Littlegourd	129	–	–	480	–	130	–	343	216	–	–	301	–	–	**1599**
Cowpea	2261	458	–	2790	1666	496	2448	889	2859	198	876	2553	176	793	**18463**
Ashgourd	–	167	–	3396	–	193	–	472	699	5241	1528	1580	–	–	**11279**
Cucumber	2361	653	–	2690	1377	496	2972	1889	3858	1198	1576	2553	276	772	**22670**
Pumpkin	334	–	56	1221	320	1244	–	1278	4518	156	242	1508	147	203	**11226**
Jlhindi	65	–	261	912	1400	1568	–	198	–	469	328	1408	309	640	**7557**
Brinjal	251	155	10	40	1301	81	–	2240	–	205	920	1104	171	530	**7997**
Chillies	08	80	83	86	200	250	–	148	158	190	131	86	91	137	**1739**
Bottlegourd	–	40	43	60	105	40	134	45	160	120	140	128	60	16	**1091**
Watermelon	–	–	–	–	–	–	–	18	–	–	–	94	–	–	**112**
Amaranthus	3749	450	700	200	2858	1012	1408	2075	1398	70	175	68	258	688	**15109**
Tomato	–	–	–	57	58	–	–	68	270	–	–	–	67	16	**536**
Ridgegourd	200	55	110	75	85	95	–	120	35	67	160	190	–	131	**1323**
Radish	–	–	–	–	–	16	–	–	–	–	–	–	–	–	**16**
Beans	–	–	–	–	–	105	–	–	–	–	–	–	300	–	**405**
Philipean Pea.	–	–	463	–	–	–	–	–	–	–	–	–	–	–	**463**

	1	2	3	4	5	6	7	8	9	10	11	12	13	14	15
Cabbage	–	–	–	–	–	814	–	–	–	–	–	–	240	–	**1054**
Peas	–	–	–	–	–	15	–	–	–	–	–	–	–	–	**15**
Cauliflower	–	–	–	–	–	20	–	–	–	–	–	–	117	–	**137**
Potato	–	–	–	–	–	6423	–	–	–	–	–	–	–	–	**6423**
Carrot	–	–	–	–	–	1561	–	–	–	–	–	–	–	–	**1561**
Beetroot	–	–	–	–	–	821	–	–	–	–	–	–	–	–	**821**
Amorphophallus	–	–	–	603	–	–	–	–	–	456	–	499	–	–	**1558**
Ginger	–	–	–	–	286	–	–	–	–	–	–	–	–	–	**286**
Banana	430	583	550	–	1240	250	–	–	–	–	530	–	–	–	**3583**
Total (MT)	12415	4017	4020	18035	15959	8651	19131	18986	21954	10266	11274	17952	3084	5082	**170836**
Area (ha)	350	120	80	315	140	100	455	440	410	120	225	250	30	65	**3100 + 975**
Productivity (MT/ha)	35	33	50	57	114	87	42	43	54	86	50	72	103	78	55

TABLE 18.2: High Yielding Vegetable varieties released by Kerala Agricultural University

S.No.	Crop	Variety	Important Characters
1.	Bitter gourd	1. Priya	High yielding, green long fruits with white stylar end recommended nationally
		2. Preethi	High yielding (39.5 t/ha) tuberculate fruits having an average weight of 310 gms. Fruits white with light green tinch, recommended nationally.
		3. Priyanka	High yielding 28 t/ha large white fruits suited for acid alluvial soils of Kerala.
2.	Snake gourd	Koumudhi	High yielding 28 t/ha large white fruited variety, suited to acid alluvial soils of Kerala.
3.	Pumpkin	Ambili	High yielding (30 t/ha) medium fruited variety with flat round fruits which are green at the immature stage.
		Suvarna	High yielding orange fleshed variety
4.	'Cucumber' Oriental pickling melon)	Sowbagya	High yielding and small to medium fruited variety
5.	Bhindi	Kiran	Fruits long straight and yellowish green
		Aruna	Fruits long red coloured
		Satkeerthi	Fruits long light green and five ribbed
6.	Amaranthus	Arun	High yielding (20 t/ha) red leaved
7.	Cowpea	1. Sarika	Trailing vegetable cowpea yield 13 t/ha, pods white with brown stylar ends and seeds black
	Cowpea	2. Malika	Trailing vegetable cowpea pods uniformly white without marking at the stylar end. Seeds brown with white speck, yield 10 t/ha
		3. KMV-1	Light green coloured trailing vegetable cowpea with long pods seeds uniformly brown coloured
	Cowpea	4. Vyjayanthi	High yielding trailing type vegetable cowpea, long violet pods with brown seeds
		5. Kanakamani	Dual purpose variety podsgreen coloured and bold grained having a length of 20 cm, ideal for homesteads
8.	Winged bean	Revathi	Photo sensitive variety yielding 20 t/ha
9.	Chilli	Jwalasakthi	Fruits pendulous long and light green with flesh, medium pungent yield 22.5 t/ha
		Jwala mukhi	Pendulous long green fruits with thick flesh

TABLE 18.3: Bacterial wilt disease resistant vegetable varieties evolved at KAU, Vellanikkara

S.No.	Crop	Variety	Important Characters
1.	Brinjal	Surya	Fruits oval, violet and medium sized recommended nationally
		Swetha	Bushy, fruits white and long recommended nationally
		Haritha	Long duration variety with long light green fruits, tolerant to phomopsis blight
		Neelima	First Fl-hybrid in the country, high yielding
2.	Chilli	Manjeri	Bushy, plant, erect fruits born in clusters, fruits light green and medium sized (4 cm)
		Ujwala	Highly pungent, fruits born in upright clusters, tolerant to mosaic
3.	Tomato	Sakthi	Semi-determinate variety with medium sized fruits, having green shoulder, susceptible to fruit cracking.
		Mukthi	Semi-determinate variety with medium sized fruit uniformly white tolerant to fruit cracking.

Per Capita consumption : 120-130 g/day

In Kerala consumption may be : < 50 g/day

But the per capita consumption of vegetables in China is 295 g/day.

Kerala-Production Scenario

Total Cropped area : 28.67 lakh ha

Area under seasonal vegetables : 15,281 ha

Area under seasonal vegetables & drum stick : 27,814 ha

Current availability (including import from other states) : 5 lakh tons/year

Internal production : 2.5 lakh tons(50%)

Present requirement/year : 15 lakh tons

Present gap in production : 12.5 lakh tons

Projections on requirement for 2000 AD : 31 lakh tons

Area required in vegetable by 2000 AD : 1.55 lakh tons (in 2 crops)

Reasons for low per capita consumption of vegetables in Kerala can be due to low productivity and production; and non-availability of vegetables at low market price. The productivity of vegetables of India is very low, compared to that of other countries.

Constraints in vegetable production

The major constraints in vegetable production in Kerala can be classified into the following four factors :

1. Specific situations of Kerala
2. Environmental/Climatological factors
3. Technological factors
4. Socio-economic factors

1. **Specific Situations of Kerala :** Homestead system of farming is predominant in the State. This system is characterised by warm humid tropical crops predominated by perennials ; low productivity of crop components ; inadequate sun light and nutrition for optimum productivity of various crops ; crop competition for water, nutrients, light etc., pest and diseases and a total neglect to the system as such. Vegetables form one of such crop components. The area under monocrops/large scale cultivation of vegetables is very less and are limited to some garden lands and paddy fallows.
2. **Environmental & Climatological Factors :** Natural calamities like drought, flood etc. also affect vegetable cultivation; and the-off season/protected cultivation also suffers due to high initial cost, high energy, sophisticated technology etc.
3. **Technological Factors**

   Lack of disease-resistance : adaptable varieties (biotic and abiotic stresses)

   Inadequate and untimely supply of seeds

   Lack of appropriate packages of inputs

   Inefficient and unbalanced supply of fertilizer applications

   Inefficient and indiscriminate use of P.P chemicals

   Lack of farm advisory services

   Pests and diseases
4. **Socio-Economic Factors :** Inefficient and uneconomic market mechanism

   Post-harvest loss due to poor transport packing, storage (25-30% loss)

   High cost of labour and inefficiency (commercial growers use family labour)

   Poor credit availability

   Lack of crop insurance

High rent of land (₹ 500-2000/-) per para or 14 cents per year to be given in advance-manuring problems

Remedies/Strategies to overcome the production problems

The remedial measures can be classified in to the following

1. Increasing area under vegetable cultivation

2. Improving productivity of vegetables
3. Improving socio-economic conditions

1. **Increasing Area** : The present gap in total requirement and production of vegetables in the State works out to 12.5 lakh tonnes; for this a total area to be put under vegetables comes to 1.2 lakh ha. Fallow lands (other than current fallows) available is only 28,038 ha. In many locations paddy lands are kept as fallows. These fallow lands can be put under vegetable cultivation.

   Another possibility to increase the area under vegetables is to promote and popularise the vegetable cultivation in homesteads. It is estimated that the total area under small holdings of 0.04 to 2.0 ha comes to 25-60 lakh ha. It is possible to produce 1.32 tonnes of vegetables/year from 0.04 ha (10 cents) area of Kitchen/nutrition gardens in homesteads. This is sufficient for ten persons per annum. Even if 50% of the total holdings come forward for nutrition garden, the present gap of 12 lakh tonnes can be covered. Other aspects need attention are-popularisation of roof/terrace garden in urban or town areas and special programmes for exported oriented vegetable cultivation.

2. **Improving productivity** : In order to improve the productivity of vegetables in the state, the following aspects become important.

   Quality seed production and timely supply of the seeds to the farmers Use of hybrid varieties adapted to Kerala with multiple resistance to pest and diseases

   Hybrids suited to each location or market preference to be developed Seed production and supply require rigorous monitoring and certification Improving the post-harvest handling & marketing methods

3. **Socio economic factors**

   Cost of production to be lowered by various methods

   Marketing, credit, purchase of inputs, processing etc. to be channelised through co-operative movements in a participatory approach by Self-Help Groups

   Consumption of traditional vegetables should be encouraged.

CHAPTER 19

LAKSH DWEEP

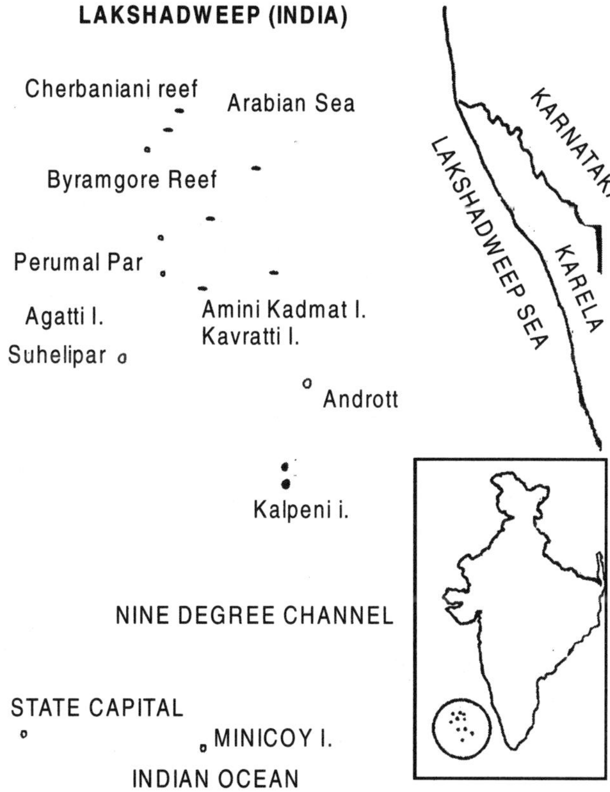

Fig. 19. (i)

This island is having 320 square kilometre area and Kavrati is its capital.It comprises of Munge small islands and is about 300-400 km from Kerala in the Laksh Dweep sea. Main occupation of people is agriculture and fishing.

TABLE 19.1: Area (ha) and production (t) under vegetables

Vegetable	Area (ha)	Production(t)
Assorted vegetables	325	368
Total	325	368

Source : LakshDweep Administration, Department of Agriculture.

CHAPTER 20

VEGETABLE GROWING IN MADHYA PRADESH (CHHATTISGARH REGION)

D.A.Sarnaik

Madhya Pradesh is situated in the centre of our country and known as largest state of Indian republic having total geographical area of 442 lakh hectares. It is predominantly an agrarian state, agriculture employing about 80% of the workforce. The State is situated under the catchment of Jamuna, Ganga, Narmada and Godavari rivers. The total cultivated area in the state is estimated to be 192.06 lakh ha out of which net irrigation area is hardly 30.06 lakh ha. Based on rainfall pattern, temperature, soil types and existing cropping patterns following 12 agro-climatic zones have been identified in the state.

(*a*) Chhattisgarh plain zone
(*b*) Baster platian
(*c*) North hill zone of Chhattisgarh
(*d*) Kymore plateau zone
(*e*) Vidhya plateau zone
(*f*) Central Narmada valley zone
(*g*) Grid zone
(*h*) Bundelkhand zone
(*i*) Satpura plateau zone
(*j*) Malwa plateau zone
(*k*) Nimar valley zone
(*l*) Jhabna hill-zone

Although vegetable cultivation is spread over the entire state, but commercial vegetable growing is primarily concentrated in Chhattisgarh plain zone and

Bundelkhand zone. Chhattisgarh plain zone comprises of Raipur, Durg, Rajnandgaon, Bilaspur, Surguja, Raigarh, Bastar and Balghat Distts. Complete information regarding hectrage under different vegetables, production status and future development plan for each distt in the zone is given in this chapter.

Unlike fruit crops, development of vegetable crops needs concerted efforts in time of both infrastructure are well as marketing. Being commercial crops, the vegetables need irrigation facilities if grown in rabi and good drainage if grown during Kharif looking into the existing status, future need and also available resources, district-wise proposals for vegetable crop development are given below:

Raipur

In case of vegetables, tomato covers the maximum area (2415 ha) which is followed by brinjal (2303 ha) and okra (1440 ha). The minimum area amongst all

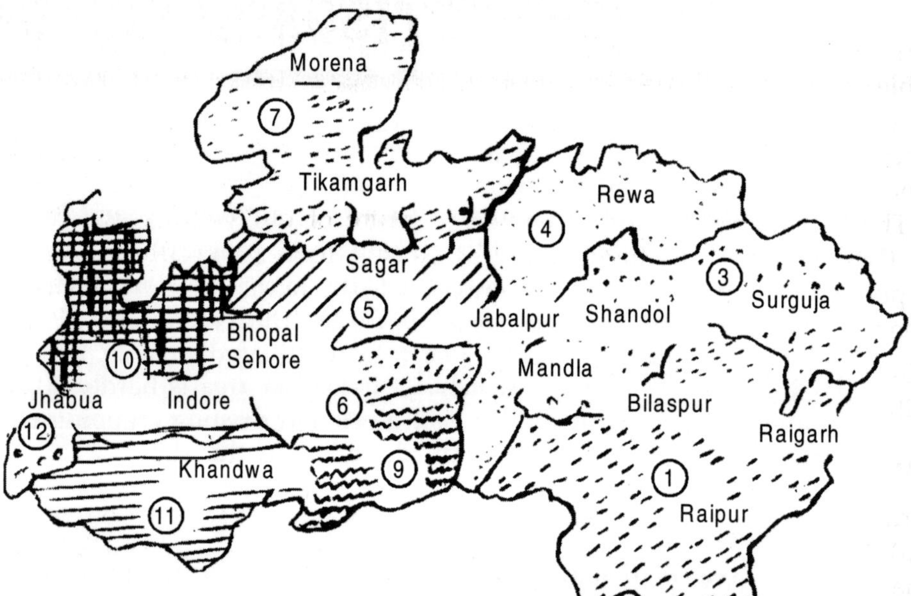

1. Chattisgarh Plain Zone Including balagharth Distric
2. Bastar Plateau Zone
3. North Hill Zone of Chattisgarh
4. Kymore Plateau and Satpura Hill Zone
5. Vindhya PlateauZone
6. Central Normada Valley Zone
7. Gird Zone
8. Budelkhand Zone
9. Satpura Plateau Zone
10. Malwa Plateau Zone
11. Nimar Valley Zone
12. Jhabua hills Zone

Fig. 20 (i) : Agro-climatic zones of Madhya Pradesh

the vegetables is occupied under pointed gourd (12 ha.) The vegetables like cauliflower, green pea, onion and cowpea are grown in area of 745, 751, 615 and 535 ha respectively in the district.

The highest (70950 tonnes) production is also harvested from tomato which is followed by Brinjal (51920 tonnes) and okra (38200 tonnes).

As there is a great potential for growing potato in the district, it is propose that an area of 175 ha during next five years under potato. The other vegetables like tomato, brinjal and okra may also be increased in an area of 100,75,125 hectares, respectively in the coming 5 years. Besides, an area of about 565 ha under other vegetables like cowpea, cluster-bean, bottle gourd, Ivy-gourd, bitter-gourd, sweet potato, onion, tomato, cauliflower, cabbage, knolkhol, ridge gourd, colocasia, pumpkin, long cucumber can also be developed in next 5 years. Table 20.1.

Durg

Brinjal occupies the highest area (1044 ha) in the district amongst all the vegetables which is followed by tomato (1005.1 ha) and okra (341 ha). Very meager area is grown under pointed gourd (3 ha), garden pea (10 ha) and Khira(ll ha) in the district. However, cauliflower (208 ha), bottlegourd (168.3 ha), cowpea (152.2 ha) cabbage (153.3 ha) and cluster bean (138.8 ha) are also grown in considerable areas. The highest production is harvested from onion (7942 tonnes) followed by Brinjal (7099.3 t/ha) and tomato (6727.3 ha). The lowest production is obtained under pointed gourd (12 tonnes), whereas production of 50 tonnes, 79 tonnes and 81.6 tonnes is obtained from garden pea, khira and drumstick, respectively.

Since there is a processing plant in Durg region, tomato has great potential for cultivation in large area up to 125 ha during next five years. (Table 20.2).

Rajnandgaon

Brinjal covers the largest area (875 ha) followed by okra (664 ha) and tomato (625 ha) amongst all the vegetables in the District. Garden pea (303 ha), Cauliflower (208 ha) and cabbage (118 ha) are also grown in a considerable area. Potato (55 ha) and bittergourd (38 ha) are grown in very small area in the district.

The highest production (18302 tonnes) is obtained from brinjal amongst all the vegetables which is followed by tomato (16179 tonnes) and onion (11482 tonnes) in the district. (Table 20.3).

Bilaspur

In Bilaspur District okra occupies the highest area (1399 hectares) amongst all the vegetables which is followed by tomato, potato and onion. Brinjal, Bitter Gourd, Colocasia and Sweet Potato are also grown in considerable area. Pointed gourd and knolkhol are also grown in a small area in the district.

Farmers of the district are also becoming aware of the benefits of hybrid seeds in vegetables in coming 5 years it is proposed to increase an area of 175 hectares

TABLE 20.1: Development Plan of Vegetable Crops in Raipur District

S. No.	Name of Vegetable Crop	Present Status (Area in ha)	Production in tonnes	Development for five years										TOTAL	
				1999-2000		2000-2001		2001-2002		2002-2003		2003-2004			
				Area (ha)	Pro (t/ha)	Area (ha)	Pro. (t/ha)	Area (ha)	Pro. (t/ha)	Area (ha)	Pro. (l/ha)	Area (ha)	Pro. (t/ha)	Ara (ha)	Pro (t/ha)
1.	Potato	320	8000	35	700	35	700	35	700	35	700	35	700	175	3500
2.	Sweet potato	446	4014	5	100	5	100	5	100	5	100	5	100	25	500
3.	Onion	615	21490	20	500	20	500	20	500	20	500	20	500	100	2500
4.	Tomato	2415	70950	25	1000	25	1000	25	1000	25	1000	25	1000	125	5000
5.	Okra	1440	38200	10	300	10	300	10	300	10	300	10	300	50	1500
6.	Brinjal	2303	51920	15	450	15	450	15	450	15	450	15	450	75	2250
7.	Cauliflower	745	22350	5	150	5	150	5	150	5	150	5	150	25	750
8.	Cabbage	421	12540	10	300	10	300	10	300	10	300	10	300	100	1500
9.	Knolkhol	318	7900	2	200	2	200	2	200	2	200	2	200	10	1000
10.	Ridgegourd	175	4375	5	50	5	50	5	50	5	50	5	50	25	250
11.	Spong gourd	109	27251	2	20	2	20	2	20	2	20	2	20	10	100
12.	Bottle gourd	185	10175	3	75	3	75	3	75	3	75	3	75	15	375
13.	Cowpea	535	80251	3	30	3	30	3	30	3	30	3	30	15	150
14.	Clusterbean	86	2890	2	10	2	10	2	10	2	10	2	10	10	50
15.	Colocasia	148	4740	2	30	2	30	2	30	2	30	2	30	10	150
16.	Ivy-gourd	90	1840	20	500	20	500	20	500	20	500	20	500	100	2500
17.	Pumpkin	178	8900	2	30	2	30	2	30	2	30	2	30	10	150
18.	Long cucumber	49	980	2	20	2	20	2	20	2	20	2	20	10	100
19.	Tinda	22	770	1	10	1	10	1	10	1	10	1	10	5	50
20.	Pointed Gourd	12	420	2	50	2	50	2	50	2	50	2	50	10	250
21.	Drumstick	73	365	2	–	2	–	2	–	2	–	2	–	10	–
22.	Kamaltal	37	37	–	–	–	–	–	–	–	–	–	–	–	–
23.	Bitter gourd	331	11545	5	75	5	75	5	75	5	75	5	75	25	375
24.	Green Pea	751	7410	5	50	5	50	5	50	5	50	5	50	25	250
25.	Khira	53	1325	2	24	2	24	2	24	2	24	2	24	10	120
26.	Other vegetables	3485	11596	3	–	3	–	3	–	3	–	3	–	15	–

TABLE 20.2: Development Plan of Vegetable Crops in Drug District

S. No.	Name of Vegetable Crop	Present Status (Area in ha)	Production in tonnes	Development for five years										TOTAL	
				1999-2000		2000-2001		2001-2002		2002-2003		2003-2004			
				Area (ha)	Pro (t/ha)	Area (ha)	Pro. (t/ha)	Area (ha)	Pro. (t/ha)	Area (ha)	Pro. (l/ha)	Area (ha)	Pro. (t/ha)	Ara (ha)	Pro (t/ha)
1.	Potato	280	2993.5	10	200	10	200	10	200	10	200	10	200	50	1000
2.	Sweet Potato	41.8	278.6	2	40	2	40	2	40	2	40	2	40	10	200
3.	Onion	161.3	7942.4	10	250	10	250	10	250	10	250	10	250	50	1250
4.	Tomato	1005.1	6727.3	25	1000	25	1000	25	1000	25	1000	25	1000	125	5000
5.	Okra	341	2046.5	10	300	10	300	10	300	10	300	10	300	50	1500
6.	Brinjal	1044	7099.3	10	300	10	300	10	300	10	300	10	300	50	1500
7.	Cauliflower	208.8	2080.6	5	150	5	150	5	150	5	150	5	150	25	750
8.	Cabbage	153.3	1247.6	5	150	5	150	5	150	5	150	5	150	25	750
9.	Knolkhol	91.50	4568.0	5	150	5	150	5	150	5	150	5	150	25	750
10.	Ridgegourd	93.80	588.0	4	40	4	40	4	40	4	40	4	40	20	200
11.	Sponge gourd	61.50	347.1	5	50	5	50	5	50	5	50	5	50	25	250
12.	Bottle gourd	168.3	848.6	5	125	5	125	5	125	5	125	5	125	25	625
13.	Cowpea	152.2	663.0	3	30	3	30	3	30	3	30	3	30	10	150
14.	Clusterbean	138.8	397.0	2	10	2	10	2	10	2	10	2	10	10	50
15.	Colocasia	34.7	228	2	30	2	30	2	30	2	30	2	30	10	150
16.	Ivy-gourd	94	862	20	500	20	500	20	500	20	500	20	500	100	2500
17.	Pumpkin	39	327	2	30	2	30	2	30	2	30	2	30	10	150
18.	Longcucumber	24	125.3	3.	30	3	30	3	30	3	30	3	30	15	150
19.	Tinda	13.5	88	2	20	2	20	2	20	2	20	2	20	10	100
20.	Pointed Gourd	3	12	0.5	13	0.5	13	0.5	13	0.5	13	0.5	13	25	65
21.	Drumstick	52.6	81.6	–	–	–	–	–	–	–	–	–	–	–	–
22.	Kamaltal	–	–	–	–	–	–	–	–	–	–	–	–	–	–
23.	Bitter gourd	106.5	482.9	10	150	10	150	10	150	10	150	10	150	50	650
24.	Green Pea	10.0	50.0	–	–	–	–	–	–	–	–	–	–	–	–
25.	Khira	11	79.0	–	–	–	–	–	–	–	–	–	–	–	–
26.	Other vegeta.	–	–	–	–	–	–	–	–	–	–	–	–	–	–

TABLE 20.3: Development Plan of Vegetable Crops in Rajnandgaon District

S. No.	Name of Vegetable Crop	Present Status (Area in ha)	Production in tonnes	Development for five years										TOTAL	
				1999-2000		2000-2001		2001-2002		2002-2003		2003-2004			
				Area (ha)	Pro (t/ha)	Area (ha)	Pro. (t/ha)	Area (ha)	Pro. (t/ha)	Area (ha)	Pro. (I/ha)	Area (ha)	Pro. (t/ha)	Ara (ha)	Pro (t/ha)
1.	Potato	55,	1181	5	100	5	100	5	100	5	100	5	100	25	500
2.	Sweet potato	136	2161	–	–	–	–	–	–	–	–	–	–	–	–
3.	Onion	464	11482	10	250	10	250	10	250	10	250	10	250	50	1250
4.	Tomato	625	16179	10	400	10	400	10	400	10	400	10	400	50	2000
5.	Okra	664	6361	10	300	10	300	10	300	10	300	10	300	50	1500
6.	Brinjal	875	18302	10	300	10	300	10	300	10	300	10	300	50	1500
7.	Cauliflower	208	4209	5	150	5	150	5	150	5	150	5	150	25	750
8.	Cabbage	118	2384	3	90	3	90	3	90	3	90	3	90	15	450
9.	Knolkhol	–	–	2	20	2	20	2	20	2	20	2	20	10	100
10.	Ridgegourd	–	–	2	20	2	20	2	20	2	20	2	20	10	100
11.	Sponge gourd	–	–	3	30	3	30	3	30	3	30	3	30	15	15
12.	Bottle gourd	61	1190	10	250	10	250	10	250	10	250	10	250	50	1250
13.	Cowpea	63	345	3	30	3	30	3	30	3	30	3	30	15	150
14.	Clusterbean	65	–	2	10	2	10	2	10	2	10	2	10	10	50
15.	Colocasia	–	–	10	250	10	250	10	250	10	250	10	250	50	1250
16.	Ivy-gourd	30	596	3	45	3	45	3	45	3	45	3	45	10	150
17.	Pumpkin	–	–	3	30	3	30	3	30	3	30	3	30	15	150
18.	Long cucumber	–	–	2	20	2	20	2	20	2	20	2	20	10	100
19.	Tinda	–	–	3	30	3	30	3	30	3	30	3	30	15	150
20.	Pointed Gourd	–	–	2	50	2	50	2	50	2	50	2	50	10	250
21.	Drumstick	–	–	2	–	2	–	2	–	2	–	2	–	10	–
22.	Kamaltal	–	–	2	–	2	–	2	–	2	–	2	–	10	–
23.	Bitter gourd	38	406	5	75	5	75	5	75	5	75	5	75	25	375
24.	Green Pea	303	1092	5	50	5	50	5	50	5	50	5	50	25	1250
25.	Khira	–	–	3	36	3	36	3	36	3	36	3	36	15	1800
26.	Other vegetables	1386	11624.7	5	–	5	–	5	–	5	–	5	–	25	–

each in Potato and Colocasia. An additional area ranging from 10 hectares to 25 hectares is proposed to be developed under important vegetables like cowpea, bottlegourd, ridge gourd and sweet potato within 5 years. Also, an area of 50 heactares is proposed to be developed in addition for growing cauliflower and cabbage. (Table 20.4)

Surguja

Surguja district is a tribal dominated district and the area of Mainpat under this district is known for *Kharif* Potato. Thus Potato is grown on large scale in this district i.e. on 3971 hectares which is followed by green peas. Tomato and Sweet Potato are also grown in 861 and 882 hectares in the district. Important vegetables like onion, okra, brinjal, cauliflower and cabbage are also grown in an area ranging from 350 to 460 hectares.

Besides, other vegetables are also grown in small area. Looking to the great scope of potato crop in the district, it is proposed to increase an additional area of 500 hectares under potato in the district. An additional area ranging from 100 to 250 hectares is also proposed in coming 5 years under Sweet Potato, Onion, Tomato, Okra, Cauliflower and Cowpea. (Table 20.5).

Raigarh

In Raigarh district tomato is most important crop and Patthalgaon town is known for tomato. An area of 1060 hectare is occupied under tomato which is followed by Potato (985 hectares) and onion (519 hectares). An area under Okra, Brinjal, Sweet Potato, Cauliflower and Cabbage is ranged from 138 to 303 hectares.

Looking to ideal climate for growing Tomato in the district it is proposed to increase an additional area of 125 hectares under Tomato and an area ranging from 15 to 25 hectares under Cauliflower, Cabbage, Brinjal, Okra, Onion, Sweet Potato and Potato. (Table 20.6)

Bastar

Brinjal is the most important crop grown in the district which is followed by green pea (213 ha), Okra (111 ha), Tomato (109 ha). Pointed gourd is grown in a small (area) Ivy-gourd and Pumpkin are grown under each Kitchen garden of the tribal losses, known as badi. The highest production (955 tonnes). is harvested from brinjal which is followed by Onion (775 tonnes) and green pea (411 tonnes). The lowest production amongst all vegetables is found under long Cucumber (1.0 tonnes) and Cucumber (3.0 tonnes) in the district. Looking to the importance of bottle-gourd, Sweet potato, Tomato, Okra, Colocasia, Green pea, Onion and Brinjal an area more than 50 hectares is proposed for further increase in next five years. (Table 20.7)

Balaghat

Potato occupies maximum area (723 ha) followed by tomato (592 ha) and Brinjal (496 ha) in the district. Pointed gourd (8 ha), Khira (12 ha) Tinda (12 ha) and Ivy-gourd (16 ha), Onion (332 ha) and Okra (238 ha) are also grown in the region. (Table 20.8).

TABLE 20.4: Development Plan of Vegetable Crops in Bilaspur District

S. No.	Name of Vegetable Crop	Present Status (Area in ha)	Production in tonnes	Development for five years										TOTAL	
				1999-2000		2000-2001		2001-2002		2002-2003		2003-2004			
				Area (ha)	Pro (t/ha)	Area (ha)	Pro. (t/ha)	Area (ha)	Pro. (t/ha)	Area (ha)	Pro. (l/ha)	Area (ha)	Pro. (t/ha)	Ara (ha)	Pro (t/ha)
1.	Potato	653.00	–	20	20	20	20	20	20	20	20	20	20	20	100
2.	Sweet Potato	164.00	–	5	5	5	5	5	5	5	5	5	5	5	25
3.	Onion	378.00	–	15	15	15	15	15	15	15	15	15	15	15	75
4.	Tomato	852.00	–	25	25	25	25	25	25	25	25	25	25	25	125
5.	Okra	399.00	–	35	35	35	35	35	35	35	35	35	35	35	175
6.	Brinjal	361.50	–	10	10	10	10	10	10	10	10	10	10	10	50
7.	Cauliflower	78.00	–	3	3	3	3	3	3	3	3	3	3	3	15
8.	Cabbage	65.70	–	10	10	10	10	10	10	10	10	10	10	10	50
9.	Knolkhol	5.00	–	–	–	–	–	–	–	–	–	–	–	–	–
10.	Ridgegourd	145.00	–	3	3	3	3	3	3	3	3	3	3	3	12
11.	Sponge gourd	–	–	–	–	–	–	–	–	–	–	–	–	–	–
12.	Bottle gourd	27.00	–	2	2	2	2	2	2	2	2	2	2	2	10
13.	Cowpea	61.00	–	2	2	2	2	2	2	2	2	2	2	2	10
14.	Clusterbean	–	–	–	–	–	–	–	–	–	–	–	–	–	–
15.	Colocasia	266.00	–	10	10	10	10	10	10	10	10	10	10	10	50
16.	Ivy-gourd	35.50	–	1	1	1	1	1	1	1	1	1	1	1	5
17.	Pumpkin	169.00	–	3	3	3	3	3	3	3	3	3	3	3	12
18.	Long cucumber	–	–	–	–	–	–	–	–	–	–	–	–	–	–
19.	Tinda	6.30	–	–	–	–	–	–	–	–	–	–	–	–	–
20.	Pointed	Gourd	2.00	1/2	1/2	1/2	1/2	1/2	1/2	1/2	1/2	1/2	1/2	1/2	2 1/2
21.	Drumstick	–	–	–	–	–	–	–	–	–	–	–	–	–	–
22.	Khira	–	–	–	–	–	–	–	–	–	–	–	–	–	–
23.	Bitter gourd	120.00	–	1	1	1	1	1	1	1	1	1	1	1	5
24.	Green Pea	–	–	–	–	–	–	–	–	–	–	–	–	–	–
25.	Other vegetable.	838.5	–	–	–	–	–	–	–	–	–	–	–	–	–

TABLE 20.5: Development Plan of Vegetable Crops in Surguja District

S. No.	Name of Vegetable Crop	Present Status (Area in ha)	Production in tonnes	Development for five years										TOTAL	
				1999-2000		2000-2001		2001-2002		2002-2003		2003-2004			
				Area (ha)	Pro (t/ha)	Area (ha)	Pro. (t/ha)	Area (ha)	Pro. (t/ha)	Area (ha)	Pro. (l/ha)	Area (ha)	Pro. (t/ha)	Ara (ha)	Pro (t/ha)
1.	Potato	3971.0	–9	100	200	100	200	100	200	100	200	100	200	500	10000
2.	Sweet Potato	882.0	–	20	400	20	400	20	400	20	400	20	400	100	2000
3.	Onion	557.0	–	50	1250	50	1250	50	1250	50	1250	50	1250	250	6250
4.	Tomato	861.0	–	10	400	10	400	10	400	10	400	10	400	50.	2000
5.	Okra	322.0	–	20	600	20	600	20	600	20	600	20	600	100	3000
6.	Brinjal	461.0	–	10	300	10	300	10	300	10	300	10	300	50	1500
7.	Cauliflower	401.0	–	20	600	20	600	20	600	20	600	20	600	100	3000
8.	Cabbage	354.0	–	5	150	5	150	5	150	5	150	5	150	25	625
9.	Knolkhol	–	–	8	800	8	800	8	800	8	800	8	800	40	4000
10.	Ridgegourd	39.50	–	–	–	–	–	–	–	–	–	–	–	–	–
11.	Sponge gourd	–	–	–	–	–	–	–	–	–	–	–	–	–	–
12.	Bottle gourd	58.0	–	5	125	5	125	5	125	5	125	5	125	25	625
13.	Cowpea	169.0	–	20	200	20	200	20	200	20	200	20	200	100	1000
14.	Clusterbean	–	–	5	50	5	50	5	50	5	50	5	50	25	250
15.	Colocasia	–	–	5	75	5	75	5	75	5	75	5	75	25	375
16.	Ivy-gourd	12.5	–	–	–	–	–	–	–	–	–	–	–	–	–
17.	Pumpkin	21.8	5	75	5	75	5	75	5	75	5	75	25	375	
18.	Long cucumber	13.3	3	2	200	2	200	2	200	2	200	2	200	10	1000
19.	Tinda	0.70	–	–	–	–	–	–	–	–	–	–	–	–	–
20.	Pointed Gourd	12.5	–	2	50	2	50	2	50	2	50	2	50	10	250
21.	Green Pea	1420.0	–	100	1000	100	1000	100	1000	100	1000	100	1000	500	5000
22.	Other vegetable.	189.0	–	–	–	–	–	–	–	–	–	–	–	–	–

TABLE 20.6: Development Plan of Vegetable Crops in Raigarh District

S. No.	Name of Vegetable Crop	Present Status (Area in ha)	Pro-duction in tonnes	Development for five years										TOTAL	
				1999-2000		2000-2001		2001-2002		2002-2003		2003-2004			
				Area (ha)	Pro (t/ha)	Area (ha)	Pro. (t/ha)	Area (ha)	Pro. (t/ha)	Area (ha)	Pro. (l/ha)	Area (ha)	Pro. (t/ha)	Ara (ha)	Pro (t/ha)
1.	Potato	985.0	19827.0	5	20	5	20	5	20	5	20	5	20	25	100
2.	Sweet Potato	303.0	4480.0	10	100	10	100	10	100	10	100	10	100	50	500
3.	Onion	519.0	9629.0	10	200	10	200	10	200	10	200	10	200	50	1000
4.	Tomato	1060.0	27-37.0	25	400	25	400	25	400	25	400	25	400	125	2000
5.	Okra	239.0	2485.0	10	300	10	300	10	300	10	300	10	300	50	1500
6.	Brinjal	290.0	8059.0	10	300	10	300	10	300	10	300	10	300	50	1500
7.	Cauliflower	138.0	3047.0	5	150	5	150	5	150	5	150	5	150	25	750
8.	Cabbage	175.0	4710.0	3	90	3	90	3	90	3	90	3	90	15	450
9.	Knolkhol	33.0	501.0	2	20	2	20	2	20	2	20	2	20	10	100
10.	Ridgegourd	24.0	223.0	2	20	2	20	2	20	2	20	2	20	10	100
11.	Sponge gourd	16.0	143.0	–	–	–	–	–	–	–	–	–	–	–	–
12.	Bottle gourd	47.0	561.0	5	50	5	50	5	50	5	50	5	50	25	250
13.	Cowpea	130.0	230.0	3	30	3	30	3	30	3	30	3	30	15	150
14.	Clusterbean	0.0	0.0	10	100.	10	100	10	100	10	100	10	100	50	500
15.	Colocasia	50.0	66.0	–	–	–	–	–	–	–	–	–	–	–	–
16.	Ivy-gourd	22.0	408.00	–	–	–	–	–	–	–	–	–	–	–	–
17.	Pumpkin	31.0	812.0	–	–	–	–	–	–	–	–	–	–	–	–
18.	Long cucumber	11.0	104.0	–	–	–	–	–	–	–	–	–	–	–	–
19.	Tinda	14.0	70.0	–	–	–	–	–	–	–	–	–	–	–	–
20.	Pointed Gourd	11.0	66.8	20	300	20	300	20	300	20	300	20	300	100	1500
21.	Drumstick	12.0	32.0	–	–	–	–	–	–	–	–	–	–	–	–
22.	Kamaltal	0.0	0.0	–	–	–	–	–	–	–	–	–	–	–	–
23.	Khira	12.0	32.0	–	–	–	–	–	–	–	–	–	–	–	–
24.	Bitter-gourd	43.0	307.0	10	100	10	100	10	100	10	100	10	100	50	500
25.	Green Pea	82.0	580.0	–	–	–	–	–	–	–	–	–	–	–	–
26.	Other vegetable.	5.0	90.0	–	–	–	–	–	–	–	–	–	–	–	–

TABLE 20.7: Development Plan of Vegetable Crops in Bastar District

S. No.	Name of Vegetable Crop	Present Status (Area in ha)	Production in tonnes	Development for five years										TOTAL	
				1999-2000		2000-2001		2001-2002		2002-2003		2003-2004			
				Area (ha)	Pro (t/ha)	Area (ha)	Pro. (t/ha)	Area (ha)	Pro. (t/ha)	Area (ha)	Pro. (l/ha)	Area (ha)	Pro. (t/ha)	Ara (ha)	Pro (t/ha)
1.	Potato	20.0	56.0	2	40	2	40	2	40	2	40	2	40	10	200
2.	Sweet Potato	69.0	32.0	15	300	15	300	15	300	15	300	15	300	75	1500
3.	Onion	40.0	175.0	5	125	5	125	5	125	5	125	5	125	25	625
4.	Tomato	109.0	775.0	10	400	10	400	10	400	10	400	10	400	50	2000
5.	Okra	111.0	374.0	10	300	10	300	10	300	10	300	10	300	50	1500
6.	Brinjal	241.0	955.0	10	300	10	300	10	300	10	300	10	300	50	1500
7.	Cauliflower	83.0	320.0	5	150	5	150	5	150	5	150	5	150	25	750
8.	Cabbage	30.	121.0	3	90	3	90	3	90	3	90	3	90	15	450
9.	Knolkhol	18.0	40.0	2	20	2	20	2	20	2	20	2	20	10	100
10.	Ridgegourd	21.0	31.0	2	20	2	20	2	20	2	20	2	20	10	100
11.	Sponge gourd	3.0	–	2	20	2	20	2	20	2	20	2	20	10	100
12.	Bottle gourd	22.0	125.0	10	250	10	250	10	250	10	250	10	250	50	1250
13.	Cowpea	33.0	90.0	3	30	3	30	3	30	3	30	3	30	15	150
14.	Clusterbean	19.0	32.0	10	500	10	500	10	500	10	500	10	500	50	2500
15.	Colocasia	31.0	94.0	5	75	5	75	5	75	5	75	5	75	25	375
16.	Ivy-gourd	14.50	40.0	5	125	5	25	5	125	5	125	5	125	25	625
17.	Pumpkin	22.0	101.0	4	60	4	60	4	60	4	60	4	60	20	300
18.	Long cucumber	1.0	1.0	–	–	–	–	–	–	–	–	–	–	–	–
19.	Tinda	6.30	–	–	–	–	–	–	–	–	–	–	–	–	–
20.	Pointed	Gourd	1.0	1.0	–	–	–	–	–	–	–	–	–	–	–
21.	Drumstick	12	6.0	2	–	2	–	2	–	2	–	2	–	10	–
22.	Kamaltal	–	–	–	–	–	–	–	–	–	–	–	–	–	–
23.	Bittter gourd	13	20.0	–	–	–	–	–	–	–	–	–	–	–	–
24.	Green Pea	213	411,0	10	100	10	100	10	100	10	100	10	100	50	500
25.	Khira	3.0	3.0	–	–	–	–	–	–	–	–	–	–	–	–
26.	Other vegetable	164	293.0	–	–	–	–	–	–	–	–	–	–	–	–

TABLE 20.8: Development Plan of Vegetable Crops in Balaghat District

S. No.	Name of Vegetable Crop	Present Status (Area in ha)	Production in tonnes	Development for five years										TOTAL	
				1999-2000		2000-2001		2001-2002		2002-2003		2003-2004			
				Area (ha)	Pro (t/ha)	Area (ha)	Pro. (t/ha)	Area (ha)	Pro. (t/ha)	Area (ha)	Pro. (l/ha)	Area (ha)	Pro. (t/ha)	Ara (ha)	Pro (t/ha)
1.	Potato	723	14245	20	400	20	400	20	400	20	400	20	400	100	2000
2.	Sweet Potato	291	2520	20	400	20	400	20	400	20	400	20	400	100	2000
3.	Onion	332	5175	10	250	10	250	10	250	10	250	10	250	50	1250
4.	Tomato	592	8555	10	400	10	400	10	400	10	400	10	400	50	2000
5.	Okra	358	2895	20	600	20	600	20	600	20	600	20	600	100	3000
6.	Brinjal	496	8226	10	300	10	300	10	300	10	300	10	300	50	1500
7.	Cauliflower	106	1234	10	300	10	300	10	300	10	300	10	300	50	1500
8.	Cabbage	33	475	10	300	10	300	10	300	10	300	10	300	50	1500
9.	Knolkhol	96	526	5	50	5	50	5	50	5	50	5	50	25	1250
10.	Ridgegourd	85	948	10	50	10	50	10	50	10	50	10	50	50	1250
11.	Sponge gourd	34	286	10	50	10	50	10	50	10	50	10	50	50	1250
12.	Bottle gourd	199	2464	20	500	20	500	20	500	20	500	20	500	100	2500
13.	Cowpea	166	1827	20	200	20	200	20	200	20	200	20	200	100	1000
14.	Clusterbean	57	688	10	500	10	500	10	500	10	500	10	500	50	2500
15.	Colocasia	244	2785	5	75	5	75	5	75	5	75	5	75	25	375
16.	Ivy-gourd	16	45	–	–	–	–	–	–	–	–	–	–	–	–
17.	Pumpkin	118	1112	10	150	10	150	10	150	10	150	10	150	50	750
18.	Long cucumber	117	524	5	50	5	50	5	50	5	50	5	50	25	1250
19.	Tinda	12	105	2	20	2	20	2	20	2	20	2	20	10	100
20.	Pointed Gourd	8	53	2	50	2	50	2	50	2	50	2	50	10	250
21.	Drumstick	30	190	–	–	–	–	–	–	–	–	–	–	–	–
22.	Kamaltal	–	–	–	–	–	–	–	–	–	–	–	–	–	–
23.	Bitter gourd	153	1056	5	75	5	75	5	75	5	75	5	75	25	375
24.	Green Pea	343	2475	10	100	10	100	10	100	10	100	10	100	100	1000
25.	Khira	12	105	5	60	5	60	5	60	5	60	5	60	25	300
26.	Other vegetable.	293	2946	–	–	–	–	–	–	–	–	–	–	–	–

CHAPTER 21

VEGETABLE GROWING IN MAHARASHTRA

S.D. Warade and Vishal Sood

1. Name of state	:	Maharashtra.
2. Total geographical area (ha)	:	307.58 lakh
3. Area under cultivation (ha)	:	214.0 lakh
4. Irrigated area (ha)	:	33.0 lakh (15.3%)
5. Area under vegetables (ha)	:	2,16,259
6. Production (t)	:	29,57,335
Productivity (t/ha)	:	11.86
Anticipated by 2000 AD (t/ha)	:	15.00

Agroclimatic Zones of Maharashtra

Maharashtra comes under torrid zone. The climate of state is mostly subtropical and dry. On an average Maharashtra having 750 mm rainfall but the range is from 500-600 mm. Mostly the rain is received from South-West monsoon upto 60-70 days and also from South East-monsoon on eastern ride, in the month of September-October. Temperature is fluctuating in summer maximum 43°C and winter upto 8°C. Western coastal areas of Maharashtra have hot and humid climate while coastal area having dry and eastern Maharashtra having hot and rainy climate. Relative humidity is about 50% but in summer upto 30%. According to rainfall soil type, cropping pattern, temperature and overall, Maharasthra is divided into nine Agroclimatic zones.

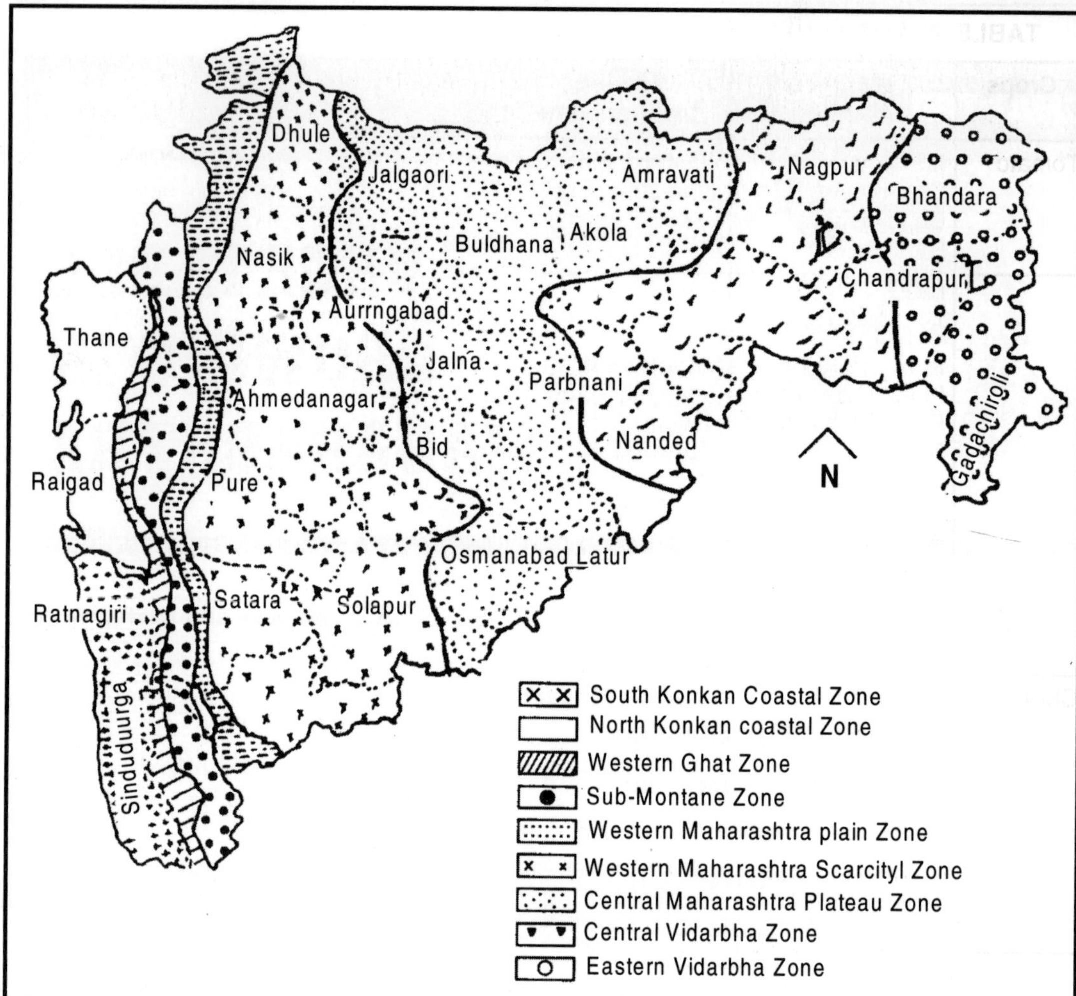

Fig. 21 (i) : Agro-climatic Zones of Maharashtra

Zone I : Southern Konkan Coastal Region : This region includes Ratnagiri and Sindhudurg districts of Maharashtra. Average rainfall 3100 mm, soil, type lateritic.

Vegetable crops : Tomato, Brinjal, Cucumber, Bittergourd, Bottlegourd, Snake gourd etc.

Zone II-Northern Konkan Coastal Region : This region includes Thane and Raigarh district. Av. rainfall 2600 mm.

Vegetable Crops : Tomato, Brinjal, Cucumber, Bittergourd, Bottlegourd, Kakrol, Okra, Leafy vegetables, Tuber crops etc.

Zone III-Western Ghat Region : This is a narrow strip region covered by Sahyadri moutain in North South direction and 2.10 lakh ha area. On an average height from mean sea level is 1000- 1900 m. Average rainfall 5000 mm and 22.25% of region is covered by forests.

TABLE 21.1: Vegetable Varieties/hybrids, Planting time and availability period

Crops	Varieties/ Hybrids	Sowing/ planting time	Availability	Major pests and disease
Tomato	**MPKV** Dhanashree, Bhagyashree, Rajshree F1	**Western Maharashtra** June-July, Sep.-Oct, Jan		Tarips, White Fly, Aphids, Fruit Borer,
	MAU ATV-1, ATV-2, ATH-1 **INTRODUCTION** Pusa Rubi, Sioux, Pusa Early Dwarf Roma Punjab Chhuhara, S-120, Pusa Gaurav, Arka Suurabh, Vasundhara Devgiri	Feb. **Marathwada** June-July, Aug-Oct, Sept-Oct, Nov-Jan **Vidharba** May-June, Aug-Sept. Dec-Jan **Konkan** May-July, Sep-Nov, Dec-Feb	Aug-Sep, Dec-Jan Apr-May Aug-Sep, Nov-Dec, Mar-Apr Aug-Oct, Dec-Feb, Mar-May	Early Blight, Later Blight, Leaf Crinkle Spotted wilt virus
Chilli	MPKV-Musal wadi Selection, X-235 Phule Jyoti, Agnirekha, Phule Suryamukhi, Phule Mukta MAU- Parbhani Tejas	**Western Maharashtra** June-July, Jan-Feb	Aug-Sept., Mar-Apr.	Thrips, mites, fruit borer Leaf curl complex Root Rot, Frui rot, Die back
	PDKV-Surakata, Jayanti KKV- Konkan Kirti **INTRODUCTION-** Pant C-l Jwala, NP-46, OCA-960, G-4, G –3	**Marathwada,** June-July Oct-Nov Jan-Feb **Vidharbha** June-July Jan-Feb	Aug-Sept. Dec.-Jan. Mar-Apr. Aug-Sept. Mar-Apr.	
Brinjal	MPKV- Vaishali, Manjri Gota, Pragati Ruchira, Krishna F1 Hybrid MAU-ABV-1 **INTRODUCTION-** Pusa Purple Round	**Konkan** May-July Sept.-Nov. Jan-Feb. June-July Sept.-Oct. Dec.-Jan.	Aug-Sept. Dec.-Jan. Mar-Apr. **Western Maharashtra** Sept.-Oct. Jan-Feb. April-May	Leaf hopper, Aphids, Mites, Fruiot

Crops	Varieties/ Hybrids	Sowing/ planting time	Availability	Major pests and disease
Pusa Purple Cluster Pusa Anuradha Kranti	Arka Nilkanth Sep-Oct, Dec-Jan.	**Marathwada** June-July, May-June **Vidharbha** May-Jun, Aug-Sept. Dec-Jan. **Konkan** May-Jun Sept-Oct. Jan-Feb.	Sept-Oct, Jan-Feb. Aug-Sept. Dec-Jan. April-May Aug-Sept. Jan-Feb. May-Jun	Little leaf, Leaf spot, Phomopsis blight
Okra	MAU-Parbhani Kranti Others-Pusa Sawni, Selection 2-2 Arka Anamika, Arka Abai Punjab-7	**Western Maharashtra** June-July Sept-Oct Jan-Feb. **Marathwada** June-July Feb-Mar **Vidharbha** Jun-Jul Jan-Feb. **Konkan** June-July Jan-Feb. Oct-Nov.		

Vegetable	Varieties/ Hybrids	Planting time	Availability	Pests and disease
Cucumber	MPKV-Himangi, Phule Shubhangi, KKV-Sheetal Others- Poona Khira, Priya F1, Pusa Sanyog F1	**Western Maharashtra** June-July Jan.-Feb. **Marathwada and Vidarbha** June-July Jan.-Feb **Konkan** June Jan.-Feb. Oct.	July-Aug. Feb.-Mar. July-Aug. Feb.-Mar. Aug.-Sept. Feb.-Mar. Nov.-Dec.	Aphids, fruit fly Powdery Mildew- Downey Mildew, Leaf spot, Wilt, CMV
Ridge gourd	Pusa Nasdar, CO_1, Local. Konkan Hanta (KKV)	**Western Maharashtra & Marathwada** June-July Jan.-Feb.	Aug.-Sept. Mar.-Apr.,	Aphids, fruit fly

Vegetable	Varieties/ Hybrids	Planting time	Availability	Pests and disease
		Vidarbha		
		May-June	July-Aug.	PM, DM Leaf spot
		Jan.-Feb.	Mar.-Apr.	
		Konkan		
		June-July	Aug.-Sept	Wilt, CMV
		Jan.-Mar.	Apr.-May	
Bitter gourd	MPKV-Hirkani, Phule Ujwala Phule Green Gold, Phule Priyanka F1 KKV-Konkan Tara Others-CO-Long white CO-Long green, ArkaHant Pusa Do Mausami Priya	**Western Maharashtra & Marathwada**		
		June-July	Aug.-Sept.	Aphids, fruit fly
		Jan.-Feb.	Mar.-Apr.	
		Vidarbha		
		May-June	July-Aug.	PM, DM, Leaf spot
		Jan.-Feb.	Mar.-Apr,	
		Konkan		
		June	July-Aug.	Wilt, CMV
		Jan.-Mar.	Apr.-May	
Bottle gourd	MPKV-Samrat Others-Pusa Summer Prolific Long, Pusa Summer Prolific Round Pusa Naveen, Pusa Meghdoot F1, Pusa Manian F1 Arka Bahar	**Western Maharashtra & Marathwada**		
		Jan.-Feb.	Mar.-Apj.	Aphid, fruit fly
		June-June	Aug.-Sept.	
		Vidarbha		
		May-June	July-Aug.	Powdery mildew
		Jan.-Feb	Mar.-Apr.	
		Konkan		
		June-July	Aug.-Sept.	Downey mildew, Leaf spot, Wilt, CMV
		Sept.	Oct-Nov.	
		Feb.	Mar.-Apr.	
Sponge gourd	Phule Prajakta (MPKV) Pusa Chikni Local	June- July	Aug.Sept.	
		Jan.-Feb.	Mar.-Apr.	
Round melon	Arka Tinda, Punjab Tinda	Jan.-Feb.	Mar.-Apr.	
		May-June	July-Aug.	
Pumpkin	Arka Suryamukhi, Arka Chandan, Large Red, Red Flesh, CO-1, CM-14 Pusa Vishwas	**Western Maharashtra & Marathwada**		
		Jan.-Feb.	May-June	
		Vidarbha		
		Jan.-Feb.	May-June	
		May-June	Sept.-Oct.	
		Konkan		
		June.July	Oct. -Nov.	
		Jan.-Feb.	May-June	

Vegetable	Varieties/ Hybrids	Planting time	Availability	Pests and disease
Water melon	Sugar baby, Anna Jyoti, Arka Manik Asahi Yamato, Local Madhu, Milon, Amrit, Sunthipti, MHW-H	**Western Maharashtra and Vidharbha** Jan.-Feb. **Marathwada** Dec.-Feb. **Konkan** Mid Oct.Dec	 Apr.-May Mar.-Apr. Jan.-Mar.	 Leaf blight, Wilt, PM, Anthracnose fruit fly
Musmk melon	Pusa Sarbati, Hara Madhu, Punjab Sunheni, Arka Jeet, Arka Rajhans	Jan.-Feb.	Apr.-May	
Cabbage	Pride of India, Golden Acre, Copenhagon Mkt, Pusa Drum Head, Early Drum Head, Late Drum Head Ganga, Pusa Synthetic, Sri Ganesh Goal, Hari Rani, Kaveri	**W. Maharashtra** Sept.-Oct. **Marathwada** June-July Sept.-Oct. **Vidarbha** Sept.-Oct. **Konkan** First week of Nov.	 Nov.-Dec. Sept.-Oct. Nov.-Dec. Nov.-Dec. Jan.-Feb.	Aphids, Diamond back moth Cabbage borer Black rot, Downy mildew, Leaf blight
Cauliflower	Pusa Deepali, Kunwari, Pusa Kataki, 61- D, Improved Japanese, Snow Ball-16, Pusa Synthetic	**W. Maharashtra** June-July Oct.-Nov. Dec-Jan. **Marathwada** June-July Sept .Nov **Vidarbha** Apr.-May June-July Sept.-Oct.	 Aug.-Sept. Dec.-Jan. Feb.-Mar. Aug.-Sept. Dec Jan. June-July Aug.-Sept. Nov.-Dec.	Aphids, Diamond back moth, Cab bage borer, Black rot, Downy mildew, Leaf bhght
Potato	Kufri Chandramukhi, Kufri Jyoti Kufri Lavkar, Kufri Sindhuri, Kufri Alankar, Kufri Badshah	**Western Maharashtra** June-July Oct.-Nov. **Marathwada & Vidarbha** Oct.-Nov.	 Sept.-Oct. Jan.-Feb. Jan.-Feb.	Leaf hopper, Aphids, Pota to tuber moth, Early blight, Late blight, Brown rot, Tomato virus X&Y

Vegetable	Varieties/ Hybrids	Planting time	Availability	Pests and disease
Carrot	Pusa Kesar, Nantes, Chan teny	**Western Maharashtra** Sept.-Nov. **Marathwada** Oct.-Nov. **Vidarbha** Sept.-Dec.	 Dec-Jan. Nov.-Jan. Oct.-Feb.	Aphids, Leaf spot, Root rot, Powdery mildew
Fenugreek	Pusa Early Bunching, Kasuri, No. 47, No- 14	**W. Maharashtra** Sept.-Mar. **Marathwada & Vidarbha** Sept.-Jan. **Konkan** Sept.-Nov.	 Oct.-Apr. Oct.-Feb. Oct.-Dec.	Aphids, Fusarium, Wilt, Leaf spot
Palak	Pusa Jyoti, Pusa All Green, Pusa Harit	**W.Maharashtra** June-July June-July **Marathwada & Vidarbha** Sept.-Jan. **Konkan** Oct.-Dec.	 July-Sept. July-Sept. Oct.-Mar. Nov.-Jan.	Leaf eating caterpillar Leaf spot
MPKV- Mahatma Phule Krishi Yidyapeeth	Rahuri	KKV-Konkan Krishi Viswavidyalya		
Onion	MPKV-N-53, Baswant-780, Phule Sufed, NT-2-4-I, N-247-9-1, Phule Suverna AADF-Agnfound Dark Red, Agnround Light Red PDKV-Selection Local White **Introduction-** Pusa, White Flat, Pusa White Round, Pusa Ratnar, Pusa Red	**W. Maharashtra** June-July Nov.-Dec. Jan.-Feb. July-Aug. **Marathwada & Vidarbha** Dec.-Jan. June-July Oct.-Nov. **Konkan** Oct.-Nov.	 Nov.-Dec. Apr.-May June-July Jan.-Mar. May-June Nov.-Dec. Apr.-May May-Apr.	Thrips, Pur pie blotch Fusarium wilt

Vegetable	Varieties/ Hybrids	Planting time	Availability	Pests and disease
Garlic	**MPKV-**Godavari, IC-49383 **Others-**G-40, G-41, Local	**W. Maharashtra** Oct.-Nov. **Marathwada & Vidarbha** 1st week Oct. **Konkan** Sept.-Oct.	Feb.-Mar. Oct.-Feb. Jan.-Feb.	Mites, Thrips, Purple blotch, Fusarium wilt
Radish	Pusa Desi, Pusa Chetaki, Pusa Reshmi, Japanese White, White Icicle, Scarlet Globe, Pusa Himani Ganesh Synthetic	**W. Maharashtra** Sept.-Nov. **Marathwada** Nov.-Feb. **Vidharbha** Aug.-Jan. **Konkan** Sept.-Oct.	Qct.-Dec. Jan.-Mar. Sept.-Feb. Oct.-Jan.	Mustard Saw Fly Aphids Sclerotiumrot, White rust, Leaf spot
KnolKhol	Early White, White Viena, Purple Top, Purple Viena, Green, King of Market	June-July Oct.-Nov. Dec-Jan.	Aug.-Sept. Dec-Jan. Feb.-Mar.	
Peas	Early Badger, Ankel Asanji, Bonneville, Jawahar, NP-29, Selection 82, VL-3, PH-1, KS-136, Selection-93	**W. Maharashtra** Sept.-Nov. **Marathwada & Vidarbha** Nov.-Feb.	Oct.-Nov. Nov.-Dec.	Podborer Stem fly, Powdery
French bean	Contander, Pusa Parvatii, Arka Komal, VL-5, Pant Anupama	June-July Sep-Oct. Jan.-Feb.	Aug.-Sept. Nov.-Dec. Mar.-Apr.	Pod borer, Stem fly, Powdery mildew, anthracnose Wilt virus
Dolichus bean	Khandeshi, Dasara, Dee pali, Konkan Bhushan (KKV), Arka Jai, Arka Vijay, Poona Red	June-July Sept.-Oct.	Oct.- Nov. Jan.-Feb.	Aphids, Powdcry mildew, Wilt
Lima bean	Local types	June-July Sept.-Oct.	Oct.-Nov. Jan.-Feb.	

Vegetable crops : Dolichus, bean, Cucurbits, Tuber crops etc.

Zone IV : Sub-mountain Region : This region is situated on the eastern slopes of Sahyadri. It includes western parts of Nasik, Pune, Satara, Sangli, Kolhapur, Area 10,289 km. Average rainfall 1700-2500 mm and more temperature 28-35°C and min. 14-19°C.

32.1 thousand ha area comes under vegetable production. Potato, onion, chilli, tomato, brinjal are main vegetable crops.

Zone V-Western Maharashtra Plains : This region includes Western side of Dhule and Sangli and middle parts of Nasik, Pune, Satara and Kolhapur. Thus region has 17.91 lakh ha area. Average rainfall 95-1250 mm. Av. max. temperature 40°C in the month of April-May. Av. min. temperature 5°C in the month of December.

Vegetable crops : Tomato, Brinjal, Chillies, Cole crops, Cucurbits, Onion, Garlic etc.

Zone Vl-Western Maharashtra Arid Region : This region includes whole Solapur, Ahmednagar districts and parts of Sangli, Satara, Pune, Dhule, Jalgaon, Nasik, Buldhana, Aurangabad, Beed, Osmanabad and Latur district. The area of region is 73.23 lakh ha and average rainfall is less than 750 mm and distribution is uneven. The area receive more rainfall two times in a year. One in June July and second in September October and dry spell 2- 10 weeks average maximum temperature 41°C during April May and average minimum temperature during 14-15°C during December.

Vegetable crops : Tomato, Brinjal, Chillies, Colecrops, Cucurbits, Onion, leafy vegetables, potato etc.

Zone Vll-Central Maharashtra Peninsular Region : It includes Parbhani, Nanded, parts of Jalana, Jalgaon, Aurangabad, Beed and Osmanabad, Latur. Average rainfall 750-950 mm. In *kharif* season 70% more rainfall is received.

Zone VIH-Central Vidarbha Region : Rainfall 950-1250 mm soil type blackish colour, heavy and black. It contains Akola, Buldhana, Wasim, Amravati, parts of Wardha, Yavatmal, parts of Nagpur.

Zone IX-Eastern Vidarbha Region : Area includes Bhandara, eastern part of Chandrapur, Garhchiroli and parts of Nagpur, Vardha. Average rainfall 1250-1700 mm. Soil type yellowish to raddish brown.

Vegetable crops : Chillies, Brinjal, Onion, Cucurbits, Cole crops etc.

Major production constrains :

(a) Biotic
1. Incidence of viral disease.
2. Incidence of Insect pests.
3. Incidence of Nematodes.

TABLE 19.2: Vegetable wise Area and production from 1991-92 to 1995-96 Area in Ha Production-in M.Ton.

Sr. No.	Name of Vegetable crop	1991-92		1992-93		1993-94		1994-95		1995-96	
		Area	Prod.	Area	Prod.	Area	Prod.	Area	Prod.	Area	Prod.
1	2	3	4	5	6	7	8	9	10	11	12
(1)	Potato	11637	232740	9859	197150	9557	117143	11363	122053	12133	119873
(2)	Onion	79124	1582450	78876	1577520	79665	1038065	82997	1200264	71254	1216207
(3)	Cabbage	8194	204250	8436	211575	11115	122985	9933	214351	8264	161202
(4)	Cauliflower	6376	127520	6035	121700	6985	136605	6426	126490	3583	71855
(5)	Tomato	25987	649675	22125	553125	43269	382274	29326	446791	28752	520147
(6)	Okra	7709	52508	5101	61212	3562	24375	5329	41015	6663	43345
(7)	Peas	5313	13255	–	–	217	599	352	1260	1116	5544
(8)	Brinjal	28742	574840	22232	444640	22232	444640	20153	311500	24742	389322
(9)	Sweet Potato	2962	44430	2095	31425	2095	31425	–	–	1527	25024
(10)	Carrot	2581	38715	1440	21600	1440	21600	–	–	1417	20630
(11)	Radish	1781	24846	1270	17825	1270	17828	–	–	996	12865
(12)	Beans	23108	96992	–	–	–	–	–	6042	17503	
(13)	Methi	5585	55850	3737	37370	3737	37370	–	–	–	–
(14)	Fenugrick	–	–	–	–	–	–	–	–	4635	35563
(15)	Cluster	bean	4286	18833	–	–	–	–	–	3737	16160
(16)	Bitter	gourd	2192	43840		–	–	–	–	1662	15793
(17)	Spinach	2123	28646	–	–	–	–	–	–	1443	9177
(18)	Cowpea	1077	11708	–	–	–	–	–	–	2719	10293
(19)	Pawata	–		–	–	–	–	–	–	644	6514
(20)	Others	19520	264284	40342	295712	40342	295712	54960	345290	34590	26516
	Total	241080	4171340	201633	3570887	225492	2737635	220847	2889022	216259	2957335

(*b*) 1. Non-availability of quality seed.

2. Irrigation facility.

3. Assured price.

4. Lack of Market Intelligence.

TABLE 19.3: District-wise area under vegetables of Maharashtra (Area in '00' ha).

1.	Mumbai sub	0
2.	Thane	53
3.	Raigad	16
4.	Ratnagiri	6
5.	Sindhudurg	6
6.	Nasik	403
7.	Dhule	53
9.	Anagar	138
10.	Pune	491
11.	Satara	257
12.	Sangli	24
13.	Solapur	78
14.	Kolhapur	42
15.	Aurangabad	26
16.	Jalna	29
17.	Parbhani	27
18.	Beed	238
19.	Nanded	10
20.	Osmanabad	51
21.	Latur	20
22.	Buldhana	49
23.	Akola	28
24.	Amravati	55
25.	Yavatmal	31
26.	Wardha	33
27.	Nagpur	154
28.	Bhandara	75
29.	Chandrapur	48
30.	Gadchiroli	7

CHAPTER 22

MANIPUR

Manipur literally means the land of the gems. This north-eastern state surrounded by Nagaland, Assam and Mizoram has an international border with Burma in the east. The state has an area of 22000 square kilo metres and Imphal is its capital, one of the oldest state capital in India. Founded about 2000 years ago, it derives its name from yum-pham meaning home- stead. Manipur formally became a part of the Indian Union in 1949 and a State in 1972.

Manipur is geographically divided into two district tracts-hills and plains. Manipur's hill ranges from parts of the Indo- Burmese Mountain arc, often referred to as the eastern arm of the Himalayas. Though pre-dominantly a hill state, it is watered by the rivers Imphal, Iril, Thoubal, Irang and Barak, which flow from north to south.

Manipur enjoys a sub-tropical monsoon climate. January is the coldest month and July the hottest. Rainfall on the whole is abundant in the state. More than 2/3rd area of the state is covered with forests of poor quality. The state is predominantly an agricultural state.

TABLE 22.1: Area (ha) and production (t) of vegetables in Manipur

	Crop	Area (ha)	Production (tonnes)
1.	Cabbage	410	12,300
2.	Cauliflower	480	9,640
3.	Other beans	–	28,000
4.	Peas	110	870
5.	Radish	–	770
6.	Tomato	290	5,800
7.	Other vegetables	160	3,120
	Total	1,450	60,500

Source : Govt. of India, Ministry of Agriculture

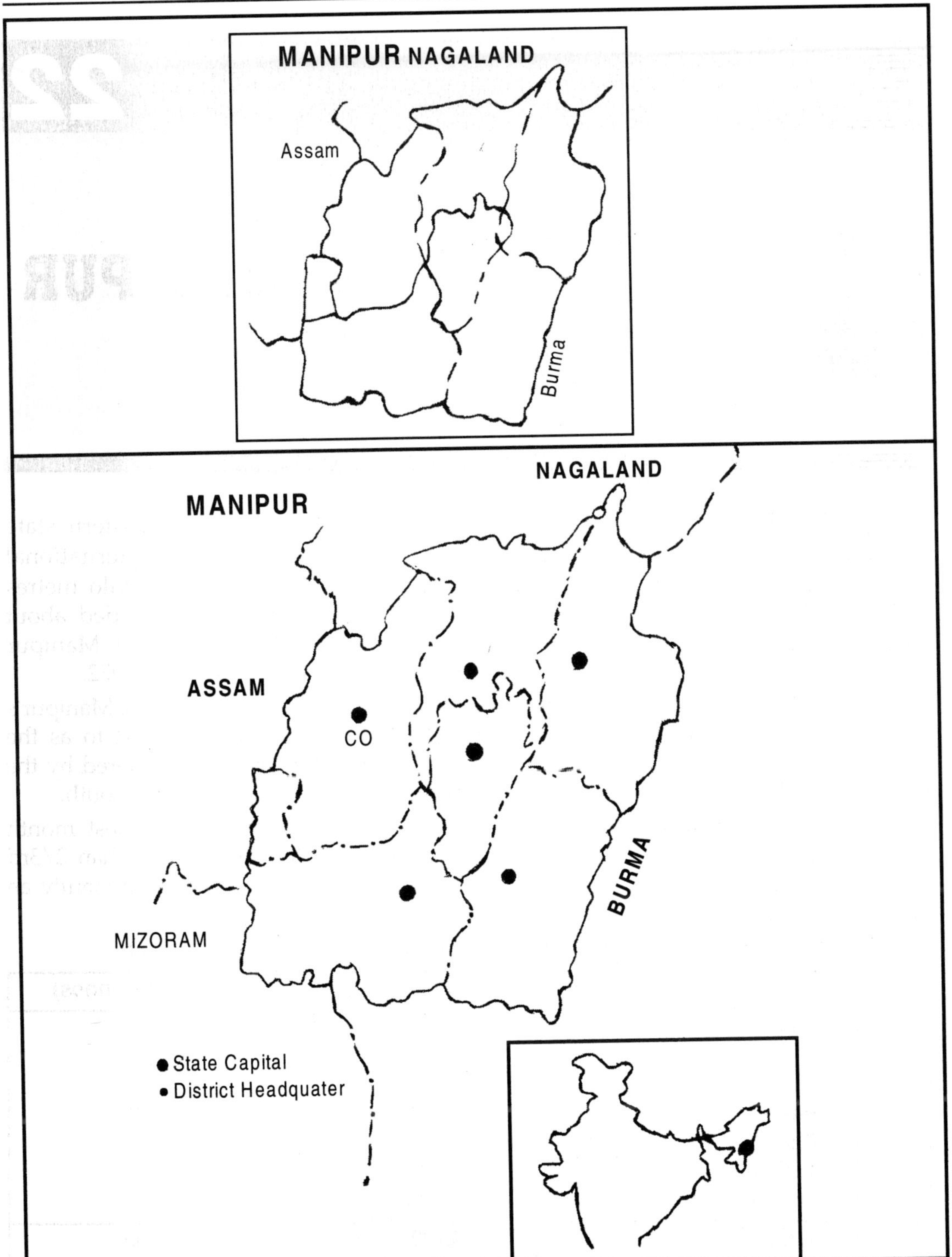

Fig. 22(i) Location map of Manipur

CHAPTER 23

MEGHALAYA

Meghalaya in north eastern India rests on the north-eastern shoulder of Bangladesh and south of the state of Assam. A part of Assam at the time of Indian independence, Meghalaya became a separate state in 1972. It covers an area of 22,429 square kilo metres.

TABLE 23.1: Area (ha) and production (t) of vegetable in Meghalaya

	Crop	Area (ha)	Production (tonnes)
1.	Bottle Gourd	350	4,640
2.	Brinjal	280	1,070
3.	Cabbage	770	7,600
4.	Carrot	180	1,400
5.	Cauliflower	600	7,130
6.	Okra	210	890
7.	Other beans	36,000	73,000
8.	Other vegetables	760	10,250
9.	Peas	180	180
10.	Radish	530	5,040
11.	Tamoto	270	160
	Total	40,130	1,11,360

Source : Govt. of India, Ministry of Agriculture

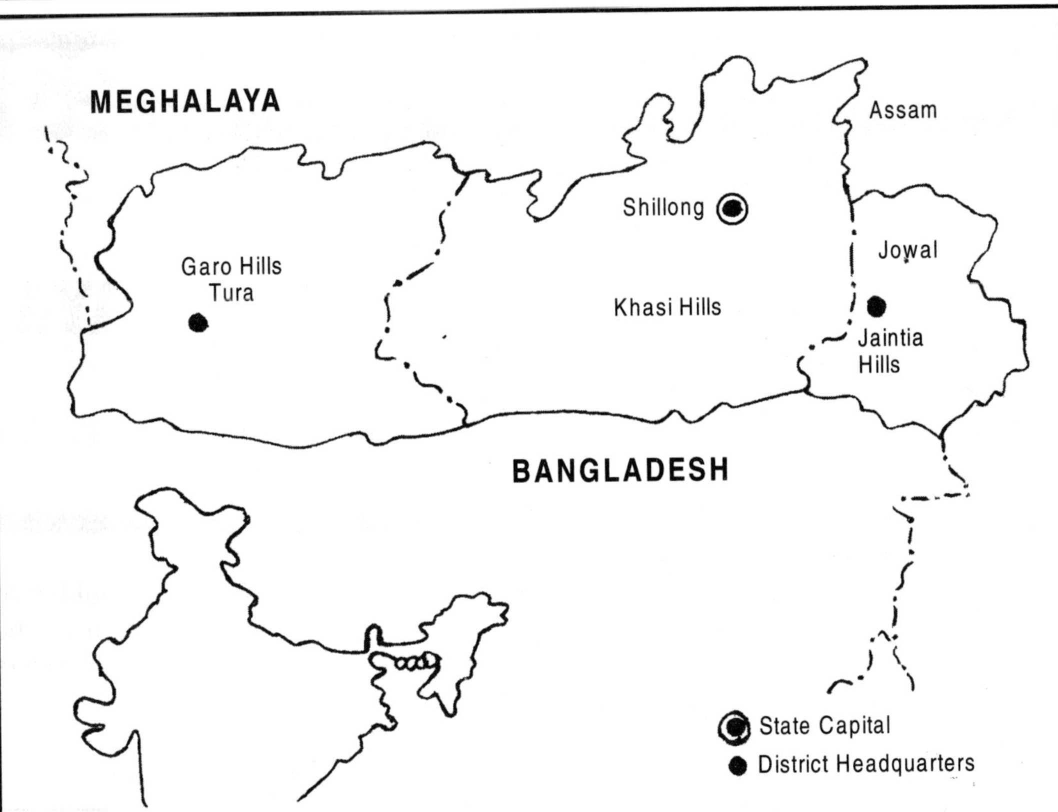

Fig 23 (i) Location map of Meghalaya

Meghalaya occupies mountainous plateau and lies in an earthquake prone area. The topography of the state is undulating landscape and sylvan surroundings. The state is drained by a number of rivers. The high altitude and the constant cloud cover keep temperatures; low throughout the year. Even in summer, the temperature does not cross 23°C. The state has been aptly named because Meghalaya means "Abode of the clouds". The hills facing south towards Bangladesh receive some of the heaviest rainfall in the world. Cherrapunjee, more famous as the rainiest place on earth.

Agriculture is the main economic activity. For long, the tribes practiced shifting cultivation but are gradually moving to more settled ways of life. The more important crops are rice and maize oranges, pineapples, potatoes, ginger, turmeric, colocasia, betel leaf and black pepper, etc. are grown. Meghalaya presents a panorama of rolling hills, pine forests, roaring waterfalls, lakes and a multitude of flora and fauna.

CHAPTER 24

STATUS AND PROSPECTUS OF OLERICULTURE IN MIZORUM

N. Sazad Thakur and K. Laxminarayana

ICAR Research Complex for NEH Region Mizoram Centre, Kolasib-796081

Mizoram, a mountainous region, is sandwiched between Myanmar in the East and the South and Bangladesh and Tripura in the West with its Northern frontiers touching Assam Manipur states. It is a store house of natural beauty with green and thick forests, rich in flora and fauna. It occupies an area of 21,081 sq km and lies between 92° 15" to 93° 29 ″ E longitude and 21° 58″ to 24° 35 ″ N latitude. The hills are steep with an average height of about 900 m. It has a sub-tropical and humid climate with a temperature range of 11° to 21° C in winter and 20° to 30° C in summer and relative humidity ranges from 45 to 95 per cent which is favourable for the growth of a large number of crops. It receives an average rainfall of 254 cm per annum but to a large extent is lost through runoff and erosion due to sloppiness, undulating topography and light textured soils.

The soils are very rich in humus content and the organic matter is more than two per cent. Heavy litterfall in Jhum land is accumulated, decomposed by microorganisms resulting in to fertility buildup, which favours the growth of all types of crops. The soils belong to Entisols, Inceptisols, Ultisols and to a little extent of Vertisols, acidic in reaction, non-calcareous, rich in organic carbon, low to medium in available N, low in available P and medium to high in available K.

The farmers in this state mainly practice 'Jhum cultivation' (Shifting cultivation).The farmers clear some forest area in the month of February-April, set it on fire and sow various crops in the months of April-June after first rain shower. They harvest the vegetables in the months of July-August, while cereal crops in the month of October- November. After getting one or two crops, they leave the Jhum land and shift to another place for cultivation.

Farmers grow cereal crops like upland paddy, maize and millets in one side of Jhum land and the remaining land is utilized for cultivation of various kinds of vegetable crops like cucumber, pumpkin, snakegourd, ashgourd, bittergourd, cabbage, cauliflower, knolkhol, gobisarson, lady's finger, brinjal, capsicum, local cowpea, beans, watermelon etc.

Out of total geographical area of 21,08,100 ha, only 4.52 percent (95,187 ha) area is under cultivation of different crops with a total production of 2.07 lakh tonnes (Anonymous, 1996). The state has an irrigation potential of 1565 ha only and rainfall is the major source of irrigation for the crops.

The, state has wide scope for cultivation of different types of vegetables. Out of total cultivated area, olericulture is practised in an area of 6564 ha (0.31%) with a total production of 50,577 t and productivity of 7.705 t/ha (Anonymous, 1996). The area under vegetable cultivation is increasing and it is anticipated that by 2000 AD it will occupy an area of 7578 ha with a production of 60,892 t.

In the steep slopes of Mizoram, pumpkin and squash occupy first place in area (19.5%) and production (40.0%), respectively (Table 24.1) and export them to other states like Assam, West Bengal, Tripura, Manipur and the adjoining countries like Myanmar and Bangladesh. The Mizo people consume the tender vines and leaves of pumpkin, bottlegourd, local mustard, Frenchbean and local cowpea as vegetables. The production of squash, pumpkin and local mustard may reach 23475, 86501 and 4950 t, respectively by 2000 AD. The present status of major vegetable crops in the state is as follows :

CRUCIFEROUS CROPS

Cauliflower

Early cauliflower varieties like early Snowball, Giant Snowball, Pusa Katki, Early Patna are sown during July-August while the late varieties like Snowball-16, Banaras, Super Snowball, Suttlers Snowball and Dania are sown during September-October. The major pests like cabbage curd borer, diamond back moth (DBM), cabbage butterfly (*Pieris* spp.) and aphid cause heavy damage to the crop. Spraying with 0.01% Deltamethrin can control these insect-pests. Diseases like lef spot, black rot and damping off prevail on the crop and controlled by treating the seeds with 0.3% Thiram before sowing.

Cabbage

Cabbage is one of the most popular vegetables among the Cole crops. Early varieties like Pride of India, Golden acre, Early Drumhead are sown in nursery during the month of August-September while the late varieties like Pusa Drumhead and late Drumhead are sown during October-November. The pests and diseases

TABLE 24.1: Area and production of vegetable in Mizoram

Sl. No.	Name	Area (ha)		Production		Productivity (t/ha.)
		1996-97	2000	1996-97	2000	
1.	Tomato (Tomato)	193	215	818	1,150	4.24
2.	Cabbage (Zikhlum)	312	330	2,134	2,686	6.84
3.	Knolkhol (Bulbawk)	101	96	409	426	4.05
4.	Turnip (Turnip)	59	65	286	372	4.85
5.	Radish (Buluih)	122	155	524	734	4.29
6.	Cauliflower (Parbawr)	117	135	682	792	5.83
7.	Local mustard (Antam)	845	950	4,120	4,950	4.88
8.	Pumpkin (Mai)	1,256	1,425	6,673	8,650	5.31
9.	Cucumber (Fanghma)	632	790	3,358	3,990	5.31
10.	Brinjal (Bawkbawn)	553	625	2,570	3,270	4.65
11.	Bittergourd (Changkha)	421	510	1,250	1,420	2.97
12.	Snakegourd (Berul)	232	250	852	900	3.67
13.	Okra (Bawrhsaiabe)	235	275	539	690	2.29
14.	French mustard (French Antam)	370	390	1,384	1,490	3.74
15.	Carrot (Carrot)	88	110	225	280	2.56
16.	Ashgourd (Maipawl	246	287	2,701	3,250	10.98
17.	Squash (Iskut)	423	520	20,170	23,475	47.68
18.	Watermelon (Dawnfawh)	69	80	438	510	6.35
19.	Muskmelon (Hmazil)	55	50	360	350	6.55
20.	Fieldpea (Motorchana)	16	15	29	32	1.81
21.	Capsicum (Sap hmarcha)	26	40	51	75	1.96
22.	Local cowpea (Behlawi)	58	75	115	180	1.98
	Others	135	190	889	1,220	6.59
	Total	6,429	7,578	50,577	60,892	7.87

Note : Parentheses indicate the local name
Source : Statistical Abstract. Department of Agriculture & Minor Irrigation, Government of Mizoram (1996).

and their control measures are similar to cauliflower. Jugindra Singh (1996) reported that tribals use raw or cooked cabbage to avoid the risk of stomach, esophagus and colon cancer.

Knolkhol

The early varieties of knolkhol are White Vienna, Earliest White and late varieties are Purple Vienna, Venus of Vienna and Pe- Tsai. Sowing seasons is July-August for early varieties and October for late varieties. Cultural practices, control measures for pests and diseases are more or less similar to other Cole crops.

Radish

It performs better in sandy loam soils containing high proportion of humus. The most popular Indian varieties in the state are Long White, Pusa Deshi, Long Red, Bombay Red, Chetki and European varieties like White Icicle, Scarlet Globe and French Breakfast. Generally these varieties are sown in the month of February-March for *kharif* and September-November for *rabi* season, respectively. European varieties are harvested 1-2 months after sowing with an average yield of 40-70 q/ha, while the Indian varieties are harvested 2-3 months after sowing with an average yield of 140-187 q/ha. Cabbage butterfly (*Pieris* spp.), mustard sawfly and mustard aphids are the common insect-pests on radish. Taproots are commonly used as appetizer or stimulant. It acts as diuretic and used in piles and gastrodynia.

Mustard

Mustard, though primarily an oilseed crop, is commonly grown as a leafy vegetable in the hills. The leaves of the plant in early stages and the young flowering stalks in the main season are used as greens. The varieties grown in state are Yellow Sarson, Banga Sarson and Lai Sarson. Lai Sarson is grown throughout the year, whereas Yellow Sarson and Banga Sarson are grown during October-November and ready for harvest at 25-30 days after sowing. Aphids and sawfly mainly infest the mustard crop. Spraying of 0.05% Phosphamidon can control these pests. The most common disease observed is white rust in this crop.

Turnip

Turnip is cultivated for its root and the greens are seldom used as vegetables but are extensively utilized as green fodder for cattle. Asiatic or Desi varieties like Pusa Sweti Pusa Kanchan and European varieties like Golden ball and Snowball are more promising. It is sown during March to end of May. Aphids and butterflies cause major damage to this crop and they can be controlled by spraying of 0.05% phosphamidon. Harvesting is done when the turnips attain a diameter of 8-10 cm

CUCURBITACEOUS CROPS

Squash

The popular varieties are Whitish Green and Dark Green in the state and are sown during February-April for early crop and June- July for late crop. The first flush of fruit is borne very early as the plant just start running to vine. These fruits are small in size and it is advisable to remove these fruits. Second flush attains a marketable size and is harvested when the fruits are still tender and somewhat hairy and seeds are soft (Yawalkar, 1985). This crop is free from insect-pests and diseases.

Snakegourd

The varieties namely Long Green, Long White and Extra long are popular and sown during April-May in *kharif* and September- October in *rabi* season. Fruits are plucked while tender and half-grown i.e. 7-8 weeks after sowing.

Ridgegourd and Spongegourd

The popular varieties namely Pusa Nasdar for ridgegourd and Pusa Chikni for spongegourd are sown during April-May in *kharif* and mid August-mid September in *rabi* seasons. Fruits are picked while green, soft and tender. Morie D'souza (1985) reported that pouring 2-3 drops of juice extracted from leaves into the nose for four days can cure jaundice.

Bottlegourd

Pusa Summer, Prolific Long, Pusa Manjari, Pusa Meghdoot are popular varieties of bottlegourd in the state. April-May and September-October are the best seasons for sowing in *kharif* and *rabi* seasons, respectively.? The crop is harvested while the fruits are still tender.

Bittergourd

The popular varieties namely Monsoon Monarch, Long Green, Pusa Do Mausmi, Long Green monsoon are grown in the state. Sowing time is February-March, June-July and October-November for mid, late and early crops, respectively. Young and tender fruits are harvested 2-3 months after sowing.

Ashgourd

The varieties namely Co-1 and Co-2 are popular and are sown during June-July. Fully ripened fruits are harvested when the peduncle withers dry and fruit becomes somewhat light as the water content is reduced.

Pumpkin

Pumpkin also known as vegetable marrow and is grown during rainy season. The varieties like Arka Suryamukhi, Arka Chandan and Co-2 are more popular and generally sown after clearing of jhum in the month of March-May. It is harvested 3 to 4 months after sowing when the fruit colour changes to yellow or orange yellow. Among the vegetables, it occupies second place in area and production after squash. Pumpkin beetle and blister beetles are the common insect-pests infesting cucurbitaceous crops and controlled by dusting of Sevin at flowering.

Watermelon

The varieties grown in the state are Arka Jyoti, New Hampshire, Midget, Pusa Bedana, Sugar Baby. Sowing time is February-March for early crop and June-July for late crop. The best time to pick watermelon is early in the morning because they remain crisp for a greater period.

Cucumber

Under Mizoram conditions, the varieties namely Chinese Green cucumber, Ridged cucumber, Apple cucumber and Pusa Sanyong are popular. Middle of the

March-May for *kharif* and middle of August-October for *rabi* crops is the best sowing time and are harvested two months after sowing.

SOLANACEOUS CROPS

Potato

It is grown in an area of around 1000 ha with a production of around 5000t. The varieties like Kufri Chandramukhi, Kufri Alankar, Darjeeling Red Round, Kufri Jyoti are being cultivated. The tubers are planted during March-April at mid and high altitude and during September-October in hills of lower altitude and harvested during July-August and January- February. The average yield is about 18 q/ha, the lowest in entire North Eastern region (Kaul, 1984). Major insect-pests like cutworms, potato tuber moth and aphids and diseases like brown rot or bacterial wilt blackleg or soft rot, Potato wart, powdery scab and late blight cause severe loss to the crop. The control measures are drenching the ridges with chrlorpyriphos @ 2.5 1/ha in 800-1000 liters of water for cutworms, 2 kg a.i./ha of carbaryl for potato tuber moth, spraying of endosulfan @2.5 1/ha against defoliators, spraying of 0.2%, streptocycline for bacterial wilt, 0.1% streptomycin sulphate for soft rot, 0.2% solution of mancozeb at 8-10 days interval for late blight, wettable sulphur or copper sulphate for wart and powdery scab disease should be followed.

Tomato

Tomato occupies a prominent place in the dietary as a protective vegetables. The varieties grown under Mizoram conditions are Pusa Ruby, Pusa Early Dwarf, Sioux, Marglobe, Roma, Italian Red pear etc. These are sown during January-March and harvested before onset of monsoon. Tomato cannot be grown successfully during the main monsoon season.

Major insect-pests infesting tomato are fruit borer, thrips, epilachna beetle and jassids. These pests can be controlled by spraying with 0.01% deltamethrin at fortnightly interval in the early stage of development of fruit. The crop is severely infested by diseases like wilt, fruit rot, damping-off, leaf curl, early and late blight. Seed treatment with 0.2% captan for fruit rot, 0.2% thiram for damping-off and weekly spraying of 0.05% endosulfan for leaf curl can control effectively. In winter crop, early blight is the major problem and spraying of Dithane Z-78 @ 0.2% is effective against this disease. However, in rainy season, late blight becomes the limiting factor. Regular spraying of Dithane M-45 @ 0.2% at an interval of 10 days protects the crop from late blight.

Brinjal

Well-drained light soils are preferable for brinjal cultivation. Brinjal is sown during April-May in Jhum land and in August-October in low-lying areas. The varieties/hybrids grown under Mizoram conditions are Pusa Purple Long, Pusa Kranti, Arka Shirish, Pusa Anmol and Krishnanagar Green Long.

The crop is generally harvested in the month of July and an average yield of 200 q/ha is obtained. The key insect-pests are fruit and shoot borers (*Leucinodes* sp.) and spraying of 0.1% endosulfan at 15 days interval check the pest population. The major disease observed is fusarium wilt, which can be controlled by periodical spraying of 0.01% carbendazim followed by crop rotations.

Chilli

In Mizoram ecosystem, chilli is well known spice since ancient times. The popular varieties grown under these conditions are K-l, K-2, Co-1, Co-2 and MDU-1. Nursery is raised during April and September-October for *kharif* and *rabi* crops, respectively and the seedlings are ready for transplanting in 40- 45 days after sowing. Flowering begins 45-60 days after transplanting and it takes another one month for green fruits. Ripe fruits are picked at an interval of 1-2 weeks.

MALVACEOUS CROPS

Lady's finger

Okra or lady'sfinger is a rainy seaosn crop and is most productive in warm moist weather conditions of Mizoram. The varieties like Pusa Sawani, and Pusa Makhamali are recommended and second fortnight of January-June and September-October is the best sowing time with a seed rate of 8-10 kg/ha. Fruit borer (*Earias* sp.), blister beetles and jassids cause severe damage to the crop and they can be controlled by spraying with 0.05% endosulfan. The diseases noticed are yellow vein mosaic and powdery mildew, which can be controlled by spraying of 0.5% karathane or 0.2% sulfex, respectively. Bhendi is widely used by tribals for treating irritant condition of the throat and improving memory and intelligence (Girija Khanna, 1982).

LEGUMINACEOUS CROPS

Frenchbean

Climber varieties like Mizo local (Kawmtlawn, Dawmthau), Kentucky Wonder, Scarlet Emperor and the dwarf varieties like Contender, Tender green, Giant Stringless and Bowntiful are popular. Sowing time is February-April and September-October for *kharif* and *rabi* seasons, respectively. *Kharif* crop is harvested from May-August and the *rabi* crop is harvested from November-January. Blister beetles, defoliating beetles and leaf folders are the major pests causing severe loss to *kharif* crops. Dusting at 15 days interval with sevin at the time of flowering control the pests. Rust and anthracnose are the main diseases of beans in the state and can effectively be controlled by spraying chlorothalonil (Kavach) (5)0.2%.

Cowpea

The varieties like Pusa Phalguni, Pusa Barsati and Pusa Dofasali are popular in the state. The leaves are sometimes used as leafy vegetables. April-May is the sowing time in Jhum lands. It is ready for harvest by August-October.

OTHER CROPS

Carrot

It belongs to the family Umbelliferae and it is grown throughout the year. The popular Indian variety Pusa Kesar and European varieties like Early Nantes, Purple Long, Chantany, Golden Heart, Tender Heart, Tender Sweet are generally grown in the state. Best time of sowing is August-November. It attains maturity when its diameter is about 2.5 to 4.0 cm and harvested in the months of October-January. The tribals for treatment of asthma, anemia, dropsy, night blindness and blood poisoning generally use carrots.

Tapioca

Tapioca or cassava belongs to the family "Euphorbiaceae" and well-drained loamy soil is ideal for its cultivation. The popular varieties like H-43, H-226, H-2304 are sown in the months of April-May. It is rotated with maize, banana, yams etc. Tapioca becomes ready for harvest at 8 to 10 months after planting. This crop is almost free from the ravages of insect-pests and diseases. The leaves are fed to the pigs and used for rearing of silk worms by the tribal people of the state.

EXPORT POTENTIAL

The vegetables grown in this state do not meet the requirements of people. Hence most of the vegetables of various types like tomato, potato, carrot, cauliflower, cabbage, knolkhol, ridgegourd, bittergourd, bhendi etc. are being imported from the neighbouring states like Assam, Meghalaya, Tripura and Manipur to meet the local demand. Squash is exported to Burma, Thailand and Bangladesh and also to Assam and West Bengal due to large production.

MAJOR PRODUCTION CONSTRAINTS

(a) **Biotic.** Most of the vegetables suffer yield losses due to insect-pests, diseases, rodents and weeds etc. The farmers due to lack of awareness and economically poor conditions do not adopt proper control measures.

(*b*) **Abiotic**

(*i*) **Climate.** Unfavourable climatic conditions like uncertainty in onset of monsoon, erratic, improper distribution, torrential rainfall, hails and high humidity during April-September and moisture stress during January-March hamper the vegetable production in the state.

(*ii*) **Soil.** Soils in Mizoram are light textured, lacking much water holding capacity, highly acidic, shallow depth and rocky layer in the sub- soil hamper the crop growth and resulting lower yields. The farmers do not use any soil amendments, thus resulting lower soil productivity.

(*iii*) **Market and transport facilities.** The state lacks proper market and transport facilities due to which the farmers are not adopting wide scale production of vegetables. Lack of link roads/connecting roads and poor transport facilities in the interior areas hamper the marketing of vegetables. This factor alone increases the marketing cost by about 43 to 85% (Kaul, 1984).

(*iv*) **Lack of awareness.** The farmers in the state are not aware about the improved technology in floriculture due to lack of training, supply of minikits/ high yielding varieties or hybrids etc.

(*v*) **Supply of inputs.** Inputs like seeds, fertilizers, pesticides etc. do not reach the marginal and small farmers in time.

(*vi*) **Storage facilities.** Most of the perishable vegetables are spoiled and rendered unfit for consumption/ market due to lack of proper storage facilities.

(*vii*) **Construction of check dams.** Construction of check dams will be helpful in storing the runoff water, which can be used for irrigation in dry spells, especially during winter and pre-monsoon season.

(*viii*) **Research.** Research on cultivation of different types of vegetables under the agro-climatic conditions of the state is required to enhance the vegetable production.

Potential areas for commercial production

The state has a wide scope for commercial production of different kinds of vegetables. The potential regions (Fig. 24 (*i*)) for vegetable production are mainly situated around Aizawl city, which is having good marketing facilities. The potential areas are :

Northern Mizoram : Bilkhawthlir, Buhchang, Phaisen, Chemphai, Bairabi, Kolasib, and Kawnpui.

Southern Mizoram : Lawngtlai, Lunglei, Serchhip, Chhingchhip, Baktawng, Saiha and Chawngte.

Eastern Mizoram: Champhai, Khawzawl, North Vanlaiphai, Hnahlan, Vaphai and Sangau.

Central Mizoram : Durtlang, Sihphir, Lungdai, Seling, Sesawng, Thingsulthliah, Khawruhlian, Mualmam, and Tuirial.

Western Mizoram : Sairang, Darlak, Mamit, Tlabung and Marpara.

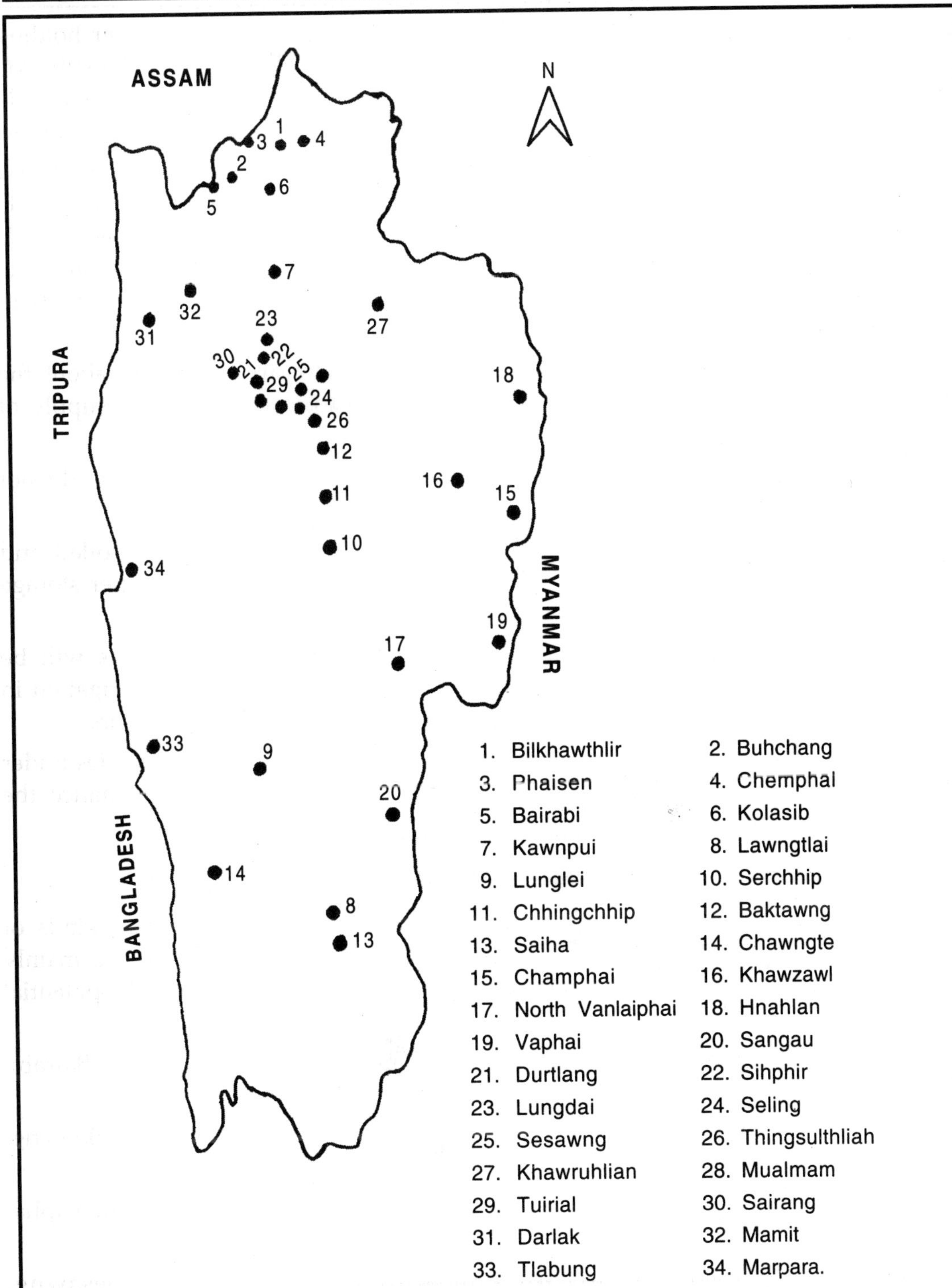

Fig. 24 (i) : Map of Mizoram depicting the potential areas for commercial production of vegetables

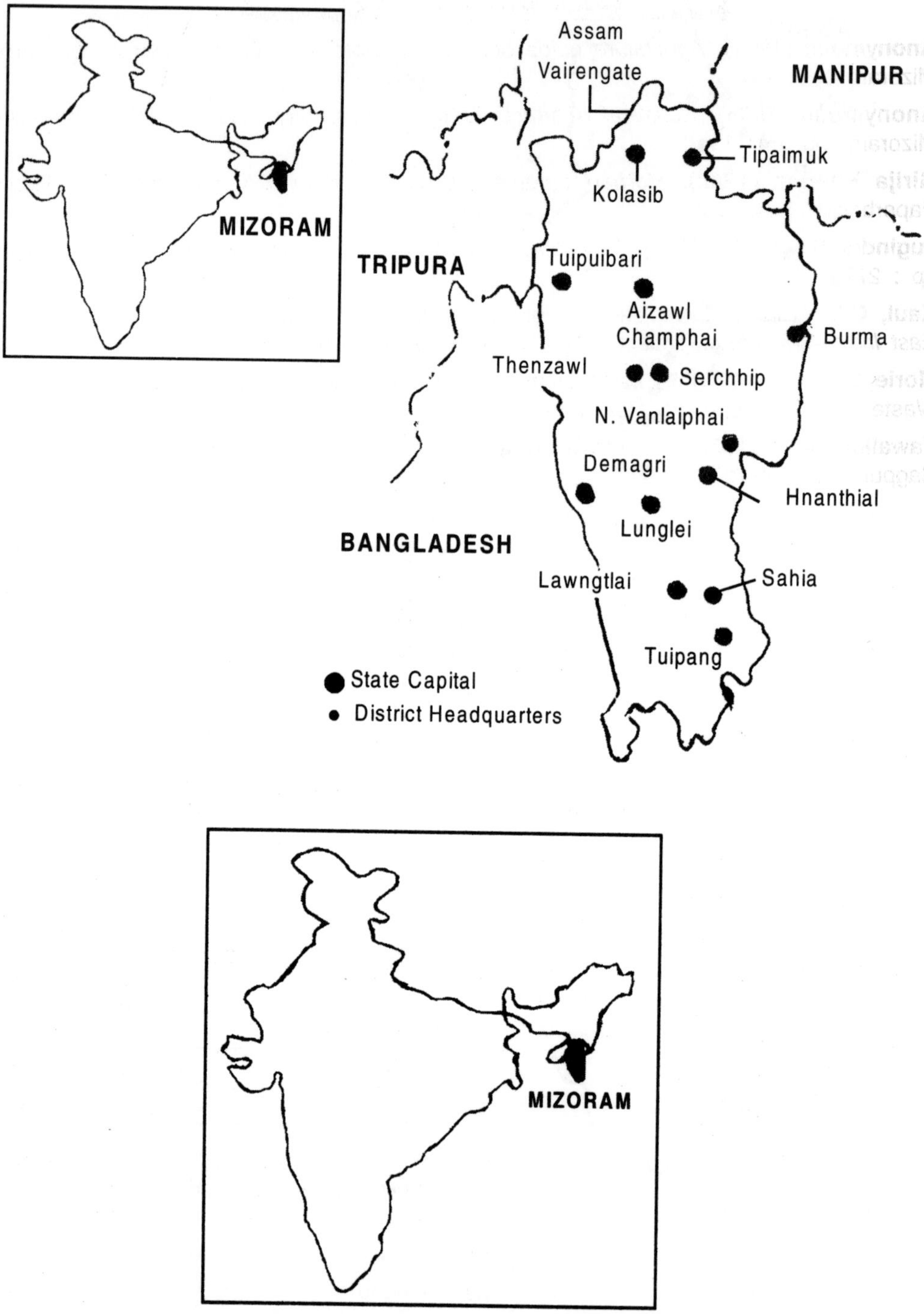

Fig. 24 (ii) Location map of Mizoram

REFERENCES

1. **Anonymous (1991).** *Agriculture guide book of Mizoram.* Pub. Department of Agriculture, Mizoram pp : 147.
2. **Anonymous (1996).** *Satistical Abstract.* Department of Agriculture & Minor Irrigation, Mizoram. pp : 44-73.
3. **Girija Khanna (1982).** *Herbal remedies, a handbook of folk medicine.* Pub. Tarang Paperbacks, New Delhi.
4. **Jugindra Singh, A. (1996).** *Vegetable in Manipur.* The Punshi Marup, Imphal, Manipur. pp : 277.
5. **Kaul, G.L. (1984).** Horticulture in North-Eastern Region. *Resource Potentials of North-East India* Vol. II Ed. Tripathi, R.S., Meghalaya Science Society, Shillong pp : 51- 60.
6. **Morie D'souza (1985).** *A book on tribal medicine.* Pub. The Society for Promotion of Waste land Development, New Delhi.
7. **Yawalkar, K.S. (1985).** *Vegetable crops of India.* Agri- Horticultural Publishing House, Nagpur, India pp: 374.

●●●

CHAPTER 25

NAGALAND

Nagaland in India's north-east, is a narrow strip of territory with an area of 16579 square kilo metres, and a population of 1.22 million. Nagaland became a full fledged state of the Indian Union in 1963. Kohima is the capital of the state. The Naga hills run through this small state with Saramati, its highest peak reaching a height of 3841 m. These mountains have some of the richest forest cover left in India.

For long, the slash and burn techniques of "Jhum cultivation" was followed. Though, only a little more than one-third of the total area in the state is cultivable and agriculture is the mainstay of the economy with 90% of the population involved in it. Development organisations and government initiatives have encouraged the people to adopt terraced cultivation, farm forestry and to plant orchards. Agriculture is the major occupation also include Sericulture and bee keeping.

TABLE 25.1: Area (ha) and proudct (t) of vegetables in Nagaland

	Crop	Area (ha)	Production (tonnes)
1.	Cabbage	500	2,000
2.	Cauliflower	200	700
3.	Other beans	60,000	38,000
4.	Peas	850	850
5.	Other vegetables	1,100	1,270
	Total	62,700	42,820

Source : Govt. of India, Ministry of Agriculture

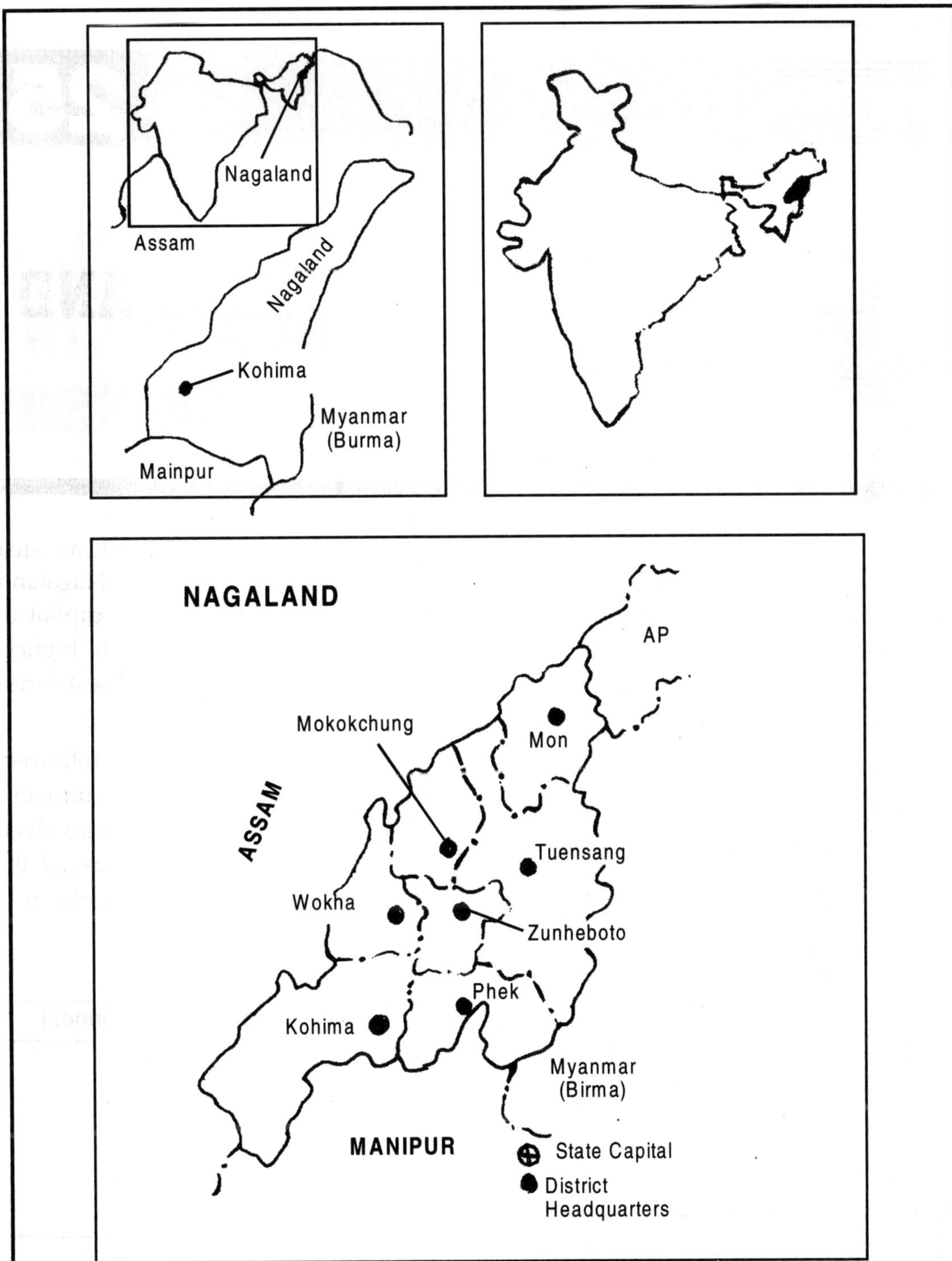

Fig. 25 (i) Location map of Nagaland.

CHAPTER 26

VEGETABLE GROWING IN ORISSA

Orissa lies in the sub-tropical belt in the Eastern Region of India between 17.52' and 22.54' North latitude and 155.4 lakh ha. Based as the prevailing agro-climatic conditions the state is divided into following different zones (Fig. 26(i)):

(*a*) North Western Platum zone

(*b*) North Central Platum zone

(*c*) North Eastern Coastal plain zone

(*d*) East and South Eastern Coastal Plain zone

(*e*) North Eastern Ghat zone

(*f*) Eastern Ghat High Land zone

(*g*) South Eastern Ghat zone

(*h*) Western Undulating zone

(*i*) West Central Table Land zone and

(*j*) Mid Central Table Land zone

Total area under vegetables in Orissa is 6.49 lakh ha with a production of 53.32 lakh tons. The detail of hectare area under important vegetable alongwith production figures is given in Table 26.1.

Major vegetable growing zones

1. **North Eastern Coastal Plain zone** : This zone comprises of three revenue Distts viz., Bilasore, Jaipur and Keonjhar/Anandpur. This zone has cropped an area of 8.75 lakh ha and about 11.6% is under vegetables. The river

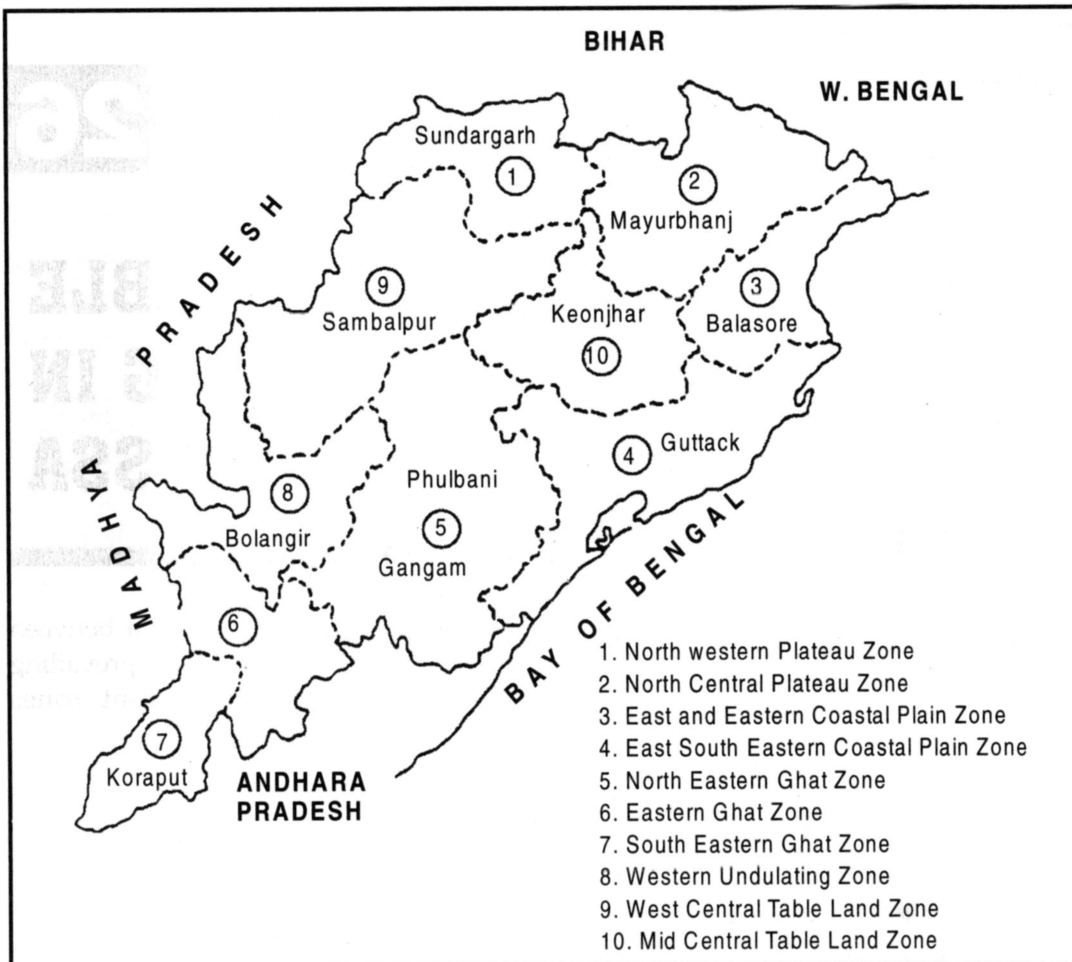

Fig. 26(i) : Agro-climatic Zones of Orissa.

basin are thickly grown vegetable areas. Brinjal, okra, tomato, potato, parwal and other cucurbit are important vegetable crops cultivated. Tejpur and Binjharpur blocks are the two major vegetable growing areas.

2. **East and South Eastern Coastal zone:** This zone covers the revenue Distts of Cuttuck, Puri and Ganjanu comprising 68 community development Blocks. This zone has net cropped area of 11.13 lakh ha out of which 0.57 lakh ha is put under vegetables. Potato, Brinjal, Tomato, Chillies and Turmeric are the major vegetables of the zone.

3. **North Eastern Ghat zone:** This zone consists of revenue districts like Phalbani, Aska, Paralakha Mundi and Rayagada. The total cultivation area is 6.06 lakh ha with cropping intensity of 148%. Aska occupies 74000 hectares under irrigation. Potato, Onion, Tomato, Okra, Cabbage are the major vegetables of the area.

4. **Eastern Ghat High land zone:** This zone has an altitude ranging from 150 to 1000 m a m s 1. This zone consists of Koraput, Nawarangpur and partly Jeypore distts. The hill scopes are locally known as Jhola lands. In Nawarngpur and Umorkote belt considerable area is suitable for vegetable cultivation. Ginger and turmeric are grown on large scale. The major vegetables of this zone area brinjal, gourds, chillies, Cole crops, tomato, beans and onion. Monsoon potatoes are grown on extensive scale. The farmers of Maliput have developed their own innovative methods of vegetable production and are able to grow vegetables round the year. About 49.60% area of this zone is occupied by vegetables covering about 1.4 lakhs ha in *kharif* arid 1.2 lakh ha in *rabi* seasons.
5. **West undulating zone:** The zone consists of entire revenue Distt of Kalahandi and partly Koraput distt. Sweet potato, Chilli, Onion and Coriander are principle vegetable/spice crops of this zone.
6. **West Central Table Land zone:** This zone consists of Sambalpur and Balangir Distts. Due to plenty of irrigation water from Hirakund canal system, vegetable cultivation is done on commercial scale.

TABLE 26.1: Area and Production of different vegetables is Orissa

	Crop	Area (ha)	Production (tonnes)
1.	Bittergourd	5230	20920
2.	Brinjal	79850	734620
3.	Cabbage	35250	408990
4.	Cauliflower	73290	564330
5.	Chilli	39850	143906
6.	Cucumber	3400	34000
7.	Garlic	7560	50220
8.	Leafy vegetable	22350	12740
9.	Okra	70260	316170
10.	Pumpkin	38645	513980
11.	Onion	43730	309460
12.	Other gourds	6750	54000
13.	Other vegetables	98065	528734
14.	Tomato	42360	508320

●●●

CHAPTER 27

VEGETABLE GROWING IN PUNJAB

J.C. Thakur

1. Name of State : Punjab
2. Total geographical area (ha) : 5033000
3. Area under cultivation (ha) : 4210000
4. Irrigated area (ha) : 3953000
5. Area under Vegetables (ha) : 110347 (1996-97)

Production (t) = 1698762

Productivity (t) = 15.39/ha

Anticiapted by 2000 AD (t) = 2038470

TABLE 27.1: Area under each Vegetable (hectares) and Proudction (tonnes) during 1996-97

	Potato	Onion	Garlic	Tomato	Brinjal	Caullflower	Total
Area	49850	3132	821	5745	2476	2898	110347
Production	870531	61008	9691	138230	36558	71337	1698762
Anticipated production by 2000 AD	1044600	73200	11630	165880	43870	85600	2038470

	Okra	Chillies	Peas	Vine Crops	Root Crops	Other Crops	Total
Area	1070	6841	13540	9331	12792	1851	110347
Production	7877	10699	81687	124848	283688	2608	1698762
Anticipated production by 2000 AD	9450	12840	98020	149820	340430	3130	2038470

Cropwise recommended varieties/hybrids, planting, times, availability period, major pests and diseases

Crop	Varieties/ hybrids	Planting time	Availability	Major pests	Major diseases	Any other
1	2	3	4	5	6	7
1. Muskmelon	*Varieties* 1. Punjab Rasila 2. Hara Madhu 3. Punjab Sunehri *Hybrids* 1. MH-10 2. Punjab Hybrid	1. *Direct sowing* Mid February 2. *Nursery* Last week of January	May June	1. Red pumpkin beetle 2. Aphids and jassids 3. Spider mite rot 4. Fruit files 6. Mosaic 7. Root-knot nematodes	1. Powdery mildew 2. Downy mildew 3. Collar rot 4. Pythium 5. Alternaria blight	Major pests and diseases are common to all cucurbits
2. Watermelon	1. Sugar Baby 2. Shipper	Mid February	June- July			
3. Summer squash	Punjab Chappan Kaddoo-1	1. Mid February 2. Mid Jan., Oct-Nov. under protection	March-May			
4. Bottle gourd	1. Punjab Round 2. Punjab Komal 3. Punjab Long	1. February-March 2. June-July 3. October-November under protection.	March to November			
5. Bitter gourd	1. C-96 2. Punjab-14	1. Feb.-March 2. June-July	1. May-June 2. September - October			
6. Sponge gourd	Pusa Chikni	1. Mid Feb.-Mar. 2. Mid May-July	1. May-June 2. Aug.-Oct.	—		

1	2	3	4	5	6	7
7. Ash gourd	Local	1. February-March 2. June-July	1. May-June 2. September - October	—		
8. Round-melon	Tinda-48	1. February-March 2. June-July	1. May-June 2. September-October March-June	—		
9. Cucumber	1. Balam Khira 2. Punjab No. 1	1. Mid February 2. October-Novem. under protection	March-June	—		
10. Longmelon	Punjab Long-melon-1	1. Mid February 2. October-Novem. under protection	March-June	—		
11. Wanga	Punjab Wanga-1	1. Mid February 2. June-July	1. April-June 2. August-October			
Tomato	*Varieties* 1. Punjab Tropic 2. S-12 3. Punjab NR-7 4. Punjab Chhuhara 5. Punjab Kcsari *Hybrids* TH-2312 TH-802	*Sowing* End October *Transplanting* Beginning December under protection	April-Mid June	1. Jassids 2. White fly 3. Fruit boreer	1. Early blight 2. Damping-off 3. Leaf curl 4. Mosaic 5. Root-knot nematodes	
Brinjal	*Varieties* 1. Punjab Bahar 2. Punjab Jamuni Gola 3. Punjab Neelam 4. Pusa Purple Long	1. October 2. November 3. February-March 4. June-July	1. March-April 2. April-June 3. May-June 4. September-December	1. Jassids 2. Hadda beetle 3. Shoot and fruit borer 4. Spider mites	1. Phomopsis-blight 2. Little leaf 3. Root- knot nematodes	

1	2	3	4	5	6	7
	5. Punjab Sadabahar Baingan 6. Punjab Barasati 7. Punjab Moti *Hybrids* 1. BH-1 2. BH-2					
Okra	1. Pusa Sawani 2. Punjab Padmini 3. Punjab- 7 4. Punjab-8	1. February-March 2. June-July	1. April-June 2. August-October	1. Jassids 2. Spotted boll-worm 3. Spider mites	1. Yeelow vein mosaic 2. Damping-off 3. Cercospora leaf spot 4. Root-knot nematodes	
Chilli	*Varieties* 1. Punjab Surkh 2. Punjab Guchhedar 3. Punjab *Hybrid* CH-1	1. October-November 2. March-April (Direct sowing-Chutki)	May October	1. Termites 2. Thrips 3. Mites 4. Aphids 5. White fly	1. Fruit rot and dicback 2. Wet rot 3. Leaf curl 4. Mosaic	
Bell Pepper	Punjab-27	October-November	April-May	-do-	-do-	
Cow Pea	Cowpea-263	1. February-March 2. June-July	1. April-June 2. August-October	1. Jassids 2. Aphids 3. Pod borer	1. Seed and seedling rot 2. Cercospora leaf spots 3. Mosaic	
Bulb crops						
1. Kharif oinion	N-53	1. Mid June 2. March (Bulb sets)	1. November December	1. Onion thnps 2. Onion maggots	1. Purple blotch 2. Downy mildew	

1	2	3	4	5	6	7
2. Rabi onion	1. Punjab Naroya 2. Punjab Selection 3. S-49 (White) 4. Punjab White 5. Punjab Red Round	1. Mid-October to Mid-November	End of May	-do-	-do-	
3. Garlic	1. Punjab garlic-1 2. Garlic 56-4	End to beginning October	End April	-do-	-do-	
Peas	*Early seson* 1. Arkel 2. Ageta-6 *Main Season* 1. Mithi Phali (Edible Podded) 2. Bonne ville 3. Punjab-87 4. Punjab-88	End- September to Mid November	End November to March	1. Pea thrip 2. Pea leaf miner 3. Pea aphid 4. Pea stem fly	1. Powdery mildew 2. Wilt 3. Root-knot nematodes 4. Collar-rot 5. Rust	
Cole Crops 1. Caulif lower	*Main season* 1. Giant Snowball 2. Punjab Giant 26 *Late season* 1. Pusa-Snow-ball-1 2. Pusa Snow-ball K- 1 3. Snowball-16	*Early season* May June *Main season* July-Aug. *Late season* End September Mid November	Sep-October Nov. December Mid January-April	1. Stemborer 2. Diamond Back moth 3. Tobacco catter pillar 4. Aphids	1. Damping off 2. Crown rot (turnip) 3. Black rot 4. Alternaria blight 5. Downy mildew 6. Stalk rot (cauliflower seed crop)	Otherwise major pests and diseases of cole & root crops are common

1	2	3	4	5	6	7
2. Cabbage	1. Pride of India 2. Drum Head Early 3. Drum Head Late	September-October	Mid January-April			
3. Broccoli	Punjab Broccoli-1	Mid August-September	End November- February			
4. Chinese Cabbage	Chinese Sarson	Mid September to Mid October	November-Feb ruary			
Root Crops						
1. Carrot	1. No. 29 2. Selection-21	August-September	December- February			
2. Turnip	1. L-I 2. 4-White 3. 4-Red 4. Golden Ball	**Asiatic** August-September **European** October-November	October-December January-February			
Radish	1. Pusa Himani 2. Punjab Safed 3. White Icicle 4. Pusa Chetki 5. Punjab Ageti	**Asiatic** August- September **European** October-November **Pusa Chetki** April- September	Throughout the Year			
Beet leaf (Palak)	1. Punjab Selection 2. Punjab Green	1. September- October 2. Mid February-March	October to May	1. Aphids	1. Cercospora leaf-spot	–
Lettuce	1. Punjab Lettuce-1	Mid September- November	November to February	—	—	—

1	2	3	4	5	6	7
Potato	*Early* 1. Kufri Chandaramukhi 2. Kufri Alankur *Medium* 1. Kufri Jyoti 2. Kufri Lalima 3. Kufri Bahar 4. Kufri Sheetman *Late* 1. Kufri Sindhuri 2. Kufri Badshah	1. Mid September-Mid October 2. First week January	*Fresh* 1. End November-March 2 May *Storage Medium* All round the year	1. Jassids 2. Aphids 3. Tobacco catter pillar 4. Cut worms	1. Late blight 2. Early blight 3. Black-scurf 4. Charcoal-rot 5. Mosaic 6. Common-scab 7. Leaf spots	

6. Export potential

(*a*) **Domestic market:** Different vegetables are sent to adjoining states of Himachal Pradesh and Jammu and Kashmir. Different vegetables are also being sent to domestic markets like Delhi, Mumbai, Calcutta, Chennai, Bangalore, Hyderabad and Ahmedabad etc. Almost all the vegetables being produced in Punjab are exported to Himachal Pradesh and Jammu and Kashmir. Potato is sent to Southern states. Tomato is sent to Delhi, dry chillies and green chillies are also being sent to the domestic market. Cucurbits, okra, pea, onion, brinjal cauliflower, cabbage, radish carrot and turnip are sent neighbouring states. Potato tubers for seed, okra and pea seed is sent to other states. Similarly muskmelon and round melon seed is sent to other states with in India.

(*b*) **Abroad:** Vegetables are being exported to foreign markets like Middle East, South East Asia, Malasia, Hong Kong, Indonesia, Japan and Singapore. The Vegetables which are being exported to these countries are potato, beans, brinjal, chillies, cauliflower, cucurbits, okra, peas, onion, garlic, leek, parsley, baby corn and coreless carrot. With the establishment of International Air Port at Amritsar the export of these vegetables will pick up from Punjab.

Seeds of vegetables like okra cauliflower, peas and muskmelon are being exported to some extent. Processed products like tomato paste, chilli, paste, canned peas, mustard sag, tomato sauce, tomato puree, garlic paste, ginger paste and carrot juice are also being exported to some extent.

7. Major Production Constraints

(*a*) **Biotic:** In muskmelon downy mildew and fruit fly are very serious particularly in hot and humid weather. In watermelon mosaic is quite serious. In summer squash mosaic is quite serious particularly in April and May. In bittergourd root-knot, fruit fly and mosaic are serious particularly during rainy season. Mosaic is also serious in cucumber during rainy season. Early and late blights are serious diseases of tomato, mosaic and root-knot nematodes are serious during rainy season and mostly the crop fails during this season. Fruit borer is also serious in tomato. Yellow vein mosaic is a serious disease of okra. Wet rot, leaf curl and mosaic are serious diseases in bell pepper and hamper its growth.

Purple blotch is a serious diseases of onion and garlic and it is particularly serious in seed crop of onion. Pea stem-fly and wilt are serious particularly in early peas, powdery mildew is also quite serious during February-March'. Stemborer and damping-off are serious problems in cauliflower. Late blight, early blight and mosaic are quite serious in potato and damage it seriously if not checked timely.

(*b*) **Abiotic:** Low temperature is the main problem during winter. Peas and cauliflower are affected by frost at pod formation and curd formation stage, respectively. Early cucurbits are also affected by low temperature. Tomato, brinjal, capsicum and chillies are susceptible to frost and should be protected at nursery and early crop stage. High temperature effects fruiting in peas, tomato brinjal and chillies etc. Low humidity and high temperature effects are harmful in above crops. Heavy rain is also harmful to many crops like early cauliflower and other crops which are grown in rainy season. Drought also affects different crops particularly the crops which are grown as rainfed and where irrigation sources are limited. Hailstorm also affects different crops particularly in early stage i.e. in February- March. Floods also affects different vegetable crops that are grown on river beds in rainy season or other crops also when there are rains which are untimely as well as heavy. Now-a-days water-logging is also causing damage to different vegetables particularly in Moga, Faridkot and Bathinda districts. Excessive salts and high pH are found in Faridkot and Bathinda districts, so only tolerant crops should be grown in these districts. Moderate temperature is needed for capsicum (bell pepper) and French bean but these conditions are not available under Punjab climate so it is very difficult to grow these crops successfully. Radish is generally a winter season crop but Pusa Chetki variety is also being grown in summer and rainy season. In onion, kharif onion varieties should be day neutral and N-53 variety is suitable for this season.

8. Topographic Regions and potential pockets for commercial production by depicting in the map of the state.

Topographic regions are given in Fig. 27 (*)

The first three districts with respect to production and area of different crops are given below :

Potato	Jalandhar, Hoshiarpur, Ludhiana.
Onion	Patiala, Ropar, Kapurthala
Garlic	Kapurthala, Patiala, Sangrur
Tomato	Kapurthala, Ropar, Hoshiarpur
Brinjal	Jalandhar, Amritsar, Kapurthala
Cauliflower	Sangrur, Amritsar, Patiala
Okra	Patiala, Amritsar, Jalandhar
Chilli	Amritsar, Jalandhar, Kapurthala
Peas	Hoshiarpur, Jalandhar, Amritsar
Vine Crops	Jalandhar, Hoshiarpur, Amritsar
Root Crops	Jalandhar, Hoshiarpur, Ludhiana
Other Crops	Kapurthala, Jalandhar, Hoshiarpur

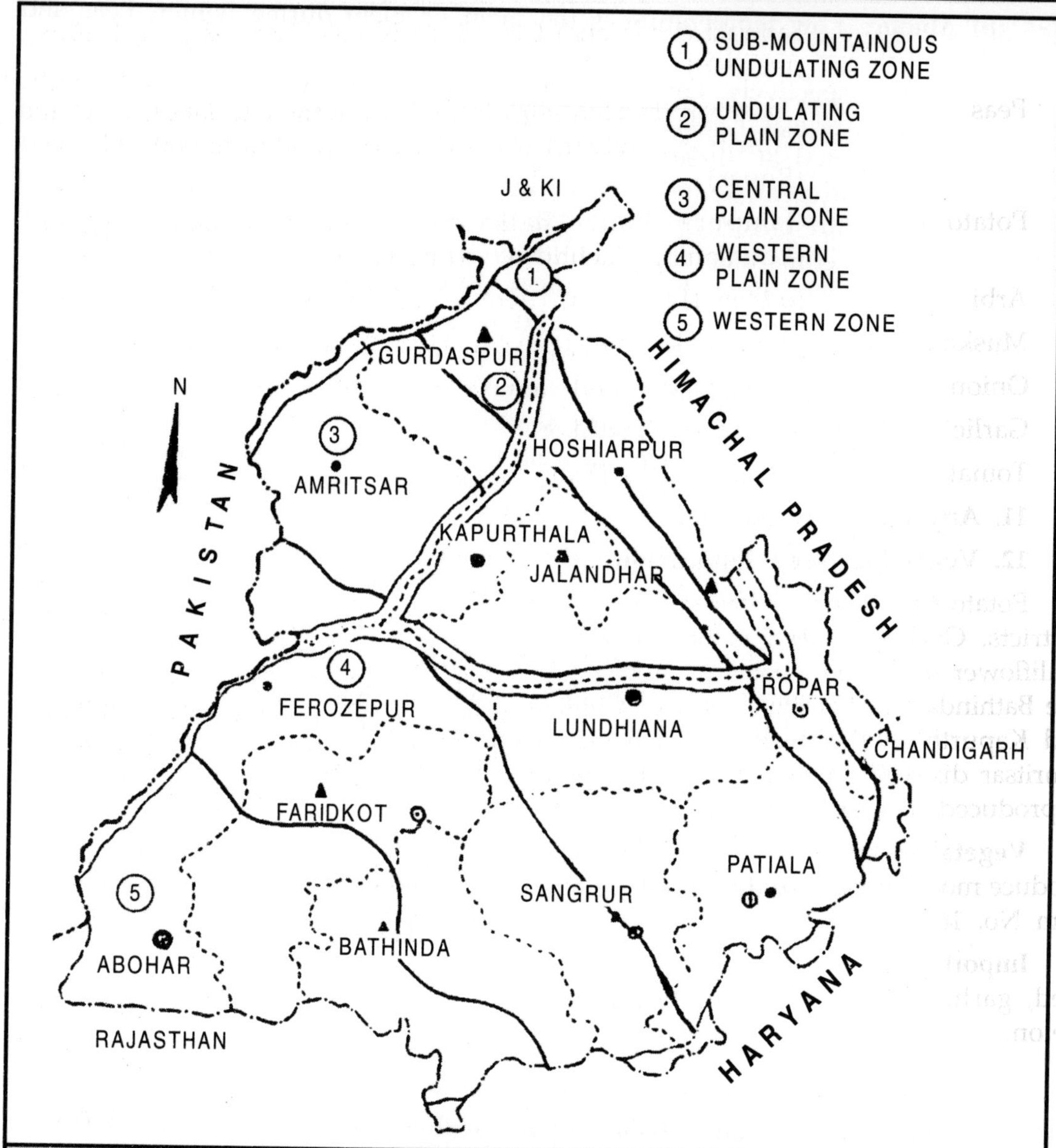

Fig. 27 (i). Agro climatic zones of Punjab

The important prockets for different vegetables are

Radish	Rajpura (Patiala), Ghanaur (Patiala), Around Gurdaspur.
Chillies	Sanaur (Patiala), Khalra (Amritsar) Bhikhiwind (Amritsar), Shahkot (Jalandhar)
Okra	Jodhan (Ludhiana), Malerkotla (Sangrur), Bir (Faridkot)
Cauliflower	Kharar (Ropar), Malerkotla (Sangrur), Phagwara (Kapurthala) Sunam (Patiala), Sultanpur Lodhi (Kapurthala),

	Samrala (Ludhiana) Dera Bada Nanak (Gurdashpur), Leelan (Jagroan)
Peas	Chabewal (Hoshiarpur), Jadla (Nawanshehar), Jandiala Guru (Amritsar), Retgarh (Patiala), Kohara (Ludhiana), Kharar (Ropar)
Potato	Rampura Phul (Bathinda), Around Moga, Jagroan (Ludhiana), Machhiwara (Ludhiana)
Arbi	Jodhan (Ludhiana), Around Jalandhar
Muskmelon	Jagroan (Ludhiana), Near Moga, Tarntarn (Amritsar)
Onion	Ghanaur (Patiala)
Garlic	Kotkapura (Fradikot)
Tomato	Ropar, Patiala (Rainy season)

11. Any other information Nil

12. Vegetable Seed Production

Potato tubers are produced for seed in Jalandhar, Hoshiarpur and Ludhiana districts. Garlic for seed is produced in Kapurthala and Patiala. Main season cauliflower seed is also being produced. Okra seed is being produced in cotton belt like Bathinda and Faridkot districts. Chilli seed is produced in Amritsar, Jalandhar and Kapurthala. Pea seed is also being produced in Hoshiarpur, Jalandhar and Amritsar districts. Muskmelon seed is produced in Ludhiana district. Radish seed is produced in Gurdaspur district.

Vegetable Area Production: Three districts which occupy more area and produce more quantity of different vegetables have been discussed previously under item No. 10.

Important Seed Vegetables: Important seed vegetables are potato tubers for seed, garlic, main season cauliflower, okra, chilli, pea, muskmelon and round melon.

●●●

CHAPTER 28

PONDICHERRY

The total area is 492 square kilo metre and Puruducherry is the capital of the union territory. It is located close to Tamil Nadu state in the Bay of Bengal. Pondicherry comprised of Karekal, Mahi and Yanam islands Karekal and Yanam are situated on the Eastern coast in Bay of Bengal and Mahi on the Western coast in Lakshdweep sagar

TABLE 28.1: Area (ha) production (t) under vegetable

Vegetable	Area (ha)	Production (t)
Assorted vegetables	142	1,128
Total	142	1,128

Source : Pondicherry Administration, Department of Agriculture

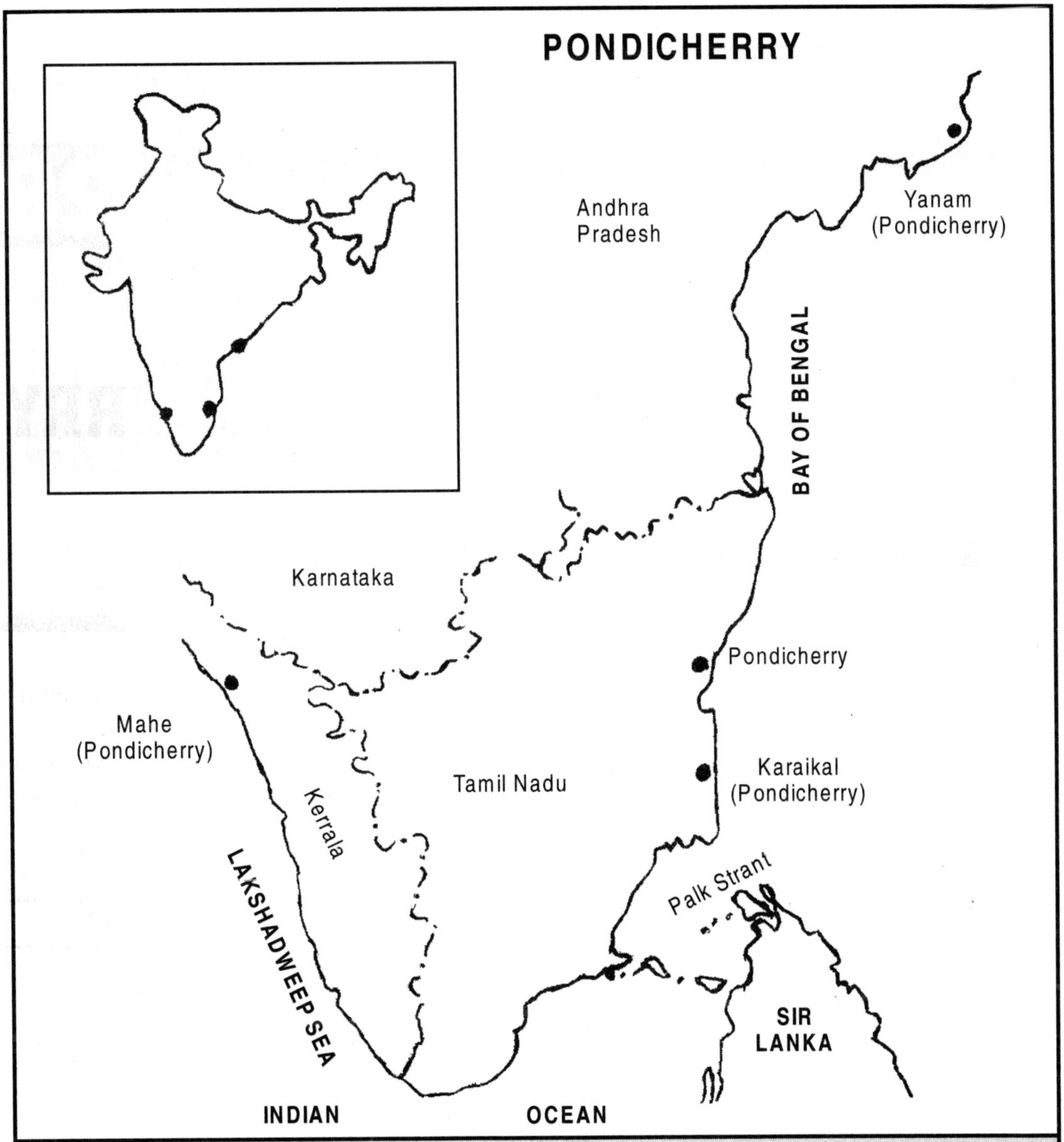

Fig. 28. (i) Location map of Pondicherry

●●●

CHAPTER 29

VEGETABLE GROWING IN RAJASTHAN

M.S. Fageria

1. Name of the state : Rajasthan
2. Total geographical area (ha) : 342 Lac
3. Area under cultivation (ha) : 180 Lac
4. Irrigated area (ha) : 40 Lac
5. Area under vegetables (ha) : 75948

   Production (t) : –356908 Mt

   Productivity : –4.6

Anticipated in 2000 AD

Area (ha)	100000 ha
Production (t)	600000
Productivity (t)	6.0

TABLE 29.1: Area, Production and Productivity of different vegetables.

Name of vegetable crops	Area in ha.	Production in (Mt)	Productivity in (Mt)	Anticipated by 2000 AD (Mt)
Potato	1553	19013	12.24	
Onion	21749	161742	7.44	
Tomato	14232	52525	3.69	
Guarfali	367	523	1.43	
Cucumber	2529	8870	3.51	
Pumpkin	485	3301	6.81	
Carrot	518	1357	2.62	
Cauliflower & cabbage	6221	17985	2.89	

Name of vegetable crops	Area in ha.	Production in (Mt)	Productivity in (Mt)	Anticipated by 2000 AD (Mt)
Tinda	3922	21681	5.53	
Ridgegourd	835	2637	3.16	
Spinach	1520	3745	2.46	
Brinjal	5461	17750	3.25	
Bhindi	3747	10757	2.87	
Pea	5730	13788	2.41	
Radish	561	2151	3.83	
Ratalu	220	1073	4.88	
Bottle guard	707	2200	3.11	
Sweet potato	2672	3491	1.31	
Others	2439	9297	3.81	
Total	75948	356908	4.6	6.0

Source : Vital Horticulture Statistics, 1996-97, published from Directorate of Horticulture, Rajasthan, Jaipur.

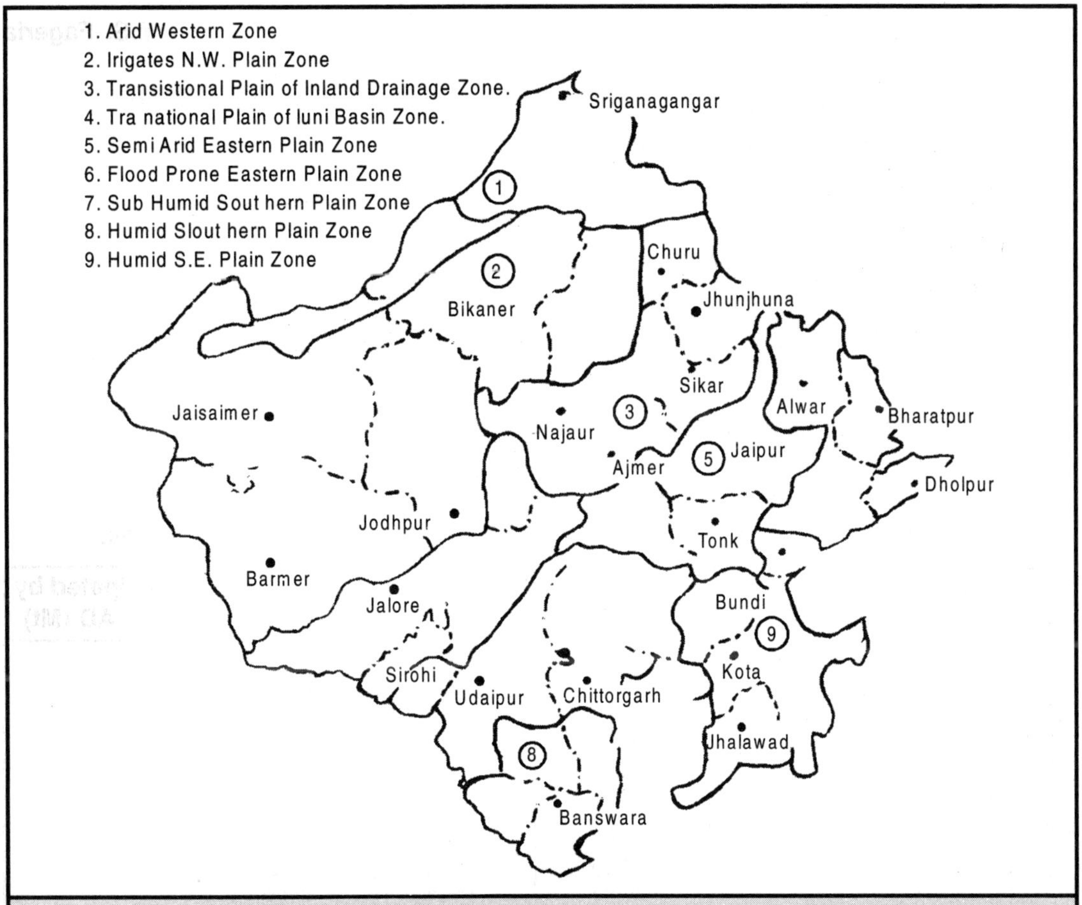

Fig. 29 (i) : Agro-climatic Zones of Rajasthan

TABLE 29.2: Classification of Climatic Zones Alongwith District Covered (Area in lacs ha.)

Argo Climatic Zones	Name of Districts	Range of Normal Rainfall (MM)	Geographical Area	Cultivated Area	Area irrigated
Arid	Ganganagar, Jaisalmer, Barmer, Jalore, Jodhpur, Bikaner, Nagaur, Sikar, Churu, Jhunjhunu and Hanumangarh	160 to 500	211	95	16
Semi Arid	Alwar, Baharatpur, S.Madhopur, Dholpur Ajmer, Jaipur, Tonk Sirohi, Pali Dausa, Karoli	520 to 690	35	35	10
Sub Humid	Jhalawar, Kota, Baran, Bundi Banswara, Dungarpur, Bhilwara, Udaipur, Chittorgarh, Rajsamand	620 to 1000	78	50	14
Total		160 to1000	342	180	40

CLIMATIC ZONES AND SUITABLE HORTICULTURAL CROPS

1. ARID WESTERN PLAIN (I-A) :

Tehsils covered :

All tehsils of Bikaner, Jaisalmer and Barmer districts, Phalodi, Shergajrh, Osion and Jodhpur Tehsils of Jodhpur distict and Dungarhgarh, Sujangarh, Ratnagarh and Sardarshahar of Churu district.

Area :

Total geographical area is 97.2 lacs ha with 34 lacs ha under cultivation is the largest zone in the state.

Soils :

Desert soils and sand dunes occupy the major areas in the desert.

Rainfall :

Average rainfall in Western part about 100 mm. and in Eastern part about 300 mm. temperature :

Maximum mean temperature during January 10.6° C to June 48.5°C and minimum mean temperature during January 2.6°C to June 28°C.

Major horticulture crops :

Ber, Pomegranate, Datepalm, Aonla, Chilli, Cumin and Isabgol, Onion, Cucrbits, Tuber crops.

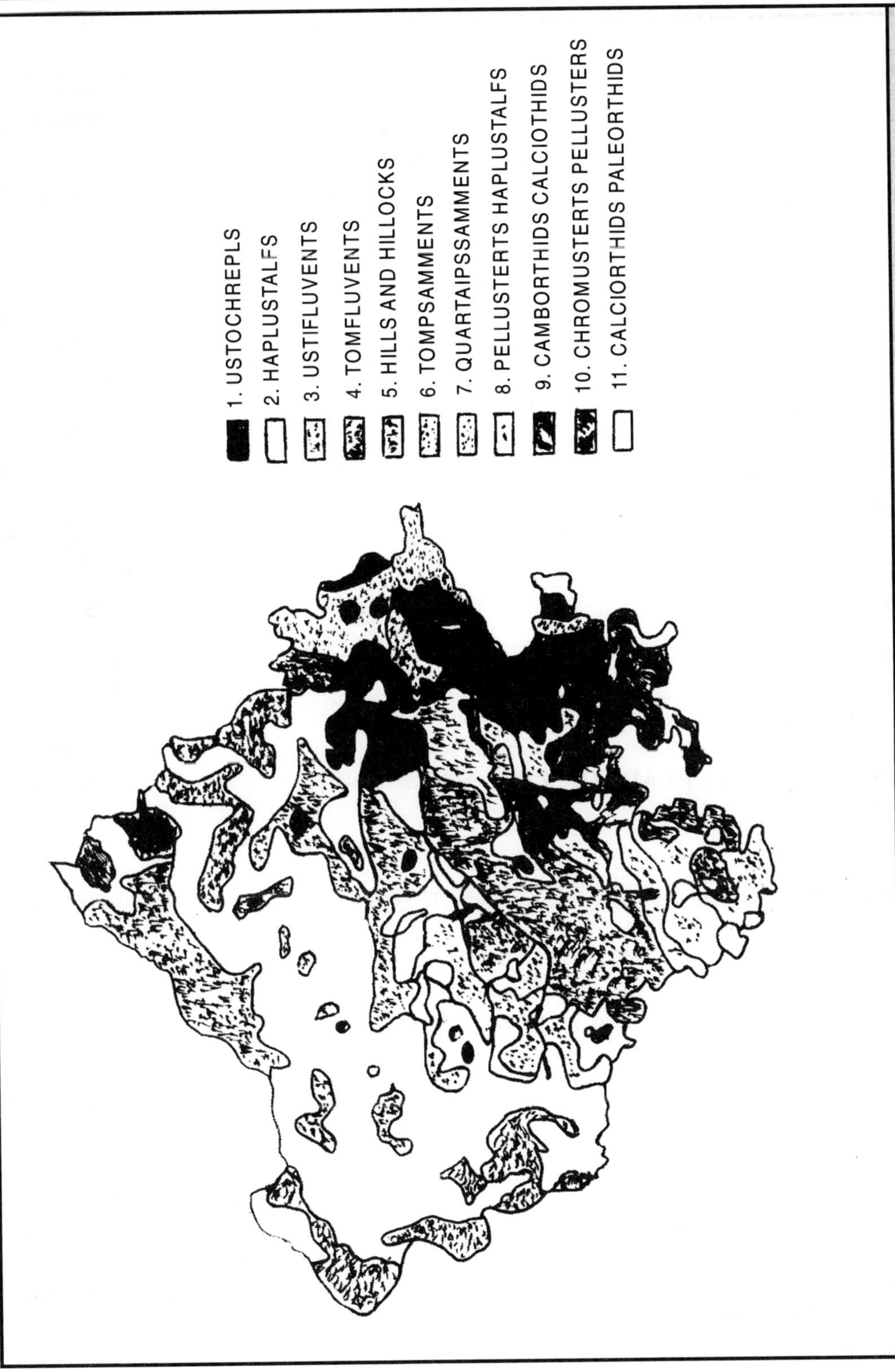

Fig. 29. (ii) Soil map of Rajasthan

2. IRRIGATED NORTH WESTERN PLAIN (I-B) :

Tehsil covered :

All Tehsil of Ganganagar and Hanumangarh district and IGNP area.

Area :

Total geographical area is 36.5 lacs ha. of which 75% is under cultivation and 17.7 m. ha. area is double cropped area.

Soil :

The soils are alluvial deposited by river Ghaggar, yellowish brown in colour, loam to silty clay loam in texture and are calcarous in nature. Generally soils are rich in exchangeable sodium ions.

Rainfall :

Annual rainfall varies from 100-300 mm. with 61.4% R.H.

Temperature :

Daily max. mean temperature varies 20.5°C during January to 42.1°C during the month of June, and daily minimum temperature varies 4.6° C during January to 28°C during the month of June.

Major horticultural crops :

Ber, Kinnow, Grapes, Malta, Mosambi, Cucurbits, Cole crops, Tomato, Chilli and Brinjal.

3. TRANSITIONAL PLAIN OF LUNI BASIN (II-B) :

Tehsil covered :

All Tehsil of Jalore and Pali districts, Reodar, Sirohi and Sheoganj Tehsils of Sirohi district and Bilara and Bhopalgarh Tehsil of Jodhpur districts.

Area :

Total geographical area is 37.7 lacs ha. or which is nearly 52% is under cultivation hereby 77% of the cropped area is rainfed.

Soil :

The soils of this zone can be broadly classified to three viz. grey brown soils, hilly soils and sandy soils. The area is prone to floods by river Luni.

Rainfall :

The rainfall of the zone is inadequate and erratic varying from 300-500 mm.

Temperature :

The mean daily maximum temperature ranges from 15-20°C in January to 45.6°C in May.

Major horticultural crops :

Among spices crops Cumin and Psllium (Isabgol) are major crops of the zone. Ber, Pomegranate, Lime among fruits and Mehandi.

4. TRANSITIONAL PLAIN OF INLAND DRAINAGE(II-A) :

Tehsil covered :

All Tehsil of Nagaur, Sikar and Jhunjhunu districts and Taranagar, Churu and Rajgarh of Churu district.

Area :

This zone covers an area of 43.2 lac ha spread over Nagaur, Sikar, Jhunjhunu and parts of Churu districts.

Soil :

In west of Aravali range the soils of the zones are sandy loam to loam and cultivation is restricted due to shallow depth and stony surface Red desert soils, saline and lithosols are found in depressions. Shifting sand dunes and undulating land topography are also found in this zone.

Rainfall and temperature :

The rainfall ranges from 300 mm in the West to about 500 mm in the East. The mean daily maximum temperature at Sikar ranges from 22°C in January to 39.7°C in May and the mean daily minimum temperature ranges from 5.3°C in January 27.5°C in June.

5. SEMI ARID EASTERN PLAIN (HI-A) :

Tehsil covered :

This zone covers all Tehsils of Ajmer, Jaipur, Dausa and Tonk districts.

Area :

This zone covers a geographical area of about 28.58 lacs hectare.

Soils :

The soils of this zone are seirogomes in the Western parts of Ajmer and Jaipur district. The alluvial soils of Western and North Western parts of Jaipur and Ajmer are modified due to increase of aeolin materials flown through gaps in Aravali ranges. Old alluvials in South Eastern parts and lithosols near the foot hills in Ajmer are also found and brown soils are found in parts of Tonk district.

Rainfall & Temperature :

The rainfall ranges from about 500 mm in the West and North- West to about 700 mm in South East. The mean daily maximum temperature range, from 8.3°C in January to 27.3°C in June.

Irrigation facility are available for 34.7 per cent of the net cropped area.

Major horticultural crops :

This zone is important for Melon and vegetables particularly Tomato, Peas and Cucumber. Ber, Guava, Aonla, Lime, Pomegranate. Almost all vegetables, particularly Cauliflower melons, Tomato, Radish and Cucurbits crops.

6. FLOOD PRONE EASTERN PLAIN(HI-B) :

Tehsil covered :

All Tehsils of Alwar, Bharatpur, Dholpur districts. Todabhim, Hindaum, Nadauti, Bamanwas, Gangapur, Karoli, Sapotra and Bonli Tehsils of Sawai Madhopur districts, and Mahuwa tehsil of Dausa district.

Area :

This zone covers a geographical area of about 27.00 lac ha spread over Alwar, Bharatpur, Dholpur and Parts of Sawai Madhopur districts.

Soils :

The soils of the zone are mainly alluvial and subject of recurring floods & water-logging. The calcareous nature of recently deposited alluvium in the soils abounding in the region.

Rainfall & Temperature :

The rainfall ranges from about 500 mm. in North West to about 700 mm. in the South-East.About 14% of the area is under irrigation.

Major horticultural crops :

The main crops of the zone are Ber, Guava, Lime, Mango, Papaya.

Vegetables :

Bhindi, Onion (specially Kharif), Tomato, Brinjal, Root & Tuber crops, cucurbits

7. SUB HUMID SOUTHERN PLAIN AND ARAVALLI HILLS (IV-A) :

Tehsil coverd :

This zone covers all Tehsils of Bhilwara and Rajsamand districts all tehsils except Dhariyawad, Salumbar and Sarada of Udaipur Pratapgarh, Arnod and Badi-Sadri of Chittorgarh districts, Aburoad and Pindwara Tehsils of Sirohi districts.

Area :

This zone covers a geographical area about 33.6 ha. Spread over Bhilwara parts of Udaipur, Chittorgarh and Sirohi districts. About 38% of the cropped area is irrigated.

Soils :

The main soil groups are yellowish brown Hilly soils, deep medium black and brown soils of saline phase.

Rainfall & Temperature :

The rainfall ranges from 500 mm in the West and North-West to about 700 mm in the South-East and above 900 mm. in the South-West. The mean daily maximum temperature of Udaipur ranges from 24.2°C in January to 38.6°C in May. Likewise, the mean daily minimum temperature ranges from 7.8°C in January to 25.3°C in June.

Major horticultural crops :

The principal crops of the zone are Guava, Limes, Aonla, Custard apple, under fruits.

Vegetables :

Tomato, Brinjal, Chilli, Spogegourd, Carrot, pea, Bhindi and Cole crops.

8. HUMID SOUTHERN PLAIN (IV-B) :

Tehsil covered :

All Tehsil of Banswara and Dungarpur district, Chhoti-Sadri, Pratapgarh, Arnod and Badi-Sadri of Chittorgarh district, Dhariyawad, Salumbar and Sarada tehsils of Udaipur districts.

Area :

The zone covers a geographical area of 17.2 lac ha spread over Dungarpur, Banswara, South-Eastern parts of Udaipur & Southern parts of Chittorgarh district.

Soil :

The soils of this zone are reddish in colour, medium textured, well drained and calcareous. There are shallow soils on hills and deep soils in the valleys.

Rainfall :

The average annual rainfall of the zone about 750 mm about 16% of cropped area is under irrigation.

Major horticultural crops :

Principal crops of the zone are Lime, Papaya, Banana, Sapota, Mango, new introduction of Litchi and coconut.

Vegetable :

Bhindi, Brinjal, Chilli, Cucurbits crops.

9. HUMID SOUTH EASTERN PLAIN (IV) :

Tehsil covered :

All Tehsils of Bundi, Kota, Baran and Jhalawar districts, Khandar and Sawai Madhopur tehsils of Sawai Madhopur districts.

Area :

The zone covers a geographical area of 29.13 lac. ha spread over Jhalawar, Kota, Bundi and parts of Sawai Madhopur districts.

Soils :

The predominent soils of this zone are black soils of alluvial origin. These are generally clay loam to clay. In some parts, soil salinity and ground water salinity have been encountered.

Rainfall and Temperature :

The rainfall ranges from 650 mm in the North West to about 1000 mm in the South East. The mean daily maximum temperature of Kota ranges from 24.5°C in January to 42.6°C in May. Similarly, the mean daily minimum temperature. May ranges from 10.6°C in January to 19.7°C. About 26% of the cropped area is under irrigation.

Major horticulture crops :

The principal crops of the zone are Aonla, guava, this zone is famous for citrus (oranges).

Vegetables :

Pea, Tomato, Brinjal, Cole crops and cucurbits.

Major Production constraints :

A. Biotic :

The most serious problems, which leads to heavy losses in yield and deteriorates quality of vegetables are as follows.

Diseases :

(*i*) Viruses	Tomato, chillies, cucurbits, okra and brinjal.
(*ii*) Powdry mildew	Cucurbits, peas
(iii) Early blight	Tomato, Potato
(iv) Wilt	Chillies
(v) Damping-off	Tomato, chillies, cauliflower
(*vi*) Purple bloch	Onion
(*vii*) Root-Knot	Tomato, Brinjal, Chillies, Okra and Karela nematode

Insects

(*i*) Shoot and fruit borer	Brinjal
(*ii*) Fruit worm	Tomato
(*iii*) White fly and spooted boll worm	Okra
(*iv*) Thrips	Onion
(*v*) White fly	Cucurbits

TABLE 29.3: Cropwise recommended varieties/hybrids, planting times, availability period, major pests and diseases

Crop	Varieties/ Hybrids	Planting/Trans-planting Time	Availability	Major pests/ diseases
Potato	Kufri Sinduri K–Alankar K–Chandramukhi K–Sheetman K–Jyoti K–Bahar K-Badshah	Mid Sept.-mid Oct	March-April	Aphids and Cutworms Black scurf Early Blight Late Blight Mosaic & leaf roll
Onion *(Rabi)* Red	Local cultivars Pusa Red Agrifound Dark Red Agrifound light red Punjab red round Arka kalyan N-53	Dec.	May	Thrips Downy mildew Blight Purple blotch
White	Udaipur-102 Pusa white flat Pusa white round Early grano	July-Aug.	Nov. Dec	
Yellow Kharif	N-53 Agrifound dark red			
Tomato	Pusa ruby Pusa early dwarf Pusa-120	Jan.- Feb. June-July	April-May Sept.-Nov.	Fruit borer Damping-off Tomato leaf curl
	Punjab Chhuhara Roma Pant Bahar Arka Vikas Hissar Arun	Sept.-Oct.	Dec-Jan	Root-knot nematode Early blight
Brinjal Long type Round type Hybrid-	PPL PPC Pusa Kranti PPR, H-4, P-8, Pusa Anmol Pant Rituraj, T-3 Arka Navneet, Pusa Hybrid-6	(i) March- April (ii) July-August (iii) Oct.-Nov.	June-July Oct-Nov. March-April	Shoot and fruit Borer Root knot nematode
Chillies	N.P.-46 A Pus Jwala Mathania long Pant C-l G-3 G-5 Hungarian Wax., Pusa Sadabahar Pant C-2, R.C.H.-l	(i) June-July (ii) March	Sept.-Nov. July- Sept.	Damping-off Leaf curl & mosaic Anthracnose Powdery mildew

Crop	Varieties/ Hybrids	Planting/Trans-planting Time	Availability	Major pests/ diseases
Bottle gourd	Pusa Summer-Prolific Long Pusa Summer-Prolific Round Pusa Manjari (F1) Pusa Meghdoot-(F1) Pusa Naveen Arka Vihar	(i) Feb.- March (ii) June-July	May-June August-Sept.	Fruit fly Mites Beetles Powdery mildew Anthracnose Downy mildew Mosaic virus
Water melon	Sugar Baby Durgapur Meetha Durgapura Kesar Arka Jyoti (F1) Madhu (F1) Matira (local)	Feb- March June-July	May-June Sept.-Oct.	-Do-
Musk-melon	Durgapur madhu Punjab Sunheri, Punjab Hybrid Arka Jeet Hara Madhu Pusa Madhuras R.M.-43	Feb.- March	April-June	-Do-
Cucum-ber	Balam khira Poinset Pusa Sanyog (F1)	(i) Feb.-March (ii) June-July	April- June August-Sept.	-Do-
Bitter gourd	Coimbtor Long Pusa do mausmi, Priya Arka Harit Pusa Vishesh Mahico Kasela Gree Long	(i) Feb.-March (ii) June-July	May-June Aug.- Sept.	-Do-
Tinda	Bikaneri Green Dil Pasand Tinda Ludhiana (S-48), Hisar Sel-1 Arka Tinda	(i) Feb.- March (ii) June-July	April-June Late Aug.-Oct.	-Do-
Cauli-flower	Early Patna Early Kunwari Pusa Katki	(i) July (ii) Aug.-Sept. (iii) Oct. to	Sept.-Nov. Nov.-Jan Jan.-Feb. Nov.	Damping-off Brown rot Black rot

Crop	Varieties/ Hybrids	Planting/Trans-planting Time	Availability	Major pests/ diseases
	Pusa Deepali Pusa early synthetic Pant Gobhi- 3 Improved			Leaf eating cater pillars, Aphids and Beetles
Mid Late	Japanese Pusa hybrid-2 Pusa Snowball K-I			
Cab-bage *Early* Late	Golden Acre Pride of India Mitra (F1) Pusa Drum Head Hybrid 10 (F1)	(i) Sept. to Oct. (ii) Oct.-Nov.	Dec- Jan. Jan.-Feb.	-do-
Okra	Pusa Sawani Pusa Makhmali Prabhani Kranti Arka Abhay Arka Anamika	(i) Feb - March (ii) June-July	April-June Aug.-Oct.	Fruit borer Root-Knot nematode Yellow vein-Mosaic virus Root rot, Powdery mildew
Peas *Early* Mid & Late	Aakil Hara bona Jawahar Matar-4 Matar ageti-6 Bonneville, Jawahar matar-1 Punjab- 48 Azad-P1 RP-3 JP-83	Sept. Nov.	Nov.-Dec. Feb.-March	Stemfly Pod borer Leaf minor Root–knot nematode Powdery mildew Seed & root rot
Palak	Pusa Jyoti All Green Jobner Green Pusa Harit	Feb. June-Nov.	March-May July-Jan.	Aphids Leaf eating- Catter pillars
Fenu-greek	Desi methi Kasuri methi	Sept.-Nov.	Oct.-Jan.	Damping-off Leaf spot Powdery mildew
Cholai	Badi cholai	Feb-March, & June-July	March-June. Aug.- Sept.	Leaf spot
Carrot	Pusa Kesar Nantes Sel-5	(i) Aug- Sept. (ii) Oct. Nov.	Oct.-Dec. Dec. Jan	Powdery mildew

Crop	Varieties/ Hybrids	Planting/Trans-planting Time	Availability	Major pests/ diseases
Radish	Pusa Chetki Pusa Rashmi Japanesse White Pusa Himani	(i) March-Aug. (ii) Sept.-Nov. (iii) Oct. mid Dec. (iv) Mid Dec.-Mid January	Sept.-Oct. Oct.-Nov. Nov.-Jan. Jan.-Feb.	Aphids, mustard sawfly Radis yellow Blac spot
Kachari (Cucu-mis call -osus)	Local (Grow Wild)	June-July (Rainfed crop)	Oct.-Nov.	
Sangari (Proso-phis cineraria	Lot of variability exists but still varieties have not been identified		Mid April to May	

(B) Abiotic

The Rajasthan state has largest desert area of the country and frequently facing scarcity of water and draught conditions in the arid and semi-arid regions which account for about 61.09% and 15.50% of the state area respectively. The state is extremely deficient in water resources which are only 1% of the country's total resources. The main constraints are as follows.

1. Unfertile soil and poor quality ground water
2. Alkaline and saline soils
3. Inadequate irrigation facilities and deficit in rains.
4. Higher temperature alongwith hot winds in summers and low temperature in winters are some crucial limitations of vegetable production.

Vegetable seed production :

Seed production of some vegetables viz; radish, spinach, chillies, okra, carrot and cauliflower (early) are being produced in the state at small scale but data of production is not available. There is great potential to produce seeds of some vegetables in the different districts of the state.

Name of crop	Districts
Spinach	Jaipur, Ajmer, Udaipur
Radish	Sriganganagar, Hanumangarh, Chomu (Jaipur)
Okra	Ajmer, Udaipur
Chillies	Tonk, Jodhpur, Pali, Jalore, Nagour, Alwar
Cauliflower (early)	Sriganganagar, Hanumangarh, Ajmer, Jaipur Onion Idaipur, Chittorgarh, Bhilwara, Sikar

Dolichus bean	Kota, Bundi, Jhalawara
Potato	Kota and Sriganganagar
Tinda	Chomu (Jaipur)
Carrot	Chomju (Jaipur)
Spinach beet, Guar	Chomu (Jaipur)
Bottlegourd	Chomu (Jaipur)
Peas	Bharatpur, Kota, Jaipur
Seed	spices Jodhpur
Bottle gourd, Cucumber, Karela	Udaipur
Turmeric, Tapioca	Udaipur

Important seed vegetable

Beet leaf, Onion, Bottle gourd, Tinda, Okra, Radish and Peas

CHAPTER 30

SIKKIM

It is a hill state close to Himalayan range with an area of 7096 square kilo metre. Its capital is Gangtok. The state of Sikkim comprised of four districts viz. East Gangtok, North Gangtok, South Gangtok (Namachi) and West Gangtok (Gialsig). Mostly the forests of Saahal, pines and Devdar are found. Agriculture is the main occupation and farmers grow potato, vegetables and spice crops-cinnamon, ginger, turmeric, cardamom and also wheat, maize, barley, rice, soya bean, etc. It was merged with India on April, 1975. It is also rich in natural mineral ores, etc.

TABLE 30.1: Area (ha), production (t) under vegetables in Sikkim state

Vegetable	Area (ha)	Production (t)
Assorted vegetables	3,000	23,000
Total	3,000	23,000

Source : Govt. of Sikkim, Department of Agriculture

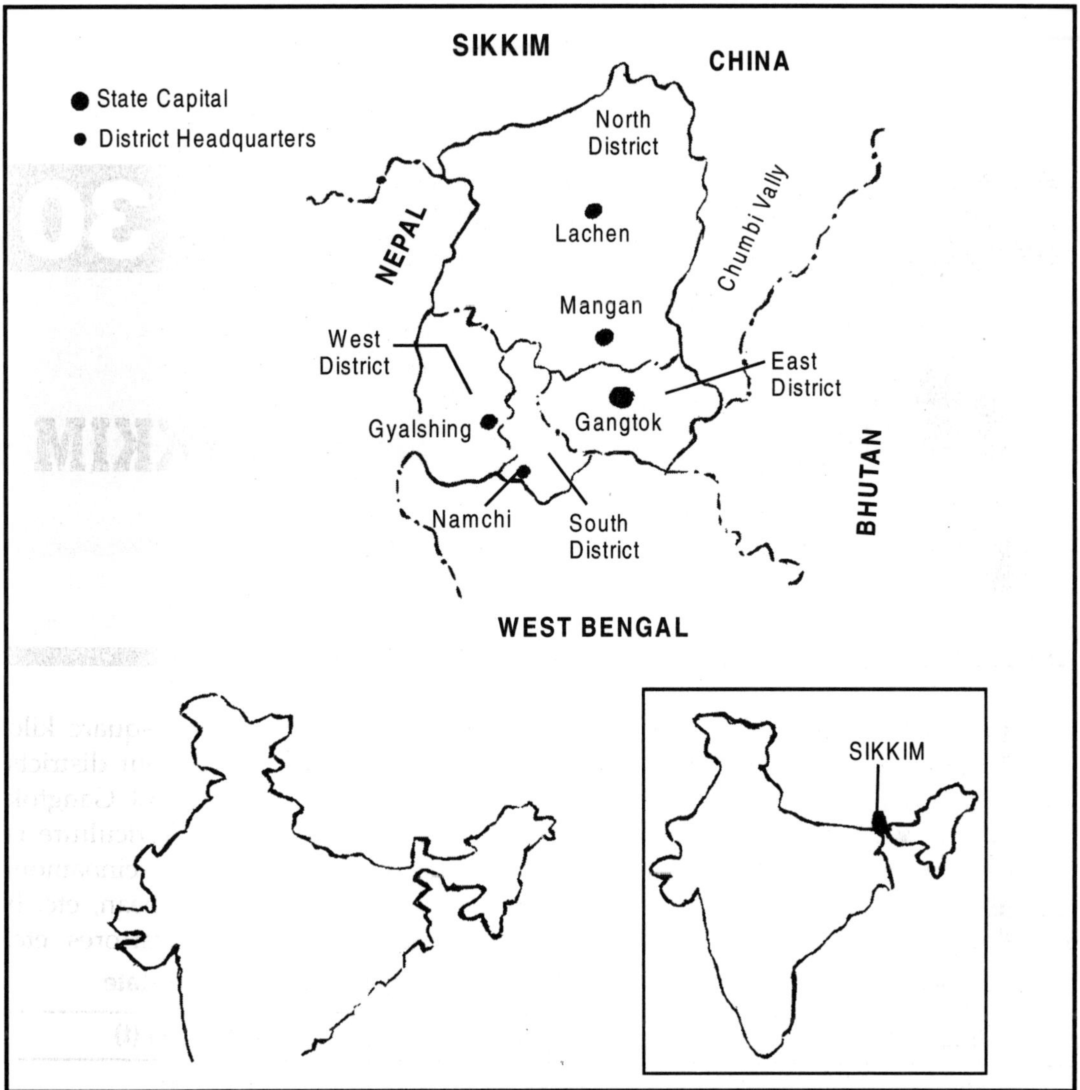

Fig. 30(i) : Location map of Sikkim

CHAPTER 31

VEGETABLE GROWING IN TAMIL NADU

V,Kantha Swamy,

Tamil Nadu is the southern most state of our country. The geographical area of the state is located between 8°5' and 13°10' N latitude and 75°15' and 80°20' East longitude. Altitude varies from 7 m to 12 m a m s 1. The climate of Tamil Nadu is basically tropical. Maximum temperature ranges from 29-30°C whereas, minimum temperature has a range of 19-27°C. Average rainfall in the state is 945 mm, however, it ranges from 600-1800 mm. Total geographical area of the state is 130.02 lakh ha out of which only 57.40 lakh ha is under cultivation. Depending upon the various agro- climatic conditions and soil profile the state is divided into seven agro-climatic zones. (Table 31.1, Fig. 31.1).

TABLE 31.1: Zonal delineations of Tamil Nadu

S.No.	Zone	Delineations
1.	North Eastern Zone	Chingleput, North Arcot, South Arcot, Aniyalur, Perambalur in Tiruchirapalli District.
2.	North Western Zone	Dharmapuri District excluding hill areas, Salem excluding Tiruchengode, Perambalur Taluk of Tiruchirapalli district.
3.	Western Zone	Periyar and Coimbatore district, Tiruchengode Taluk of Salem, Karur Taluk of Tiruchirapalli and Northernpart of Madurai.
4.	Cauvery Delta Zone	Tanjore district and Musiri, Thiruchirapalli, Lalgudi, Tharaiyar, Kulithalai Taluks of Tiruchirapalli distict, Aranthangi Taluk of Pudukottai, Chidambaram and Kattumannarkoil taluks of South Arcot district.

S.No.	Zone	Delineations
5.	Southern Zone	Ramanathapuram and tirunelveli district, Dindigul, Natham, Melur, Tirumangalam, Madurai North and South, Pudukkottai district.
6.	High Rainfall Zone	Kanyakumari district.
7.	High Altitude and Hilly Zone	Nilgiris, Shevroys, elagiri-Javachi, Kollimalai, Pachdi Malai, Annamalais, Palnis and Podhezai Malai.

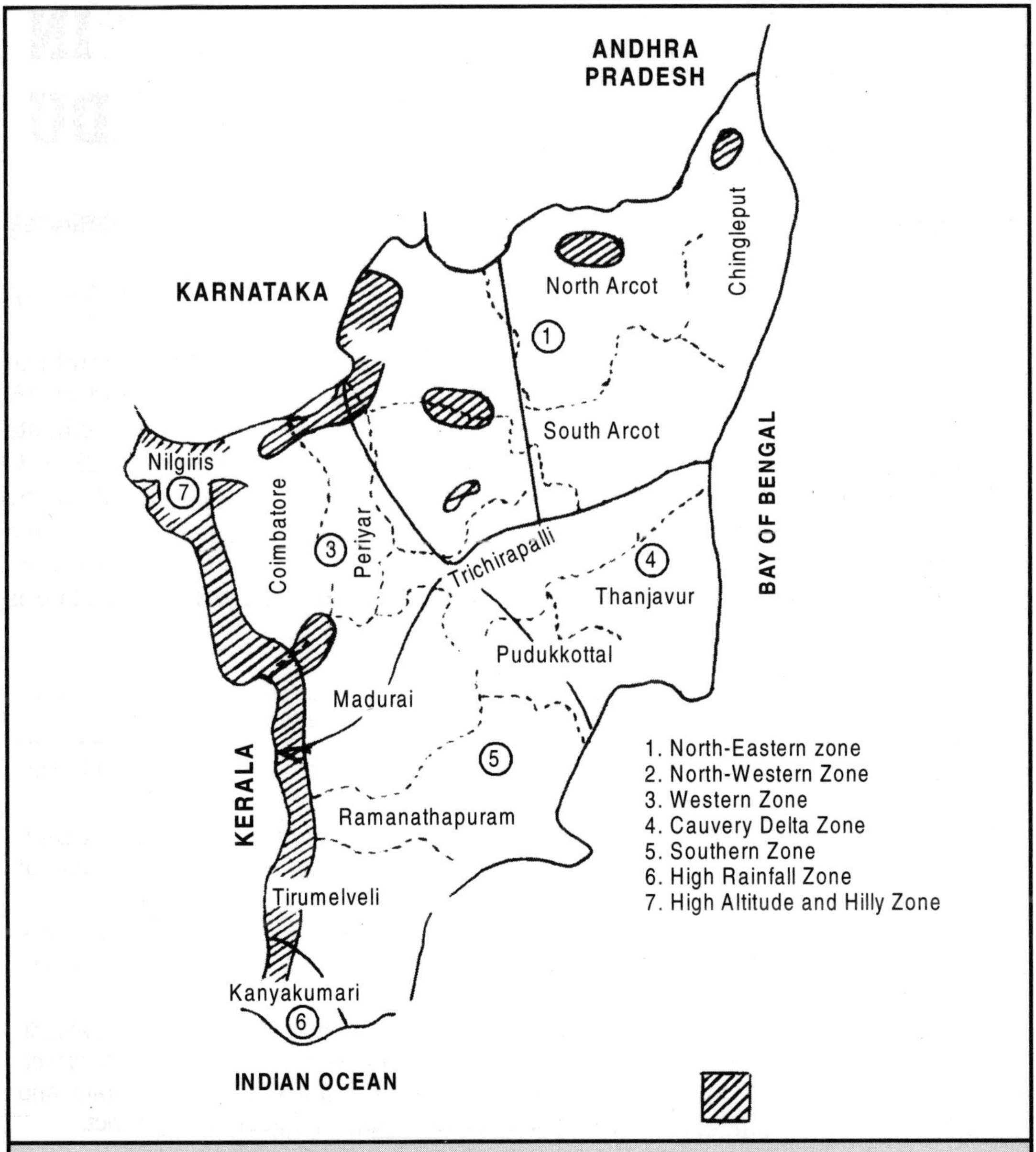

Fig. 31(i) Agro Climatic zones of Tamil Nadu

Horticultural zones and district-wise predominanty grown crops

Horticulturally the state can be divided into five horticultural zones. Various districts representing each zone and have been shown in Table 31.2. In Tamil Nadu, fruits and vegetables cultivation significantly contribute to the state agricultural income. However, vegetable cultivation is spread over the entire state but some district particularly Cuddalore and Villupuram, Salem, Namakkal, Maduria, Dirdigul and Nilgiris are most suitable for commercial vegetable cultivation. District-wise information regarding soil type, normal rainfall and its distribution pattern, and principal horticultural crops grown, has been delieated in Table 31.3.

Area and production of vegetables

In Tamil Nadu, tapioca, onion, tomato, brinjal and bhindi occupy major share of total area under vegetable cultivation. It can be seen in Table 31. 4, that there has been a inclining trend in the area under many vegetable w e f 1980-81, however, few vegetables particularly potato, sweet potato, cabbage etc. witnessed decrease in the area. In the year 1994-95 vegetable cultivation was done or an area of 174818 ha with total production of 4597932 tonnes. Which gave average productivity of 25.16 t/ha. Table 31.5 clearly depicts the percentage share of each vegetable in respect of area and production in the state as well as the predominant districts and their percentage contribution in area under each crop. District-wise area under various vegetable crops has also been given in Table 31.6.

Rank of Tamil Nadu at National level in terms of Area and Production

Tamil Nadu contributes significantly in respect of area and production under principal vegetable crops particularly tomato, onion and brinjal at National level. The detail has been given in Table 31.7.

Availability period of horticultural crops

Due to tropical climatic conditions in Tamil Nadu many vegetables are available round the year in the state. Complete detail of availability periods of fruits, vegetables, spices condiment and plantation crops has been given in Table 31.8.

Vegetable improvement work

Tamil Nadu agricultural University with its head quarter at Coimbatore has been contributing significantly for the promotion of vegetable cultivation in the State. The State Agricultural University has released as many as 73 promising varieties in 32 different vegetables grown in the state. Complete list of varieties released by the Tamil Nadu Agricultural University is given in Table 31.9.

TABLE 31.2: Tamil Nadu

Horticultural Zones

ZONE–I	ZONE–II	ZONE–III	ZONE–IV	ZONE–V
1. Whole of Kanchipuram & Thiruvallur	1. Whole of Vellore	1. Pudukottai, Keeranur and Thirumayam taluks of Pudukottai District	1. Whole of Kanayakumari District	1. Whole of Nilgiris District
2. Cuddalore & Villupuram	2. Thiruvannamalai	2. Whole of Madurai & Theni	2. Shenkottai & Tenkasi Taluks of Tirunelveli District	2. Shevrnya, Kolli Hills, Pachannalars of Salem District
3. Thanjavur	3. Dharamapuri	3. Dindigul		3. Kodaikanal taluk of Dindigul
4. Nagapattinam & Thiruvarur	4. Salem	4. Ramanathapuram		
5. Tiruchi, Musiri, Lalgudi and Kulithalai of Tiruchirapalli District	5. Erode	5. Sivagangai		
6. Aranthangi Taluk of Pudukottai Distric	6. Coimbatore	6. Virudhunagar		
	7. Karur, Ariyalur, Thuraiyur, Perambalur, Udayarpalayam, Manaparai Taluks of Tiruchi District	7. Tirunelveli		
		8. Tuticorin		

*Depending Upon the Agro Climatic "Conditions and Soil Profile". The State can be divided into five horticultural zones.

Source : Techno Economic Feasibility Study for Development of Horticulture in Tamil Nadu Agricultural Finance Corporation Ltd., Bombay

TABLE 31.3: District Wise Soil Type/Normal Rainfall/Predominently Grown Plants

District	Soil Type	NORMAL RAIN FALL				Horticultural Plants Predominently Grown
		Winter	Summer	South West	North East	
		Jan.-Feb.	Mar.-May	June-Sept.	Oct.-Dec.	
(1)	(2)	(3)	(4)	(5)	(6)	(7)
Kanchi puram & Thiruvallur	Red Loam, Black Soil Sandy Coastal	35.5	76.4	422.0	631.4	Fresh fruits, Ladys' Finger, Pumpkin, Flowers.
Cuddalore & Villupuram	Red Loam Black Soil, Sandy Coastal	50.4	106.2	392.0	588.1	Jack Fruit, Tapioca, Brinjal, Pumpkin, Sweet Potato, Cashew
Vellore	Black Soil	23.2	102.1	448.8	379.3	Mango, Lady's Finger, Beans, Yam, Flowers
Thiruvannamalai	Black Soil	36.5	112.7	468.4	457.1	Flowers
Salem & Namakkal	Red Loam Black Soil	23.1	159.3	346.1	313.0	Guava, Orange, Pear, Pineapple, Greens, Tapioca, Turmeric, Pepper, Cloves, Coffee, Arecanut
Dharmapuri	Red Loam, Black Soil	19.0	160.2	366.2	311.6	Mango, Grapes, Greens, Tapioca, Tomato, Potato, Carrot, Cabbage, Betelvinc
Erode	Red Loam, Red Sandy Soil	21.5	147.6	183.4	307.6	Beans, Yam, Turmeric, Garlic
Coimbatore	Red Loam, Red Sandy Soil	25.6	135.1	158.3	328.2	Tomato, Beans, Beetroot, Turmeric, Tea, Arecanut
Madurai & Theni	Red Loam, Black Soil	35.8	153.2	250.8	387.3	Guava, Mango, Grapes, Sweet Potato, Beet Root, Cabbage, Greens, Tamarind, Cardamom, Tea

(1)	(2)	(3)	(4)	(5)	(6)	(7)
Dindigul	Red Loam, Black Soil	39.2	158.1	229.2	407.5	Lime, Guava, Orange, Grapes, Pineapple, Pear Beans, Onion, Potato, Tamarind, Garlic, Grapes Ginger, Coffee, Flowera
Ramana thapuram	Red Loam, Black Soil, Sandy Coastal Alluviam	67.4	122.7	135.3	501.6	Chillies
Tiruchir-appalli Karur & Perambalur	Red Loam	34.2	125.1	266.5	397.8	Banana, Lime, Jack Fruit, Sweet Potato, Pumpkin, Onion, Brinjal, Carrot, Beans, Coriander, Cashew
Nagapat-tinam & Thiruvarur	Red Loam, Sandy Coastal Alluviam	81.5	107.6	277.9	762.9	Minor Horticultural Crops
Thanjavur Coastal	Red Loam, Sandy Crops Alluviam	59.9	114.8	319.8	528.0	Minor Horticultural
Pudikottai	Red Loam	52.0	117.6	342.4	398.8	Pineapple, Cashew
Virud-hunagar	Red Loam, Black Soil	52.6	164.3	169.7	425.1	Coriander
Sivagangai	Red Loam, Black Soil	45.9	135.8	329.3	393.7	Cashew
Tirunelveli	Red Loam, Black Soil	90.8	169.0	140.5	484.4	Banana, Lime, Cloves, Cocoa
Tuticorin	Red Loam, Black Soil	62.0	110.9	59.9	429.4	Banana, Yam, Chillies Coriander, Cardamon
Kanya-kumari	Sandy Coastal Alluviam	50.2	321.5	559.1	526.0	Jack Fruit, Tamarind, Ginger, Cloves, Arecamul, Cocoa
The Nilgiris	Red Loam, Black Soil, Lateritic Soil, Red Sandy Soil	62.5	278.1	1022.3	494.1	Orange, Citrus Fruits, Pear, Potato, Carrot, Beetroot, Cabbage, Pepper, Ginger, Cardamom, Tea, Coffee

TABLE 31.4: Vegetables Area (in Ha) 1980-81 - 1995-96 (P)

	80-81	81-82	82-83	83-84	84-85	85-86	86-87	87-88	88-89	89-90	90-91	91-92	92-93	93-94	94-95	95-96 (P)
VEGETBALES																
1. TAPIOCA	53264	4852	48338	57322	61410	47112	47635	67367	65968	75423	76431	85543	7412	85412	85983	77625
2. ONION	22595	7913	8583	21959	23054	19774	18004	19457	22617	24572	22185	26630	22278	24596	28488	21439
3. TOMATO	—	—	10904	9952	9592	12532	12878	11970	13553	14587	15715	13834	17481	20445	21055	21519
4. BRINJAL	8784	7327	7159	7002	7389	7441	7189	6125	6879	6347	7218	7715	8054	8941	8836	8174
5. POTATO	10456	10131	9533	9535	8417	7773	8336	8728	6799	8680	5310	4917	5411	5816	4781	3802
6. BHENDI	2913	2155	1681	2309	2236	2022	3168	2203	2325	2189	3147	3065	3417	3969	4355	4292
7. GREENS	1183	6178	951	1078	1458	1552	1418	1367	1124	1134	904	1525	1744	1196	2566	2596
8. CARROT	480	454	393	585	848	919	1637	1787	1252	18876	2332	2542	2691	3081	2398	2610
9. SWEET POTATO	4352	4099	3456	4048	4538	3625	2985	2215	3845	2996	2276	2327	2130	2644	2218	1511
10. YAM	1142	827	562	906	1367	1336	1193	812	1311	1311	1033	1086	1270	1105	1918	1367
11. BEANS	966	1300	1259	1436	1107	1658	1984	1792	1375	1588	1286	2537	1864	1380	1723	1735
12. CABBAGE	1244	1578	1705	1864	1770	1627	2335	2281	1799	1595	1056	1166	1373	1201	944	906
13. PUMPKIN	N.A.	N.A.	N.A.	N.A.	N.A.	N.A.	N.A.	285	N.A.	816	562	1275	630	737	860	652
14. BEET ROOT	484	492	579	560	417	437	681	506	470	661	551	555	709	817	628	730

NA: Not Available

TABLE 31.5: Horticultural Crops-Area, Production, Productivity, Percentage of Share and Predominent Districts in Tamil Nadu 1994-95

	Name of Crop	Area (ha)	Pro-duction (M.T.)	Pro-ductivity	0% of Share in Area	0% of Share in Pro-duction	Predominent District & Their % of Share in Airea I	II	III
	VEGETABLES								
1.	Tapioca	85983	3117460	36.26	49.18	70.89	Salem & N(40)	Villupuraml(13)	Kanyakumari (11)
2.	Onion	28488	294270	10.33	16.30	6.69	Salem & N(21)	Dindigul(18)	Trichy K&P (18)
3.	Tomato	21055	232430	11.04	12.04	5.28	Salem & N(33)	Coimbatore (16)	Dharmapuri (12)
4.	Brinjal	8836	115300	13.06	5.05	2.62	Salem & N(24)	Dindigul(10)	Madurai & T (9)
5.	Potato	4781	83790	17.53	2.74	1.91	Nilgiris (50)	Dindigul (46)	Dharmapuri (3)
6.	Bhendi	4355	38020	8.73	2.49	0.86	Salem & N(38)	Tirunelvell (8)	Kanchipuram &T(8)
7	Greens	2566	12830	5.00	1.47	0.29	Tuticorin (38)	Cuddalore (16)	Madurai & T (11)
8	Carrot	2398	52756	22.00	1.37	1.20	Nilgiris (2)	Dindigul (67)	Vellore (29)
9.	Sweet Potato	2218	37260	16.80	1.27	0.85	Villupuram (18)	Trichy K&P (17)	Tirunelveli (13)
10.	Yam	1918	47950	25.00	1.10	1.09	Vellore (35)	Erode (30)	Tuticorin (16)
11.	Beans	1723	8615	5.00	0.99	0.20	Dindigul (52)	Erode (11)	Coimbatore (8) Tutl. (8)
12.	Cabbage	944	107620	114.00	0.54	2.45	Nilgiris (62)	Dharmapuri (29)	Madurai & T (8)
13.	Pumpkin	860	18060	21.00	0.49	0.41	Dindigul (30)	Trichy KP (28)	Kanchipuram&T(II)
14.	Beet Root	628	13816	22.00	0.36	0.31	Madurai&T (57)	Nilgiris(24)	Coimbatore (10)
15.	Other Vegetables	8065	217755	27.00	4.61	4.95	Dindigul (20)	Trichy K&P (10)	Madurai &T (8)
	Total Vegetables	174818	4597932	25.16					
	Total vegetables (except Tapioca)	88835	1280472	14.41	50.82	29.12			

TABLE 31.6: Area of Vegetables 1995-96 (Provisional)

	Tapioca	Tomato	Onion	Brinjal	Bhendi	Potato	Carrot	Gerens	Beans	Sweet Potato	Yam	Cabbage	Beetroot	Pumtroot	Other vegetables	Total vegetables
1. Kanchipuram, Thiruvallur	243	25	1	483	267	–	–	88	5	220	3	–	–	60	357	1752
2. Cuddalur	6775	2	71	339	58	–	–	356	–	95	–	–	–	12	240	7948
3. Villupuram	8949	39	149	232	155	–	–	185	–	251	32	–	–	31	62	10065
4. Vellorc	23	759	95	603	215	1	–	86	27	7	205	4	–	21	687	2733
5. Thiruvanna-malai	53	141	99	255	60	–	–	10	36	27	99	–	–	68	79	927
6. Salem Namakkal	31582	6ll9	5289	1960	1553	–	–	308	12	45	4	–	–	35	424	4733
7. Dharmapuri	9381	3765	212	321	58	163	56	94	88	45	10	345	64	20	323	14945
8. Coimbatore	877	3738	1940	564	359	–	–	30	390	–	11	2	66	182	528	8687
9. Erode	2854	401	1859	364	151	40	–	13	151	3	587	–	2	13	472	6910
10. Karur	231	117	92	80	9	–	–	–	–2	55	8	–	–	52	354	1198
11. Tiruchirapalli	4718	224	1197	140	64	–	–	12	79	67	–	–	–	5	48	6554
12. Perambadur	1663	92	2764	162	15	–	–	19	26	68	–	–	–	77	350	5236
13. Pudukottai	21	2	–	87	14	–	–	–	–	3	2	–	–	15	16	160
14. Thanjavur	55	3	7	159	51	–	–	5	2	–	106	–	–	14	267	669
15. Nagai, Thiruvarur	374	–	–	40	32	–	–	31	17	9	–	–	–	3	48	554
16. Madurai	51	2025	1151	725	269	–	278	74	78	5	26	445	4	600	5731	Theni_
17. Dindigul	163	2812	3150	751	373	869	722	13	744	63	–	14	38	7	2250	11969
18. Ramnad	–	7	2	24	19	–	–	6	–	–	–	–	–	–	16	74
19. Virudhunagar	17	291	1070	203	78	–	–	58	9	39	57	–	–	7	87	1916
20. Sivagangarm	26	4	45	142	4	–	–	5	5	–	4	–	–	–	3	238
21. Thirunelvell	217	575	1372	303	299	–	–	39	15	101	33	–	–	18	265	3207
22. Tuticorin	23	375	904	174	167	–	–	955	20	138	165	–	2	4	278	3205
23. The Nilgiris	74	–	–	–	–	2729	1832	3	35	17	36	517	113	–	856	6210
24. Kanyakumari	9255	3	–	63	22.	–	–	2	–	–	–	–	–	4	97	9446
Total	77625	21519	21439	8174	4292	3802	2610	2596	1735	1511	1367	906	730	652	8707	157666

TABLE 31.7: Area, Production, Productivity and Rank of Tamil Nadu at National Level (Year 1994-95)

VEGETABLES							
1.	Tomato	21055	7	232430	8	11.04	17
2.	Brinjal	8836	10	115300	11	13.05	12
3.	Bhendi	4355	12	38020	12	8.73	9
4.	Onion	28488	5	294270	8	10.33	16
5.	Potato	4781	17	83790	15	17.53	7
6.	Cabbage	944	18	107620	8	114.00	1

Source : National Horticulture Board-year Book-1997

TABLE 31.8: Availability Period of Horticultural Crops

	Crop	Jan.	Feb.	Mar.	Apr.	May	June	July	Aug.	Sept.	Oct.	Nov.	Dec.
	FRUITS-SEASON												
1.	Banana	√	√	√	√	√	√	√	√	√	√	√	√
2.	Mango			√	√	√	√						
3.	Lime	√	√	√			√	√	√	√		√	√
4.	Guava	√	√	√	√	√	√	√	√	√	√	√	√
5.	Orange (Mandarin)											√	√
6.	Jack Fruit			√	√	√	√	√					
7.	Grapes				√	√			√	√			
8.	Pear					√	√	√	√	√	√	√	√
9.	Pineapple	√	√	√	√	√						√	√
10.	Sapota		√	√	√	√	√			√	√		
11.	Custard Apple									√	√	√	
12.	Mangosteen								√	√	√		
13.	Papaya	√	√	√	√	√	√	√	√	√	√	√	√
14.	Pomegrante	√								√	√	√	√
15.	Water Melon						√	√	√				
16.	Apple				√	√	√	√	√	√			
17.	Plum				√	√	√	√	√				
	VEGETABLES SEASONS												
1.	Tapioca				√	√	√	√	√				
2.	Onion	√					√	√					
3.	Tomato	√	√	√	√	√	√	√	√	√	√	√	√
4.	Brinjal	√	√	√	√	√							√
5.	Potato	√	√	√	√			√	√				√

	Crop	Jan.	Feb.	Mar.	Apr.	May	June	July	Aug.	Sept.	Oct.	Nov.	Dec.
6.	Lady's Finger						√	√	√	√	√	√	
7.	Carrot	√										√	√
8.	Beans	√	√	√	√								√
9.	Cabbage	√	√	√	√	√	√	√	√	√	√	√	√
10.	Radish	√	√	√						√	√	√	√
11.	Beet Root											√	√
12.	Pumpkin												√
13.	Cauliflower	√	√	√							√	√	
14.	Capsicum					√	√	√					
15.	Cucumber				√	√	√						
16.	Green Peas	√	√	√	√	√	√	√	√			√	
17.	Mushroom	√	√	√					√	√	√	√	√
18.	Spinach	√	√	√	√	√	√					√	√
	SPICES & CONDIMENTS SEASONS												
1.	Chillies	√	√	√	√	√	√	√	√	√	√		√
2.	Coriander	√	√										
3.	Turmeric	√	√										
4.	Tamarind			√	√								
5.	Cardamom	√											√
6.	Pepper	√	√	√									
7.	Garlic		√	√									
8.	Ginger								√	√	√	√	
9.	Cloves			√	√	√	√						
	PLANTATION CROPS SEASONS												
1.	Cashew			√		√							
2.	Tea	√	√	√	√	√	√	√	√	√	√	√	√
3.	Coffee	√	√									√	√
4.	Betelvine	√	√	√	√	√	√	√	√	√	√	√	√
5.	Arecanut	√					√	√					
6.	Cocoa	√			√	√	√			√	√	√	√

TABLE 31.9: List of vegetable varieties released from Tamil Nadu Agricultural University

S.No.	Crop	Varieties
1.	Tomato	CO.1, CO.2, CO.3, PKM. 1, Paiyur 1, COTH (Hybrid)
2.	Brinjal	CO.1, CO.2, MDU.I, PKM.I, PLR.I, KKM.I
3.	Chillies	CO.1, CO.2, CO.3, PKM.I, PKM.I KI, K2, MDU.I PLR.I
4.	Bhendi	CO.1, CO.2 (Hybrid), CO.3 (Hybrid), MDU.I

S.No.	Crop	Varieties
5.	Onion	CO.1, CO.2, CO.3, CO.4
7.	Tapioca	CO.2, CO.2, CO.3
8.	Sweet potato	CO.1, CO.2, CO.3
9.	Pumpkin	CO.1, CO.2
10.	Bittergourd	CO.1, MDU.1
11.	Ashgourd	CO.1, CO.2
12.	Snakegourd	CO.1, CO.2, PKM.1, MDU.1 (Hybrid)
13.	Ribbedgourd	CO.1, CO.2, PKM.1
14.	Bottelgourd	CO.1
15.	Drumstick	PKM.1
16.	Radish	CO.1
17.	Beetroot	OPTY.1
18.	Garlic	OPTY.1
19.	Cucumber	CO.1
20.	Colocasia	CO.1
21.	Dioscorea	CO.1
22.	Coleus	CO.1
23.	Butterbeans	KKL.1
24.	Moringa bean	KKL.1
25.	French beans	CO.1
26.	Pole beans	TKD.1
27.	Water melon	PKM.1
28.	Palak	Ooty.1
29.	Potato	CO. Simla
30.	Dolichos beans	CO.1
31.	Carrot	Ooty.1
32.	Cauliflower	Ooty.1

●●●

CHAPTER 32

TRIPURA

Tripura is one of the state constitute the NEH Region in the eastern part of India. The total area of the state is 10,486 square kilometer and Agartala its capital. It was declared full fledged state in 1972. The state is comprised of three districts viz. North Tripura (Dharamnagar), West Tripura (Agartala) and South Tripura (Udayapur). The main occupation of the people is agriculture including spice and vegetable growing.

TABLE 32.1: Area (ha) and production (t) under vegetables in Tripura

Vegetable	Area (ha)	Production (t)
Other vegetables	22,500	1,74,000
Total	22,500	1,74,000

Source : Govt. of India, Ministry of Agriculture.

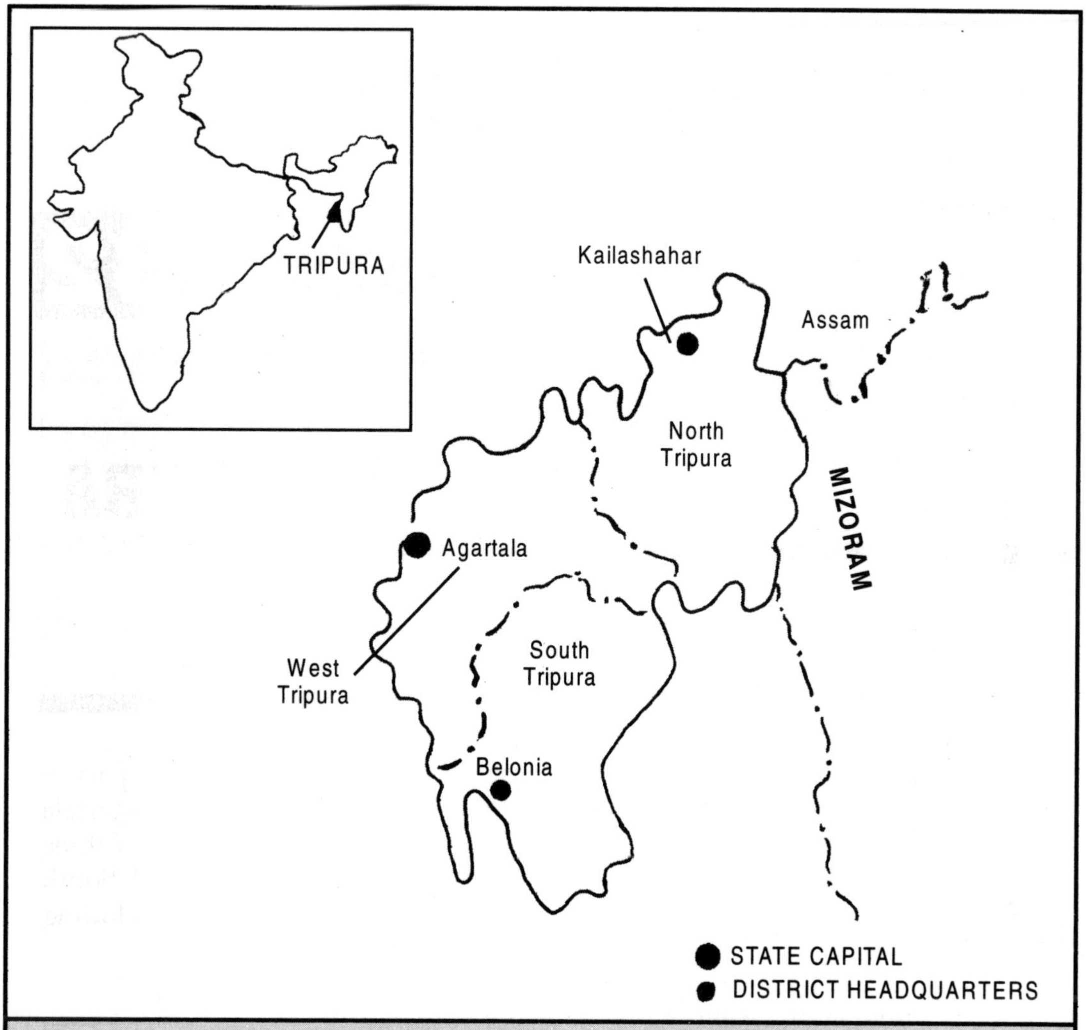

Fig. 32(i) Location Map of Tripura

●●●

CHAPTER 33

VEGETABLE GROWING IN UTTAR PRADESH

Hari Har Ram

Uttar Pradesh, one of the largest State in India, is located between 23°501-3°028°N latitude and 771 41 - 84° 381 E longitude. The state is spread over an area 2.94 lakh km, out of which 1.72 lakh km is under cultivation. In the State about 60% of the total cultivated area is under irrigation. Tubewells are the main source of irrigation. Based on rainfall pattern, temperature, soil types and existing cropping pattern the State is divided into following ten agroclimatic zones.

Hill Zone

This zone includes Uttar Pradesh, Chamoli, Pauri-Garhwal, Tihri Garhwal, Dehradun, Pithoragarh, Almora and hilly regions of Nainital. The hill region on the basis of altituditional variation can be categorised as sub-tropical (250-1200 m a m s 1), sub-temperate (1200-1700 m), temperate (1200-3500 m) and alpine zone (3500 m and above). Different vegetables including potato are cultivated in an area of 14000 ha.

Bhabar and Tarai Zone

It is a narrow strip of land at the foot hills of Himalayas covering northern part of Saharanpur, Bijnor, Rampur, Moradabad, Pilibhit, Bareilly, Lakhimpur, Kheri and plains of Nainital.

Western Plain Zone

This area represents regions between two important rivers Ganga and Yamuna and considered to be the most fertile area of the state. Saharanpur, Muzaffarnager, Meerut, Ghaziabad and Bulandshahar are included in the zone.

Mid-Western Plain Zone

This zone includes Bijnor, Muradabad, Rampur, Barielly Pilibhit and Badaun. This zone has an area of 23.1 lakh ha under cultivation., The total are under vegetable crops in the zone is 43.8 thousand ha. Out of which 19% is occupied by onion, 15% by Cole crops and 9% by Tomato.

South Western Semi-Arid Zone

This zone comprises of Aligarh, Etah, Mainpuri, Mathura and Agra. This zone has net irrigation area of 1285848 ha which is 61.88% of the net cropped area. About 30000 ha area is covered under potato.

Central Plain Zone

This zone comprises Lakhimpur, Kheri, Sitapur, Hardoi, Ferukhabad, Etawa, Kanpur, Unnau, Lucknow Rae-Bareli, Fatepur and Allahabad. The major areas of this zone have got alluvial soils.

Bundelkhand Zone

Thiz zone represents Thansi, Lalitpur, Banda, Hamirpur and Jalaun districts. This zone has net irrigated area of 453842 ha which is 24.5 per cent of the total net cropped area.

North-Eastern Plain Zone

This zone is located in North of the Saryer river and comprises Gonda, Bahraich, Basti, Gorakhpur and Deoria. Thc soils of the zone are mainly of alluvial nature. Vegetables almost suited to soils and crops like turmeric, spices and tuber crops are commercial cash crops of this regions.

Eastern Plain Zone

This zone lies between Saryu and Ganga rivers. The major distts. included in this zone are Barabanki, Faizabad, Sultanpur, Jaunpur, Azamgarh, Ballia, Ghazipur and Varanasi. This zone has got irrigated area of 1478941 ha with shares 54.8% net cropped area of the zone.

Vindhyan Zone

This zone covers Mirzapur and parts of Allahabad and Varanasi distts. Among all the zones, this is the smallest zone. Most of the area in the zone is undulated and rocky.

Although any of vegetables are grown throughout the state for home consumption as well as local markets, however intensive cultivation on commercial scale is confined only to U.P. hills, and geographical regions adjacent to Ghaziabad, Mccrut, Bynor, Moradabad, Barcely, Sahjahanpur, Badaun, Lucknow, Sultanpur, Faizabad, Basti, Jaunpur and Banaras. Uttar Pradesh contributes maximum share

TABLE 33.1: Crop-wise recommended varieties/hybrids, planting time, availability period, major pests and diseases in U.P.

Crop	Varieties/Hybrids	Planting time	Availability	Insects	Diseases
			Plain		
Cucumber	Japanese Long green & Poinsette	April-Oct.	June-July (R) & Feb-March (S)	Red pumpkin beetle & aphids	Powdery mildew & cucumber mosaic virus.
Muskmelon	Hara Madhu, Pusa Madhuras, Durgapur Madhu, Punjab Hybrid & Pusa Rasraj	Jan.-Feb. (river bed) & March	April-June	Red pumpkin beetle, aphids & fruit-fly	Powdery mildew, Fusarium wilt & cucumber mosaic virus
Watermelon	Sugar baby	Jan.-Feb. (R) March	April-June	—	Fusarium wilt
Pumpkin & Squashes	Local varieties, Australian Green & Pusa Vishwas	June-July & March	Round the year	Aphids, Red pumpkin beetle & fruit-fly	Powdery mildew & cucumber mosaic virus
Bottle-gourd	Pusa Summer Prolific Long, Pusa Summer Prolific Round, Pusa Naveen, Punjab Komal, Kalyanpur Long Green & Warad	May-July & March	July-Nov. & Aprl-June	Red pumpkin beetle, Aphids & fruit-fly	Powdery mildew.
Bitter gourd	Pusa Do Mausami, Pusa Vishesh, Kalyanpur Barahmasi, Kalyanpur Sona & Jaunpuri (Local)	March & May-July	April-Sep. & April	Fuirt Fly	Powdery mildew.
Luffa	Pusa Nasadar, Pusa Sadabahar, Pusa Chikni & Kalyanpur Chikni	July-March	May-Nov.	Aphids	Powdery mildew
Cauliflower	Pant Subhra, Pant Gobhi-4, Pusa Synthetic, Pusa Deepali, Pusa Snowball-1, Pusa Snowball-2 & Pusa Snow ball-K1	June-Oct.	Sept.-March	Cater-pillar (Diamond Back moth), Cut worms & Aphids	Black leg, Rhizoctonia, Alternaria leaf spot, Club-root, black rot, Bacterial wilt & soft rot.

Crop	Varieties/Hybrids	Planting time	Availability	Insects	Diseases
Cabbage	Golden Acre, Pride of India, Pusa Mukta & Pusa Drum Head	Sep.-Nov.	—	Diamond back moth, Caterpillar, cutworm Butterfly caterpillar & Aphids	Cabbage yellows, Black rot, Black leg, Mildew, Rhizoctonia & Black spec.
Knol-khol	White Vienna, Early Purple Vienna & Large Green	Sept.-Oct.	Dec.-Feb.	Aphids	Black leg, Club root, Altcrnaria leaf spot & Fusarium wilt.
Tomato	Pusa Ruby, US 101, HS-102, HS-110, Hisar Arun, Hisar Laliina, Hisar Lalit, Hisar Anmol, KS-2, SL-120, Pant T-3, Narendra Tomato-2, Narendra Tomato-1, Pusa Hybrid-2, Naveen, R upali & Avinash-2	July-Aug. & Nov.-Feb.	Round the year	Fruit worm, Jassids, Tobacco caterpillar, White fly & Root knot nematode	Daming-off, root rot, Late blight, Buckeye, Fruit rot, Early blight, Leaf curl virus, Fusarium wilt & Tobacoo mosaic virus
Brinjal	Pusa Purple Long, Pusa Purple Cluster, PH-4, Pusa Kranti, Pusa Hybrid-6, Punjab Barsati, Pant Samrat,Pant Rituraj, Pant Brinjal Hybrid-1, Azad Kranti, Pant Brinjal Hybrid-1 & NDBH-1	July-July, Nov.-Dec. & March	—	Epilachn a beetle, Jassids, Leaf roller Stem Fruit borer, Root knot nematodes	Damping-off, Phomo-psis blight, Alternaria leaf spot, bacterial wilt & Little leaf.
Chilli	Pant C-l, Pusa Jwala & Agni	June-July Dec.-Jan.	Round the year	Thrips, Aphids, Mites & Root knot Nematodes	Damping- off, Anthraconose, fruit rot, Leaf curl, virus & Fusarium wilt
Bell pepper	California Wonder Bharat, Indira, Heera	Aug.-Nov.	Nov.-Dec. & April-June	Aphids & cut worms	Cercospora leaf spot, Ancheracnose, Fruit rot & Phytophthora blight.

Crop	Varieties/Hybrids	Planting time	Availability	Insects	Diseases
Radish	Japanese White & Pusa Chetki Radish	Aug.- Jan.	Oct.-April	Aphids & Mustard Saw-fly	Alternaria blight, White rust & mosaic virus.
Carrot	Pusa Kesar & Nantes	Aug.-Dec.	Oct.-March	Carrot rust- fly	Bacterial softrot, Watery soft rot & Black rot
Turnip	Pusa Chandrima, Pusa Swarnima, Purple Top White Globe, Golden Ball, Pusa Kanchan & Pusa Sweti	Sep.-Dec.	Dec.-Feb.	Aphids & Mustard saw-fly	Alternaria leaf spot, phyllody & Turnip yellow mosaic virus
Pea	Arkel, Pant Sabji Matar-3, Matar Ageta-6, Early Badger, VL-Ageta Mater-7, Bonneville, Azad Pea-1 & Narcndera Vegetable Pea-1	Oct.-Nov.	Jan.-March	Aphids, Pod borer, Pea weevil & Leaf minor	Powdery mildew & Rust
French Bean	Contender, Pusa Parvati, VL Boni Bean-1 Pant Anupma & Pant Bean-2	Sep.-Oct. & Feb.	Nov.-Jan. & April-May	Bean aphids, Jassids, Stem fly & Pod borer	Anthracnose Cercos-pora leaf spot, Root rot & Bean common mosaic virus, Rust
Cow pea	Pusa Phalguni, Pusa Barsati, Pusa Do Phasali, Pusa Komal (Sel-1552) & Narendra Lobia-1	July-Feb. & March	Oct.-Nov. & May-June	Aphid, Jassids & pod borer	Anthracnose Die back, Powdery mildew, Bacterial blight & Mosaic.
Onion	Pusa Red, Pusa Ratnar, Agrofound Dark Red, Kalyanpur Red Round, Pusa Madhvi, Pusa White Round & Pusa White Flat	Oct.-Nov.	Round the year	Thrips	Onin Smut & Purple Blotch.

Crop	Varieties/Hybrids	Planting time	Availability	Insects	Diseases
Okra	Parbhani Kranti Pusa A-4	June-July & Feb.-March	Aug.- Oct. & April-June	Jassids & Pod borer	
HILLS					
Tomato	Lower-hills Mid-hills	Feb-Mar.Apri April-May	June-Aug.	**Note :** The varieties, insects and diseases for hills situations are almost the same as applicable to plains.	
Chilli	Valleys & mid-hills	April	July-Aug.		
Capsicum	-do-	Feb.-March	April	June-July, July-Aug.	
Brinjal	-do-	April	July-Aug.		
Cabbage	Valleys	mid & high-hills	July-Aug. June	Oct.-Nov. Sept.-Oct.	
Cauliflower	Mid-hills	April	July-Aug.		
French Bean	Valleys & mid-hills	April & Aug. June	July & Aug. Sept.		
Peas	Valleys & high-hills	Aug. Nov.-Dec.	Oct.-Nov. Apr.-May		
Radish	Mid & high-hills	Apr.-June	June-Aug.		

R = Rainy season, S = Summer season and RB = River bed.

in country's vegetable production. Total area under vegetables is estimated to the tune of 12.6 lakh ha with the production of 10.2 million tons. Information regarding different varieties/hybrids grown, planting time, availability and major insect-pests is given in Table 33.1.

Export potential

(*a*) **Domestic market:** The off-season vegetables and some normal season vegetables are sent to local markets within U.P. itself. The potential markets outside U.P. are Delhi for vegetables grown in Western U.P. and U.P. Hills and Calcutta for the vegetables grown in the Eastern U.P.

(*b*) **Abroad :** On a limited scale,- French bean, bitter- gourd and onion produced in U.P. are exported to Gulf countries.

Major production constraints :

(A) Biotic

(*i*) Fruits and shoot borer in brinjal

(*ii*) Bacterial wilt in brinjal

(*iii*) Leaf curl virus and tobacco mosaic virus in tomato

(*iv*) Late blight, fruit rot and fruit borer in tomato.

(*v*) Anthracnose and fruit rot in chilli.

(*vi*) Jassids in chilli and okra.

(*vii*) Pod borer in French bean and okra.

(*viii*) White mold in French bean.

(*ix*) Cucumber mosaic virus and Powdery mildew in cucurbit.

(*x*) Fruit-fly in cucurbit.

(*xi*) Purple blotch and thrips in onion.

(B) Abiotic constraints

(*i*) Inadequate organic matter.

(*ii*) Inadequate availability of farmyard manure/compost.

(*iii*) Inadequate technical know how on riverbed cultivation.

(*iv*) Excessive rains and waterlogging for *kharif* vegetables.

(*v*) Low temperature stress.

(*vi*) High temperature stress.

Vegetable Seed Production

Vegetable seeds of important vegetable varieties namely : Pant Samrat, Pant Rituraj, Pant Brinjal, Hybrid-1, Narendra Brinjal Hybrid-1, Narendra Brinjal-225, Azad Kranti (Brinjal); Pant Subhra, Pant Gobhi-4, (Cauliflower); Pant Anupama,

Pant Bean-2, (French bean); Pant Bahar, Pant Tomato-3, Narendra Tomato-1, Narendra Tomato-2, Pusa Ruby (Tomato); Arkel, Azad pea-1, Pant sabji Matar-3, NDVP-4 (Vegetable pea); Pusa Komal, Narendra Lobia-1 (Cow pea) 4; Parbhani Kranti (Okra); Japanese White, Pusa Chetki (Radish; Pusa Kesar (Carrot); Kalyanpur Long Green, Pusa Naveen (Bottlegourd), Kalyanpur Sona (Bittergourd), Pusa Chikni (Luffa), Pant C-l, (Chilli), etc. is being produced at GBPUAT, Pantnagar; CSAUAT, Kanpur; NDUAT, Narendranagar, Faizabad and Project Directorate of Vegetable Research, Varanasi.

Besides these public sector institutions, the seeds of vegetables are also being produced by private seed growers in the areas adjoining to Bareilly, Faizabad, Jaunpur and Varanasi. The seed of temperate vegetables is being produced Vivekanand Parvatiya Krishi Anusandhansala, Almora, Hill Campus Ranichauri and establishments of Department of Horticulture, Govt. of U.P. A few private sector seed companies like Indo- American Hybrid Seeds, Mahyco and Pro-Agro are also involved in the activities related vegetable seed production.

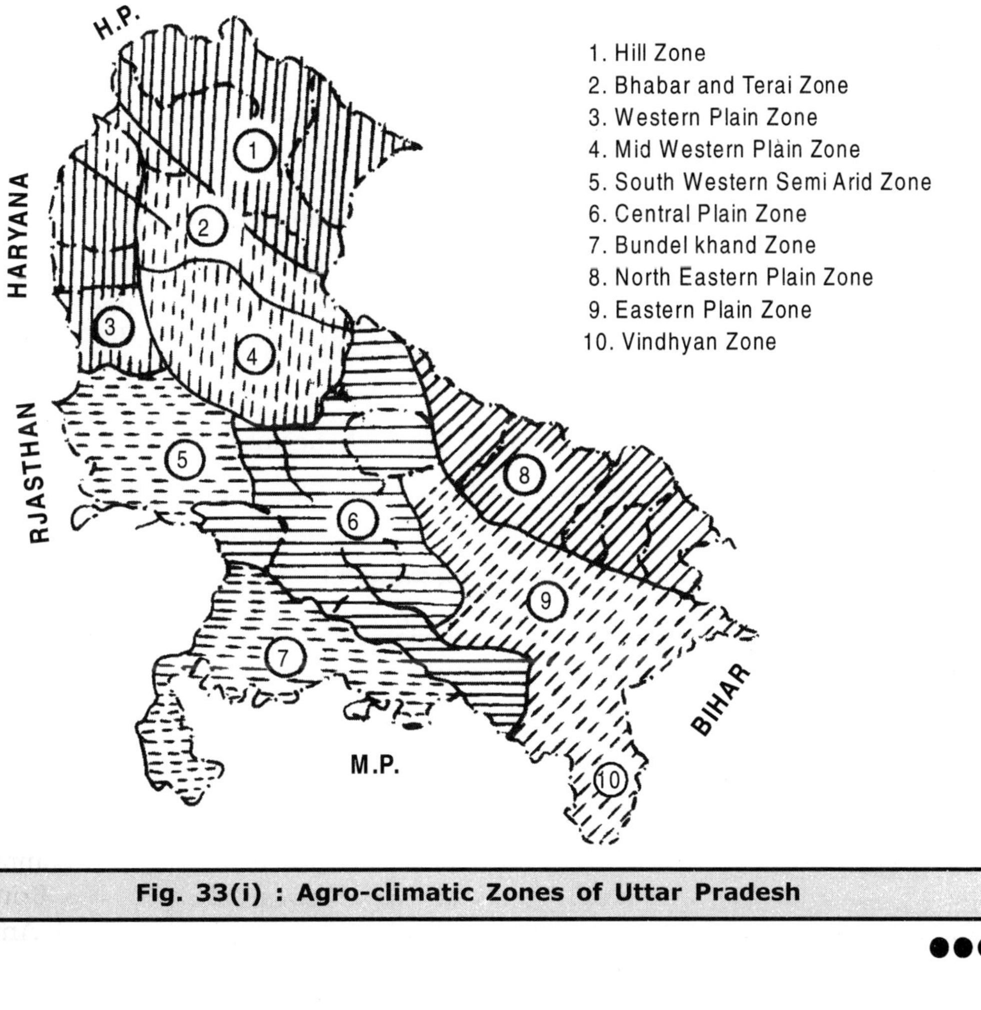

Fig. 33(i) : Agro-climatic Zones of Uttar Pradesh

●●●

CHAPTER 34

VEGETABLE GROWING IN WEST BENGAL

P. Hazara

1. Name of State : West Bengal
2. Total geographical area : 8.85 million hectare
3. Area under cultivation : 5.60 million hectare
4. Irrigated area : 2.20 million hectare
5. Area under vegetables : 5.1 lakh hectare (excluding potato)
6. Total vegetable production : 53.91 lakh ton.
7. Productivity : 10.5 ton per hectare
8. Area under potato : 2.6 lakh hectare
9. Total potato production : 60 lakh ton
10. Productivity : 23 ton per hectare
11. Area under each vegetable (approximate)

TABLE 34.1: Area and Production of different Vegetables

Crop	Area ('000 ha)	Production ('000t)
Brinjal	89.4	911.60
Okra	48.6	323.20
Cabbage	46.6	747,00
Cauliflower	41.7	641.50
Pumpkin	35.1	360.00

Crop	Area ('000 ha)	Production ('000t)
Tomato	24.6	355.50
Onion	23.4	258.00
Watermelon	13.5	91.20
Other cucurbits (mainly pointed gourd, bottlegourd, bittergourd, ridge gourd, Wax gourd and cucumber)	56.3	453.50
Other vegetables crops*	130.8	453.50
Total	510.0	5391.00

* (mainly chilli, radish, amaranthus, palak, Indian spinach, cowpea, hyacinth bean, pea, French bean, Carrot and garlic).

TABLE 34.2: Cropwise recommended and cultivated varieties/hybrids, planting times, availability period, major pests and diseases

Crop	Varieties/hybrids	Planting time	Avbailability	Major pests and diseases
Brinjal	Mostly local varieties, some good performing improved varieties are Pusa Purple Long, Pusa Purple cluster, Pant Rituraj, Muktakeshi, Black Beauty, Pusa Kranti (widely diverse local varieties are good performing)	April-May for summer-rainy crop, Sept-October for autumn-winter crop (main season)	Almost throughout the year (abundance from July-Oct and Nov-March.	Bacterial wilt, Phomopsis blight, Fusarium wilt, Little leaf, Fruit & shoot borer and Epilachna beetle and nematode
Okra	Pusa Sawani, Parvani Kranti, Punjab 7, Arka Anamika & some hybrids	Late Nov. to Dec. for spring summer crop & May-July for summer-rainy crop	March to May June to Sept.	Yellow vein mosaic Jassids & spotted boll worm
Cabbage	Golden Acre, Pride of India, Pusa Mukta, Green Express and hybrids (good hectarge)	Sept-Oct for early crop (main crop & Nov-Dec. for late crop	November to March	Downey mildew, Fusarium Yellowing, club root, blackrot, cabbage borer & diamond back moth.
Cauli-flowers	Pusa katki, Pusa Deepali, Early Patna, Pant Subhra, Dania, Pusa Snowball-1 (seeds collected mainly from Hajipur, Bihar are also sold under different brand names)	July-August for early crop, August-Sept. for mid season crop (main crop) and Nov. for late crop	October to March	-do-

Crop	Varieties/hybrids	Planting time	Avbailability	Major pests and diseases
Tomato	Pusa Ruby, Punjab Chuhara, ArkaVikash, Pant T3, Arka Saurav, Pusa Gaurav and mostly hybrids (some are Abinash- 2, Naveen, ARTH 3 etc.)	August-Sept, for early crop, Sept-Oct for autumn-winter (main crop) & December for late crop	November to March	Early blight, Fusarium wilt, bacterial wilt, leaf curl Fruit borer and nematode
Onion	Pusa Red, Patna Red, Nasik Red, N-53 and some local varieties	October to January (mostly Dec)	March to May (abundance April-May)	Purple blotch, bas al rot and bacterial soft rot
Watermelon	Sugar baby, Arka Jyoti, Durgapur Meetha, Arka Manik	December	Late March to May	Downey mildew Anthracnose Red pumpkin beetle, fruitfly.
Pumpkin	Widely diverse local cultivars	Oct-Nov. & May-June	Feb to April (mostly stored for late marketing) & Aug. to Oct.	Fruit rot Red pumpkin beetle
Pointed gourd	Widely diverse local cultivars	October (Planting of both vine & root cuttings)	Feb-Sept.	Phytopthora rot of both vine & fruit, Fruitfly.
Cucumber	Poinsette, different local cultivars & few hybrids	November for Spring-summer crop (most profitable) & March for summer-rainy crop	March-May and June to Sept	Downey mildew, Anthracnose, Powdery mildew, fruitfly.
Other gourds, (bottle gourd, bitter gourd, ridge gourd, etc.)	Mostly local varieties, some identified var. are Phule BG-6, Priya, Pusa Domousumi, MC -84 Arka Uchha (bitter gourd), Pusa Naveen (bottle gourd), Pusa Nasdar (ridge gourd)	December-January for spring summer crop & March- June for summer-rainy crop	March to October	-do-
Chilli	Pusa Jwala, Pant C-l, Bhagyalakshmi, Andhra Jyoti, NP 46-A	Widely diverse local varieties	Oct-Nov. for main crop and May-June for rainy crop. Almost throughout the year	Fruit rot and dieback, leaf spot and leafcurl
Cowpea	BCKV-1, BCKV -2 (determinate/semi determinate fleshy podded type), (Sel Tm3, Birsa Sweta, Asparagus bean (viny sesquipedalis type)	Feb-March for summer crop, Augu st-Oct. for autumn crop	April to July & Sept. to December	Cercospora leaf spot, bacterial blight, bean yellow mosaic, April, pod borer.

Crop	Varieties/hybrids	Planting time	Avbailability	Major pests and diseases
Hyacinth bean	JDL 79, K6 802, HD-18, and some JDL 37, local types	July-August	Nov. to March	Yellow mosaic, Aphid, pod borer.
Pea	Arkel, Bonnevile, Meteor, Perfection New Line	Late October to Nov.	December to March	Fusarium wilt, Powdery mildew, Aphid, Pod borer.
Radish	Pusa Deshi, Pusa Chetki, Pusa Reshmi. Pusa Himani, Chinese Pink, Contai Long and local asiatic types	July-November	August to March	Alternaria, blight, Aphid, mustard saw fly
Palak	All- Green, Pusa Jyoti, Jobner Green, Banerjee's Giant	July-December	August to March	Cercospora leaf spot
Amaranthus	Widely diverse local varieties of mostly *A. tricolor*	Feb. to Sept.	Almost throughout the year	No serious disease and pests

Export potential

(*a*) **Domestic market** : Huge possibility exists for the vegetables grown in West Bengal. Already large quantities of tomato and chilli grown in terai zone (northern district of West Bengal) are directly transported to Delhi for onward marketing. Andaman and Nicobar islands depends heavily on the vegetables grown in West Bengal. Similarly Assam is a good domestic market for the vegetables grown (main by) in Cooch behar district (north bengal). Successful cultivation of all the vegetables is possible in this state due to existence of all the agroclimates. So domestic market can be substantially increased by proper planning.

(*b*) **Abroad** : At present, substantial quantity of different vegetables are exported to Bangladesh (mainly potato, onion, tomato, sweet pepper etc.) and Bhutan (most of the vegetables) by transborder activities. So export data is not available.

Bright possibility exists for exporting Okra, Chilli, bottle-gourd, Sweet pepper, slicing cucumber, gherkhin, baby corn, garlic, bittergourd, tomato, etc. to Bangladesh, Sri Lanka, Maldives, gulf and other countries.

Any other information : Agroclimatic zones of West Bengal and their characteristics are given separately. (fig. 34(i) and Table 34.3)

Vegetable seed production : Separate directorate of Horticulture has been created recently. State Government is taking initiatives for seed production of some vegetable crops like tomato, brinjal, okra, chilli, onion and cauliflower.

TABLE 34.3: Agroclimatic zones of West Bengal and some characteristics

Zone	Districts	Rainfall (mm)	Temperature (°C)		Soil types	pH of the soil	Remarks
			Max.	Min.			
Hill Zone	Darjeeling district (except Siliguri Sub-division) and northern fringe of Jalpaiguri District.	2500-3000 received mostly during June-Sept.	20-26	2-15	Porous, coarsely loam, light textured, high organic matter	5.0-6.0	Aluminium toxicity, boron and molybdenum deficient soil
Terai	Jalpaiguri, Coochbehar, Siliguri sub-div. of Jalpaiguri & Islampur sub-div. of North Dinajpur.	3220 (maximum during April-May)	32-35	7-23	Relatively coarse textured sand, loam to silty clay often mixed with gravels & pebbles	5.0-6.5	Dark brown top layer, moderately undulating
Old Alluvial Zone	South & North Dinajpur Malda Baradhman Medinipur (E)	2000	28-33	16-26	Heavier in texture, soil is acidic to neutral	5.0-7.0	Soft fertile in south part and light in north part.
New Alluvial Zone	Nadia, Murshidabad, hooghly, Howrah	1400-1600	28.5-33.5	13.9-25.4	Soil is deep fertile, Gengetic soil & neutal in reaction	6.5-7.0	Soil-mostly fertile
Coastal saline Zone	South 24-Parganas, Medinipur (some Eastern parts)	1800	27-32	18-26	Heavy clay rich in Na, Mg. Ca, P and organic matter	6.5-7.5	EC-3.0 to 18X) mm hos soil fertile
Red & laterite Zone	Bankura, Birbhum, Medinipur (Western part), Purulia	1000-1300	28-39	15.8-27	Coarse textured with honeycomb type of ferrogenous, well drained undulated moderately to strongly acidic.	4.5-7.5	So porous low water holding capacity, low organic matter, fertile to less fertile

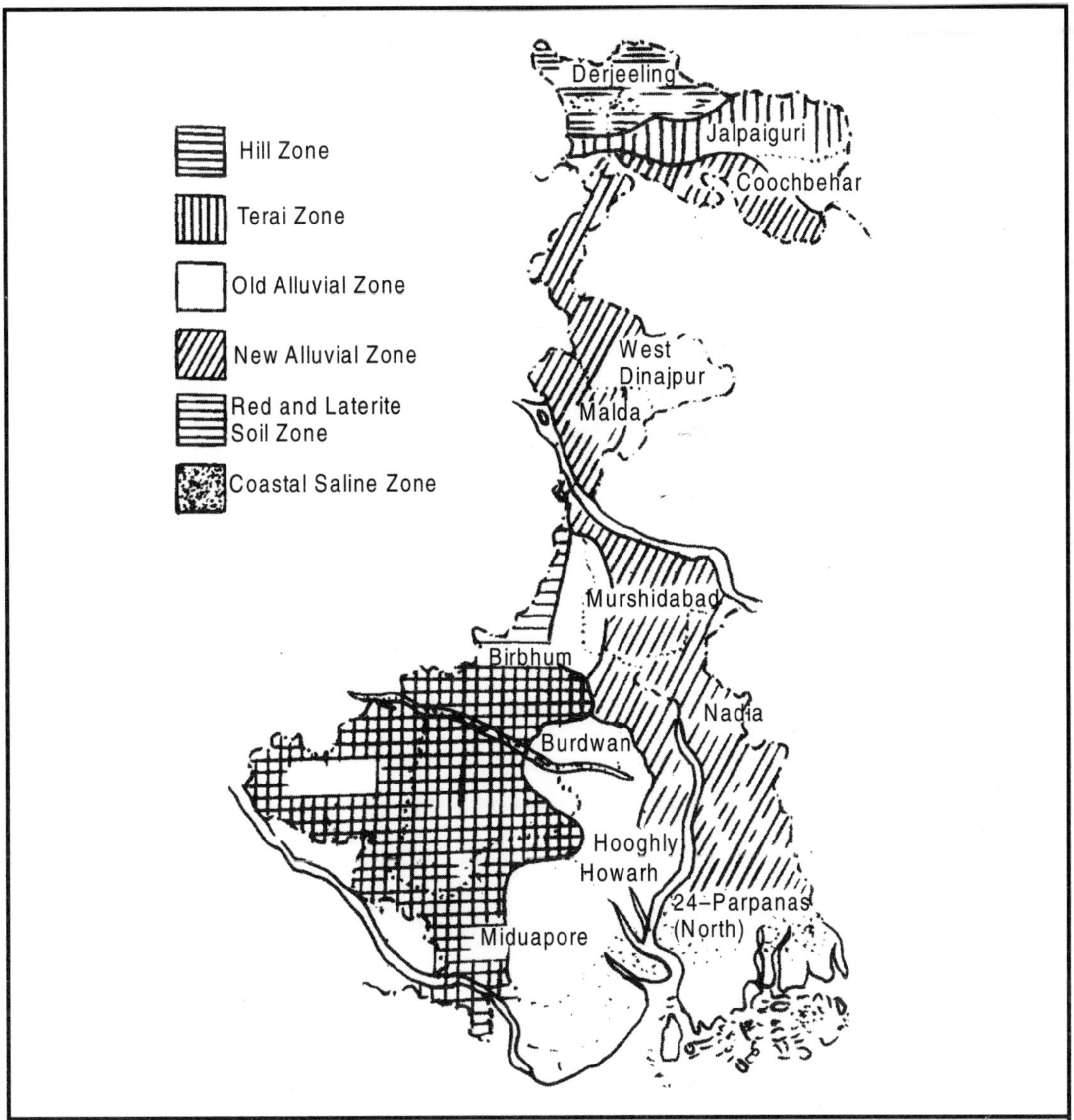

Fig. 34(i) Agro-climatic Zones of West Bengal.

ANNEXURES

ANNEXURE-I

LIST OF PVT. SEED COMPANIES

LIST OF PVT. SEED COMPANIES

M/S. Ankur Seeds Pvt. Ltd., 27, New Cotton Market Layout Nagpur- 44018.

M/S. Maharashtra Bharat Seed Corporation BA 22-24 Phase-II Magalpuri Industrial Area, Delhi-110 034.

M/S. Excel Industries Ltd., 184-187, Swami Vivekanand Road, Jogeshwari, Bombay-400 102.

M/S. Hoechst India Ltd., (Seed Division) 54-A, Andheri East, Bombay- 400 093.

M/S. Heritage Seeds Pvt. Ltd., PB No. 63, Bhadgaon Road, Pachora, Jalgaon - 424 201 (MS).

M/S. J.K. Seeds, 20, Palgah Colony, Behind Anand Theatre, SP Road Secundrabad-500 003.

M/S. Nath Seeds Ltd., Nath House Nath Road, PB No. 318, Aurangabad-431 005

M/S. Navaritis India Ltd., Seed House 1170/27, Revenue Colony, Shivajee Nagar, Pune- 411 005 (MS).

M/S. Pure Seed Genetics International Pvt. Ltd., New Delhi - 110 008.

M/S. Proline Seeds Corporation Ltd., 5-3-964 First Floor B. Block,

M/S. Bajosheetal Seeds Pvt. Ltd., PB-77 A-2, Old MIDC Jalna - 431203.

M/S. Century Seeds Pvt. Ltd., 85, Indira Market Old Sabzi Mandi, Delhi-110 007.

M/S. Golden Seeds Pvt. Ltd., B-22A, Block B, Bridge Main Building, KR Cross Yediyur-Banglore-82.

M/S. Harsa Ram Seed Corporation, 100, Indira Market, Old Sabzi Mandi, Delhi 110 002.

M/S. Indo-American Hybrid Seeds, PO Box No. 7099, 17th Cross 2nd 'A' Main K.R. Road, Banashankri Second Stage, Banglore - 560 070.

M/S. Maharashtra Hybrid Seed Co. Ltd., Plot No. B-4 Industrial State, JALNA - 431 203 (MS)

M/S. Namdahri Seeds, Bidadi-562 109, Banglore, Karnataka.

M/S. Nandi Seeds, 22, Tank Bund Road, Aparna Complex Banglore-' 560 009

M/S. Pocha Seeds Pvt. Ltd., PO Box 55, Near Sholepur Bazaar, Pune- 411 040.

M/S. Pro-Agro Seed Company Ltd., 498, W Nagar HMT Layout, Fasi Jung Lane Nizom Sahi Road, Hyderabad -500 095. AP.

M/S. Rallis India Ltd., PB No. 166, 21, DS Marg. Bombay-400 001.

M/S. Sai Seed Corporation, Opp. Sub Station, Karimnagar Road, Metpolly -505 325. AP

M/S. Sungrow Seed Ltd., 207, Aradhna Bhavan, Azadpur, New Delhi-110 033.

M/S. Welcome Seeds Pvt. Ltd., 209, Lusa Tower, Azadpur Complex, Delhi-110 033.

M/S., Maharashtra Hybrid Seed Co. Jalna, Maharashtra.

M/S. Suttind Seeds Pvt. Ltd.,K 26, Cannaught Circus, (Opp. Plaza Cinema) New Delhi- 110-001.

M/S Verma Seed Co. Pvt. Ltd. 53, Kasagran, Barali, (U.P).

M/S Globe Nursery, Tower 4, College Street Market Barabazar, Calcutta-7.

M/S Kisan Seed Store, Chaura maidan, Ludhiana.

M/S Harayna Seed Bhandar, Rajguru Market, Hisar.

M/S Haryana Seed Development Corporation, Chandigarh.

Ganganhalli Ext., Banglore- 560 032.

M/S. Sandoz India Ltd., Seed Division, Sandoz House Dr. AD Road Worli Bombay-400 018.

M/S. Sultan Seeds, Sultan Seed Farm, Manwarabad, Srinagar- 190 001.

M/S Sunseeds India Ltd., 80 feet Main road, RT Nagar, Banglore- 560 032.

M/S. Nirankari Seeds, GT Road Chauhan Nagar, Mandi Dabwali, Sirsa-125 104.

M/S. L.U. Naulakha and Sons, Krishi Bhawan, Bhawani Pant Pune.

M/S. Unicorn Seeds Pvt. Ltd., 1-7-139/3 SD Road, Secundrabad, Andhra Pradesh - 500 003.

M/S Bankim Prasad Ghosh & Co., 54, Dharamtalla Road, Hawara.

M/S Navjeevan Hybrid Seed Corporation, New Market, Jalana

M/S Public Seed Store, Sabjee Mandi, Amritsar.

M/S Pioneer Seeds, Banglore.

M/S Parag Seed Supply Co., Daraganj, Allahabad. (U.P.)

M/S Gujarat State Seed Corporation, Gandhinagar, Gujarat.

ANNEXURE-II

ICAR INSTITUTES/ NATIONAL RESEARCH CENTRES

ICAR INSTITUTES/NATIONAL RESEARCH CENTRES/ NATIONAL BUREAUX/PROJECT DIRECTORATES ETC.

Sr. No.	Name & Address	Telephone Number (s)	Fax	Telegraphic Address	E-mail
1.	Indian Council of Agriculture Research (ICAR), Krishi Bhavan, Dr. Rajendra Prasad Road, New Delhi-110001	011-3388991-5 (PABX)	011-3387293	AGRISEC (for K.B.) AGRIKAB (for K.A.B.)	
2.	Central Avian Research Institute (CARI), Izatnagar-243122 (Uttar Pradesh)	0581-440484, 447261	0581-447321	POULTRY	cavri @ × 400. nicgw.nic.in.
3.	Central Agricultural NDRA Research Institute for A & N Group of Islands (CARIANG), Andaman-Nicobar and Lakshadweep Group of Islands, Post Box No. 181, Port Blair-744101 (Andamans)	03192-33276,50436	03192-33281	KRISHIKE	cariangi @ × 400.nicgw.nic.in
4.	Central Arid Zone Research institute (CAZRI), Jodhpur-342003 (Rajasthan)	0291-740584, 740485	0291-740706	SUSHKH-SHETRA	cazri @ × 400. nicgw.nic.in

Sr. No.	Name & Address	Telephone Number (s)	Fax	Telegraphic Address	E-mail
5.	Central Institute of Agricultural Engineering (CIAE), Nabibagh, Berasia Road, Bhopa-62038 (Madhya Pradesh)	0755-534016, 530980, 537191	0755-534016	KRIYANTRA	ciae @ × 400.nicgw.nic.in
6.	Central Institute of Brackishwater Aquaculture (CIBA), 141, Marshalls Road, Egmore, Chennai-600008 (Tamil Nadu)	044-8554891	044-8554851	MONODON	ciba @ × 400.nicgw.nic.in
7.	Central Inland Capture Fisheries Research Institute (CICFRI), Barrackpore-7431 01 (West Bengal)	033-5600177, 5601190	033-5600388	FISHSEACH	cicfri @ × 400. nicgw.nic.in
8.	Central Institute for Cotton Reseach (CICR), Panjari Farm, Wardha road, Nagpur - 440010 (Maharashtra)	07103-75536,75538	07103-75529	KAPASSANS-THAN	cicr @ × 400. nicgw.nic.in
9.	Central Institute of Freshwater LT Aquaculture (CIFA), P.O. Kaushalyagang, Bhubaneswar-751 002 (Orissa)	00/4-463421, 463446	0674465407	AQUACU	cifa @ × 400. nicgw.nic.in
10.	Central Institute of Fisheries Education (CIFE), Jaiprakash Rd., 7-Bunglows, Versova, Mumbai-400061 (Maharashtra)	022-6363404, 6361446-8	022-6361573	FISHINST	cife @ × 400. nicgw.nic.in
11.	Central Institute of Fisheries Technology (CIFT), Willingdon Island, Matsyapuri P.O., Kochi-682029 (Kerala)	0484-66680, 667727	0484-668212	FISHTECH	cift @ × 400. nicg.nic.in

Sr. No.	Name & Address	Telephone Number (s)	Fax	Telegraphic Address	E-mail
12.	Central Institute of Postharvest Engineering & Technology (CIPHET), PAU Campus, Ludhiana-141004 (Punjab)	0161-808669	0161-808670	CIPHET	ciphet @ × 400. nicw.nic.in
13.	Central Institute for Research on Buffaloes (CIRB), Sirsa Road, Hisar-125001 (Haryana)	01662-35975,39604	01662-39604	BUBALINEX	ciro @ × 400. nicgw.nic.in
14.	Central Institute of Research for Cotton Technology (CIRCOT), Post Bag No. 16640, Adenwala Road, Matunga, Mumbai-400019 (Maharashtra)	0224146002, 4127273	0224130835	TECH-SEARCH	circot @ × 400. nicgw.nic.in
15.	Central Institute for Research on Goats (CIRG), P.O. Farah, Mathura-281122 (Uttar Pradesh)	0565-763380	0565-763246	VETEX	cirg @ × 400. nicgw.nic.in
16.	Central Institute for Subtropical Horticulture (CISH), Raebareli Road, P.O. Dilkusha, Lucknow-226002 (Uttar Pradesh)	0522-440424	0522-440626	MANGO-SEARCH	cish @ × 400. nicgw.nic.in
17.	Central Institute of Temperate Horticulture (CITH), P.O. Sanatnagar, Srinagar, Kashmir-190005 (Jammu&Kashmir)	0194-433104	0194-43178	HORT-SEARCH	cith @ × 400. nicgw.nic.in
18.	Central Marine Fisheries Research Institute (CMFRI), Post Bag No. 1603, Ernakulam, Cochin-682014 (Kerala)	0484-394798, 394909	0484-374818	CADALMIN	

Sr. No.	Name & Address	Telephone Number (s)	Fax	Telegraphic Address	E-mail
19.	Central Plantation crops Research Institute (CPCRI), Kasaragod-671124 (Kerala)	0499-430333, 480894-6	0499-430322	RESEARCH	cpcri @ x 400. nicgw.nic.in
20.	Central Potato Research Institute (CPRI), Shimla-171001 (Himachal Pradesh)	0177-225073, 224830	0177-224460	POTATO-SEARCH	cpri @ x 400. nicgw.nic.in
21.	Central Research Institute for Dryland Agriculture (CRIDA), Santoshnagar, Saklabad P.O., Hyderabad-500659 (Andhra Pradesh)	040-4530177, 4530161	040-4531802	DRYLAND	crida @ x 400. nicgw.nic.in
22.	Central Res. Inst. for Jute & Allied Fibres (CRIJAF), Nilgung, Distt. 24-Parganas (North), Barackpore-743101 (West Bengal)	033-5606124	033-5600415	JUTRE-SE ARCH	crijaf @ x 400. nicgw.nic.in
23	Central Rice Research Institute (CRRI), Cuttack 753006 (Orissa)	0671-643015, 642445-50	0671-641744	RICE (PBX)	crri @ x 400. nicgw.nic.in
24.	Central Soil Salinity Research Institute (CSSRI), Zarifa Farm, Kachhwa Road, Karnal-132001 (Haryana)	0184-290501	0184-290480	SALINITY	cssri @x 400. nicgw.nic.in
25.	Central Soil & Water Conservation Research & Training Institute (CSWCRTI), 218, Kaulagarh Road, Dehradun-248195 (Uttar Pradesh)	0135-758564	0135-754213	SOILCONS	cswcrti (aix400. nicgw.nic.in
26.	Central Sheep & Research Institute (CSWRI), (Teh. Malpura, Distt. Tonk), Via Jaipur Avikanagar-304501 (Rajasthan)	01437-25212/8162	01437-8163	SHEEPINST	cswri @ x Wool 400.nicgw.nic.in

Sr. No.	Name & Address	Telephone Number (s)	Fax	Telegraphic Address	E-mail
27.	Central Tuber Crops Research Institute (CTCRI), P.B No. 3502, Sreekariyam, Thiruvananthapuram -695017 (Kerala)	0471-448431, 448551-4 (PABX)	0471-550063	TUBER-SEARCH	ctcri @ × 400. nicgw.nic.in
28.	Central Tobacco Research Institute (CTRI), Rajah-mundry 533105 (Andhra Pradesh)	0883-465995	0883464341	TABSEARCH	ctri @ × 400. nicgw.nic.in
29.	Directorate of Maize Research (DMR), Cumming's Laboratory, IARI, Pusa, New Delhi-110012	011-5782372, 5772105	011-5768195	KRISHIPUSA	
30.	Directorate of Oilseeds Research (DOR), Rajendranagar, Hyderabad-500030 (Andhra Pradesh)	040-4015222, 4015331	040-4017969	SODH-TELHAN	pdoilseed @ × 400. nicgw.nic.in
31.	Directorate of Rice Research (DRR), Rajendranagar, Hyderabad-500030 (Andhra Pradesh)	0404015120, 4015036-9	040-4015308	RICE	pdrice @ × 400. nicgw.nic.in
32.	Directorate of Water Management Research (DWMR), P.O. Phulwari Sharif, WALMI Complex, Patna-801505 (Bihar)	0612-452231	0612-452232	JALPRAB-ANDH	pdwm @ × 400. nicgw.nic.in
33.	Directorate of Wheat Research (DWR), Post Box 158, Agarsain Marg, Kunjpura Road, Karnal-132001 (Haryana)	0184-252390, 251830	0184-251390	WHEAT	dowr @ × 400. nicgw.nic.in

Sr. No.	Name & Address	Telephone Number (s)	Fax	Telegraphic Address	E-mail
34.	High Security Animal Disease Laboratory (HSADL), 1010, Kalpana Nagar, Bhopal-462021 (Madhya Pradesh)	0755-587542			
35.	Indian Agricultural Research Institute Pusa, New Delhi-110012	011-5787461, 5754595 5766420	011-5751719,	KRISHIPUSA	rbsingh @ iari. ernet. in (IARI),
36.	Indian Agricultural Statistics Research Institute (IASRI), Library Avenue, Pusa, New Delhi-110012	011-5741479	011-5741479	AGRIRESTA	Iasri @ × 400. nicgw.nic.in
37.	ICAR Research Complex for Goa (ICARRCG), Ela, Old Goa-403402 (Goa)	0832-286181	0832-286249	RESEARCH	icar @ goa. nic.in
38.	Indian Grassland & Fodder Research Institute (IGFRI), Gwalior-Jhansi Road, Jhansi-284003 (Uttar Pradesh)	0517-444771	0517-440833	GHASAN-USANDHAN	igfri @ × 400. nicgw.nic. in
39.	Indian Institute of Horticultural Research (IIHR), Hassaraghatta Lake Post, Bangalore -560089 (Karnataka)	080-8466353, 8466471	080-8466291	HORT-SEARCH	iihr @ × 400. nicgw.nic.in
40.	Indian Institute of Pulses Research (IIPR) Kanpur-208024 (Uttar Pradesh)	0512-250264	0512-252582	DALHAN-SODH	iipr @ × 400. nicgw.nic.in
41.	Indian Institute of Sugarcane Research (IISR), Rae Bareli Road, Post Dilkusha, Lucknow-226002 (Uttar Pradesh)	0522–80726, 480735-7	0522-480738	GANNAA-NUSANDHAN	iisr.@ × 400. nicgw.nic.in

Sr. No.	Name & Address	Telephone Number (s)	Fax	Telegraphic Address	E-mail
42.	Indian Institute of Spices Research (IISR), P.B. No. 1701, Marikunnu P.O., Calicut-673012 (Kerala)	0495-370294, 371410	0495-370294	RESEARCH	iisrspices @× 400 nicgw.nic.in
43.	Indian Institute of Soil Science (IISS), Nabi Bagh, Berasia Road, Bhopal-462038 (Madhya Pradesh)	0755-730946, 734487	0755-733310	SOILINST	iiss @ × 400. nicgw.nic.in
44.	Indian Lac Research Institute (ILRI) P.O.Namkum, Ranchi-843010 (Bihar)	0651-520202, 520117	0651-520202	LACCUM	ilri @ × 400. nicgw.nic.in
45.	ICAR Research Complex for NEH Region (IRCNEHR), Umroi Road, Barapani, Shillong-793103(Meghalaya)	0364-64257, 64335 222922	0364-64288,	AGRI-COMPLEX	rcneh @ × 400. nicgw.nic.in
46.	Indian Veterinary Research Institute in (IVRI) Izatnagar-243122 (Uttar Pradesh)	0581-447069, 447185	0581-447284	VETEX	ivri @ × 400. nicgw.nic.
47.	National Academy of Agricultural Research Management (NAARM), Rajendranagar, Hyderabad-500030 (Andhara Pradesh)	040-4015070	040-4015912	NAARM	katyal @ katyalnaarm. ernet.in
48.	National Bureau of Animal Genetic Resources (NBAGR), P.O. Box No. 129, Makrampur Campus, G.T. Road (Baldi) Bye Pass, Karnal-132001 (Haryana)	0184-253918	0184-253654	GENETICS	nbagr @ × 400. nicgw.nic.in

Sr. No.	Name & Address	Telephone Number (s)	Fax	Telegraphic Address	E-mail
50.	National Bureau of Plant Genetic Resources (NBPGR), Pusa Campus, New Delhi-110012	011-5783697, 5739575	011-5731495	GERMPLASM	nbpgr @ × 400. nicgw.nic.in
51.	National Bureau of Soil Survey & Land Use Planning (NBSSLUP), Shankarnagar PO: Amravati Road, Nagpur-440010 (Maharashtra)	0712-532386, 534545,543678	0712-522534, 5727813	SOILNDBRU	brij @ × 400. nicgw.nic.in
52.	National Centre for Agricultural Economics & Policy Research (NCAP), Library Avenue, Pusa, New Delhi-110012	011-5563396	011-5571986		
53.	National Centre for Integrated Pest Management (NCIPM), Lal Bahadur Shastri Bhavan, Block K-I, IARI Campus, Pusa, New Delhi-110012	011-5765935	011-5765472	INTEGPEST	ncipm @ × 400. nicgw.nic.in
54.	National Dairy Research Institute (NDRI), Karnal-132001 (Haryana)	0184-2528009, 259002, 254372	0184-250042	DAIRY-SEARCH	ndri @ × 400. nicgw.nic.in
55.	National Embryo Biotechnology Centre for Animal Production (NEBCAP), NDRI Campus, Karnal-132001 (Haryana)				
56.	National Institute of Animal Genetics (NIAG) P.O. Box No. 129, Karnal-132001 (Haryana)	0184-32918			

Sr. No.	Name & Address	Telephone Number (s)	Fax	Telegraphic Address	E-mail
57.	National Institute of Animal Nutrition & Physiology (NIANP), S.R.S. NDRI Campus Adugodi P.O., Bangalore - 560030 (Karnataka)	080-5532119, 5711303-4	080-5711420		nianp @ × 400. nicgw.nic.in
58.	NationalInstitute of Research on Jute & Allied Fibre Technology (NIRJAFT), 12, Regent Park, Calcutta-700040 (West Bengal)	033-4711807, 4710192	033-4712583	JUTLAB	jtrl @ × 400. nicgw.nic.in
59.	National Research Centre for Agroforestry (NRCAF), Pahuj Dam, Gwalior Road, Jhansi-284003 (Uttar Pradesh)	0517-448213-14	0517-442364	KRISHIV-ANIKI	nrcaf @ × 400. nicgw.nic.in
60.	National Research Centre on Arid Horticulture (NRCAH), 10th Mile Stone Ganganagar Road, Beechwal, Bikaner-334003 (Rajasthan)	0151-544917	0151-526354	UDYANS-HODH	nrcah @ × 400. nicgw.nic.in
61.	National Research Centre for Banana (NRCB), 44, Rama linga Nagar, South Extn., Vayalur Road, Trichy- 620017 (Tamil Nadu)	0431-770797, 771299	0431-70564	HORT-SEARCH	nrcbanana @ × 400. nicgw.nic.in
62.	National Research Centre on Camel (NRCC), P.B. 07, Jorbeer, P.O. Shivbari Bikaner-334001 (Rajasthan)	0151-522183, 529070	0151-522183	CAMCENTRE	nrccamel @ × 400. nicgw.nic.in
63.	National Research Centre for Cashew (NRCC), Puttur, D.K. Karnataka-574202 (Karnataka)	08251-21530, 20902	08251-24350	CAJUKEN-DRA	nrccashew @ × 400.nicgw.nic.in

Sr. No.	Name & Address	Telephone Number (s)	Fax	Telegraphic Address	E-mail
64.	National Research Centre for Citrus (NRCC), Seminary Hills, Nagpur-440006 (Maharashtra)	0712-527813, 530572	0712-5278133	CITRUS-SEARCH	nrccitrus @ × 400.nicgw.nic.in
65.	National Research Centre for Coldwater Fisheries (NRCCWFC), Shilwa Hills Nursery, Roop-nagar, P.B. No. 28, Haldwani- 263139 (Uttar Pradesh)	05942-47279, 27280	05942-47279	MAHSEER	
66.	National Research Centre for Equines (NRCE), Sirsa Road, Hisar-125001 (Haryana)	01662-32787, 32748	01662-33217	EQUINE	nrcequine @ × 400.nicgw.nic.in
67.	National Research Centre for Grapes (NRCG), P.B. No. 3, Manjri Farm Post, Solapur Road, Pune-412307 (Maharashtra)	020-814245, 814246	020-814246	HORT-SEARCH	nrcgrapes.mah .nic.in
68.	National Research Centre Groundnut (NRCG), Ivnagar Road, P.B.No. 5, Junagadh-362001 (Gujarat)	0285-651550	0285-651550	GNUT-SEARCH	nrcg @ × 400. nicgw.nic.in
69.	National Research Centre for Mithun (NRCM), ICAR Research Complex, Jharnapani Distt., Kohima-797106 (Nagaland)	03862-32341		MEDNA-GALAND	nrcmithun @ × 400. nicgw.nic.in
70.	National Research Centre for Mush-rooms (NRCM), Chambaghat, Solan-173213 (Himachal Pradesh)	01792-30451	01792-30451	MUSHRO-OMSEARCH	

Sr. No.	Name & Address	Telephone Number (s)	Fax	Telegraphic Address	E-mail
71.	National Research Centre for Medicinal & Aromatic Plants (NRCMAP), Boriyavi Taluka Anand-387310 (Gujarat)	0268-78602	0268-78601	MEDPLANTS	
72.	National Research Centre for Meat & Meat Products (NRCMMP), C/o IVRI Campus, Izatnagar-243122 (Uttar Pradesh)	0581-447069, 447185	0581-447284	VETEX	nrcmeat @ × 400.nicgw.nic.in
73.	National Research Centre for Orchids (NRCO), ICAR Research Complex for North-Eastern Hills Region, Regional Station, Tadong, Gangtok-737102 (Sikkim)	03592-31717, 57954 (Farm)	03592-31717	AGRI-COMPLEX	orchids@×400. nicgw.nic.in
74.	National Research, Centre for Oilpalm (NRCO), Door No. 1-66- D, Shatvahana Nagar, Gooravarma, Eluru, West Godavari Dist-534003 (Andhra Pradesh)	08812-75409, 75495	08812-75531	PALM-SEARCH	
75.	National Research Centre for Onion & Garlic (NRCOG), Rajghrunagar, Distt. Pune-410505 (Maharashtra)	02135-24056, 22026	02135-24056	HORT-SEARCH	nrconion @ × 400. nicgw.nic.in
76.	National Research Centre on Plant Biotechnology (NRCPB), IARI, PUSA, New Delhi-110012	011-5788783, 5711554			rps @ biciari.ren.nic.in
77.	National Research Centre on 24688 Rapeseed-Mustard (NRCRM), Sewar, Bharatpur-321303 (Rajasthan)	05644-24688, 26855	05644-25566,	SAR-SONSODH	prk @ nrcrm.raj.nic.in

Sr. No.	Name & Address	Telephone Number (s)	Fax	Telegraphic Address	E-mail
78.	National Research Centre for Sorghum (NRCS), Rajendranagar, Hyderabad-500030 (Andhra Pradesh)	040-04015225, 4015349	040-4016378	SORGHUM	nrcsorghum @ × 400.nicgw.nic.in
79.	National Research Centre for Soybean (NRCS), Khandwa Road, Indore-452001 (Madhya Pradesh)	0731-476188	0731-470520	SOYSEARCH	nrcsoya@ × 400 nicgw.nic.in
80.	National Research Centre for Women in Agriculture (NRCWA), 93, Dharama Vihar, Khandgiri P.O., Bhubaneswar - 751030 (Orissa)	0674-471013	0674-471448		
81.	National Research Centre for Weed Science (NRCWS), 215, Ravindra Nagar, Adhartal, Jabalpur-482004 (Madhya Pradesh)	0761-330701, 331701, 330538	0761-332329, 342158	WEED-SCIENCE	nrcwccd @ × 400. nicgw.nic.in
82.	National Research Centre on Yak (NRCY), Dirang, West Kameng-790101 (Arunachal Pradesh)	218, 220, 259		YAKSEARCH	nrryak & × 400. nicgw.nic.in
83.	Project Directorate on Biological Control (PDBC), PB. No. 2491, Hebbal Bellary Road, HA Farm Post, Bangalore-560024 (Karnataka)	080-3414220 3117930	080-3331961	BIOSUPP-RESSION	pdr>lc@ × 400. nicgw.nic.in
84.	Project Directorate Cattle (PDC), PH-7, Pallavpuram, Phase-II, Modipuram, Meerut-250110 (Uttar Pradesh)	0121-570268	0121-571471	CATTLES EARCH	pdcattlc @ × on 400. nicgw.nic.in

Sr. No.	Name & Address	Telephone Number (s)	Fax	Telegraphic Address	E-mail
85.	Project Directorate for Cropping Systems Research (PDCSR), Modipuram, Distt. Meerut-250110 (Uttar Pradesh)	0121-S70708, 570095,571539	0121-571548	AGRISYSTEM	pdcsr @ × 400. nicgw.nic.in
86.	Project Directorate on Poultry (PDP), APAU Campus, Rajendranagar, Hydrabad-500030 (Andhra Pradesh)	040-4015650, 4015651-2 (PABAX) 4017000	040-4017002	POULTEX	pdpoultry @ × 400. nicgw.nic.in
87	Project Directorate of Vegetable Research (PDVR), 1-Gandhi Nagar, Naria, Sunderpur, Varanasi-221005 (Uttar Pradesh)	0542-635247, 635236	0542-318504	VEGRES	pdvcg @ × 400. nicgw.nic.in
88.	Sugarcane Breeding Institute (SBI), Coimbatorc-641007 (Tamil Nadu)	0422-472986, 472971	0422-472923	GANNAP-RAJANAN	sbi-col @ × 400.nicgw.nic.in
89.	Vivekanand Parvatiya Krishi Anusandhan Shala (VPKAS), Almora-263601 (Uttar Pradesh)	05962-30208, 30060	05962-31539	VII.AB	vpkas @ × 400.nicgw.nic.in
90.	Water Technology Centre for Eastern Region (WTCER), Chandrasekharpur, Bhubancswar-751 012 (Orissa)	0674-440060, 440010, 440481	0674-441651	WATERTECII	wtccr @ × 400. nicgw.nic.in

***VEGETABLE RESEARCH MANDATE**

●●●

ANNEXURE-III

STATE AGRICULTURAL UNIVERSITIES

Sr. No.	Name & Address	Telephone Number (s)	Fax	Telegraphic Address
1.	Assam Agricultural University (AAU), Jorhat- 785 013 (Assam)	0376-320965	0376-320919, 325344	AGRIVARSITY
2.	Acharya N.G. Ranga Agricultural University (ANGRAU), Rajcndranagar, Hyderabad-500 030 (Andhra Pradesh)	040-4015035, 230781	040-4015031	AGRIVARSITY
3.	Birsa Agricultural University (BAU), Kanke, Ranchi-834006 (Bihar)	0651-455850, 304389	0651-304451, 203744	
4.	Bidhan Chandra Krishi Vishwa Vidyalaya (BCKW), PO Krishi Viswavidyalaya, Mohanpur-741 252 (West Bengal)	033-5879772	03473-22275, 22277	KRISHIBIDHAN
5.	Central Agricultural University (CAU), Iroisemba, Imphal-795 001 (Manipur)	0385-310636	0385-310636	AGRIVARSITY
6.	CCS Haryana Agricultural University (CCSHAU), Hisar-125 004 (Haryana)	01662-31640, 37721 (PBX)	01662-34952	AGRIVARSITY

Sr. No.	Name & Address	Telephone Number (s)	Fax	Telegraphic Address
7.	C.S.Azad University of Agri. & Tech. (CSAUAT), P.O. Nawabganj, Kanpur-208 002 (Uttar Pradesh)	0512-294557	0512-210408	
8.	Gujarat Agricultural University (GAU), Sardar Krushinagar-385 506 (Gujarat)	02748-78222, 78147	02748-78261, 78262	KRUSHICAMP
9.	G.B. Pant University of Agri. & Tech. 33663 (GBPUAT), Pantnagar-263145 (Uttar Pradesh)	05946-33333, 33500,	05946-33473,33608	PANTVARSITY
10.	Himachal Pradesh Krishi Vishwa Vidyalaya (HPKVV) Palampur- 176 062 (Himachal Pradesh)	01894-30521	01894-30511	HIMKRISHI
11.	Indira Gandhi Krishi Vishwa Vidyalaya (IGKW), Labhandi, Krishak Nagar, Raipur-492 012 (Madhya Pradesh)	0771-425219,497012	0771-424532	IKRISHI
12.	Jawaharlal Nehru Krishi Vishwa Vidyalaya (JNKW), Krishinagar, Adhartal, Jabalpur-482 004 (Madhya Pradesh)	0761-343606, 340361	0761-342719	KRISHIVISWA
13.	Kerala Agricultural University (KAU), P.O. Vellanikkara, Thrissur-680 654 (Kerala)	0487-370034	0487-370019	AGRIVARSITY
14.	Konkan Krishi Vidyapeeth (KKV), Dapoli-415 712 (Maharashtra)	02358-82064	02358-82074	KONKANAGRI
15.	Marathwada Agricultural University (MAU), Parbhani-431 402 (Maharashtra)	02452-45002, 23801-5,7,8 (EPABX)	02452-235812	UNIVERSITY

Sr. No.	Name & Address	Telephone Number (s)	Fax	Telegraphic Address
16.	Mahatma Phule Krishi Vidyapeeth (MPAU), Rahuri-413 722 (Maharashtra)	02426-43208	02426-43302	KRISHIVID
17.	Narendra Dev University of Agriculture and Technology (NDUAT), Narendranagar, Kumarganj, Faizabad-224 001 (Uttar Pradesh)	05270-62032	05270-62118	AGRIVARSITY
18.	Orissa University of Agriculture and Technology (OUAT), Bhubaneswar-751 003 (Orissa)	0674402677	0674-407780	AGRITECH
19.	Punjab Agricultural University (PAU), Ludhiana-141 004 (Punjab)	0161-401794, 400955	0161-400945	AGRIVARSITY
20.	Punjabrao Deshmukh Krishi Vidyapeeth (PKV), Krishinagar, Akola-444 104 (Maharashtra)	0724-25365	0724-58219	UNIVERSITY
21.	Rajendra Agricultural University (RAU), P.O. Pusa, Pusa-848 125 (Bihar)	06274-74226	06274-74266	
22.	Rajasthan Agricultural University (RAU), Bikaner-334 001 (Rajasthan)	0151-523977 (Bilcaner) 0294-61977 (Udaipur)	0151-250336	AGRIVARSITY
23.	Sher-e-Kashmir Univ. of April. Sci. & Tech. (SKUAST), Rail Road, Jammu Tawi, Jammu-180 004 (J&K) (Nov.-Apr.)	0191-433417,434883	0191434883	AGRISITY
	Sher-e-Kashmir Univ. of Agril. Sci. & Tech. (SKUAST), Shalimar Campus, P.O. Nishat, Shrinagar-191121 (J &K) (May-Oct.)	0194-530450		AGRISITY

Sr. No.	Name & Address	Telephone Number (s)	Fax	Telegraphic Address
24.	Tamil Nadu Veterinary & Animal Sciences University (TANUVAS), Vepery High Road, Chennai-600 007 (Tamil Nadu)	044-5371574,584954	044-5371576	UNIVVET
25.	Tamil Nadu Agricultural University (TNAU), Coimbatore-641 003 (Tamil Nadu)	0422-431222,431788	0422431672	FARMVAR
26.	University of Agricultural Sciences (UAS), Gandhi KVK Campus, P.B. No. 2477, Bangalore-560 065 (Karnataka)	080-3332442	080-3330277	UNIVAGRIS
27.	University of Agricultural Sciences (UAS), Krishinagar, Dharwad-580 005 (Karnataka)	0836-347783,347958	0836-348349	UNIVAGRIS
28.	West Bengal University of Animal & Forestry Sciences (WBUAFS), 68, Khudiram Bose Sarani, Belgachia, Calcutta-700 037 (West Bengal)	033-5563450	033-5571986	
29.	Dr. Y.S. Parmar University of Horticulture & Forestry (YSPUHF), via Oochghat Solan-173 230 (Himachal Pradesh)	01792-52363,52357	01792-52242,52259	VANUDYAN

●●●